Saints & Scientists

Richard T. Wootton

Saints & Scientists
Published by EduTech
1992

ISBN 0-9633242-0-9 Hardback edition.
ISBN 0-9633242-1-7 Paperback edition.
Second Printing (1993)

Library of Congress
Catalog Card Number
92-90491

Published by:
Edutech Corp.
3066 So. Mollera St.
Mesa, AZ, 85210
602-831-1632

Printed by:
Cox Printing
Mesa, Arizona

TABLE OF CONTENTS

CHAPTER V: MORE TESTS OF SCIENCE-MORMONISM HARMONY

CHAPTER VI: SCIENTISTS' BELIEFS ON MAJOR CONTROVERSIES

CHAPTER VII: HOW TROUBLED WERE UTAH SCIENTISTS BY SCIENCE-RELIGION CONTROVERSY?

CHAPTER VIII: RELIGIOUS BELIEFS OF UTAH SCIENTISTS: 1955-1992

GRAPHS AND EXHIBITS

Definitions

Scientists, 1955 Study: This study was done by the author about the Utah born scientists listed in the 1949 volume of American Men of Science. The data in Chapters V, VI, and VII report the results for those scientists in 1955. Appendix A Tables detail those results.

Scientists, 1992 Study: This study was of the scientists graduated from Utah Universities and listed in the 1990 volume of American Men and Women of Science, also done by the author. Its results are compared with those of 1955 in Chapter VIII and in some Tables of Appendix A. The 1992 data are inserted in the Tables as rows labelled "1992".

Other Churches' Believers: Utah scientists who indicated on the questionnaire that they were other than Mormons and that they possessed a conviction regarding the divinity of Jesus of either "Fair", "Strong", or "Very Strong". This was 32.3 percent of non-Mormon Utah scientists in 1955.

Fair Believers: Utah scientists who indicated "Fair" degree of conviction of the Divinity of Jesus and/or that Joseph Smith was inspired by God in the formation of Mormonism.

Strong Believers: Utah scientists who indicated "Strong" conviction of the Divinity of Jesus and/or that Joseph Smith was inspired by God in the formation of Mormonism.

Very Strong Believers: Same as above, but indicating "Very Strong" as their conviction.

Nominal Members: Those Utah scientists indicating "No Such Conviction" or "Weak" conviction that Jesus was Divine.

Science-Mormon Religion Harmony: The hypothesis critically tested by most of the questionnaire items is as follows: Scientific minds can harmonize science with the Mormon religion. "Harmony" is further defined by the questionnaire items and answers.

An item in the questionnaire sent to the scientists was worded as follows: "Which best represents your method of reading the 'Standard Works'? (1) Take them literally, (2) Interpret them with reason, (3) View them skeptically, (4) Some combination of these."

This choice provides context for the definitions of "Literal", "Interpretive", and "Skeptical". These three words are used repeatedly in the book as labels for three viewpoints held by scientists and others about the understanding of scriptures. What follows may help the reader understand these terms.

Literal: There are two distinctively different Webster's definitions for "Literal". The one listed first is: "Actual words in **ordinary** meaning rather than in figurative, symbolic, or explanatory" senses. This is the meaning intended in this book.

The second dictionary definition is: "Real, accurate, unvarnished", i.e. "true". This book never intends "Literal" to mean this second definition of "real" or "true". To do so here would "beg the question", that is, be circular rather than addressing the real question.

The answers by scientists suggest that most of them understood the meaning to be "actual words in ordinary meaning rather than symbolic", as intended in the book. Those who might have thought it meant "real" and "true" would have been moved toward choosing "Literal", if they were "Believers" in scriptures as true. Support for the "Literal" was thus raised by an unknown extent by any scientists using "Literal" as a synonym for "true".

The "actual words in ordinary meaning" definition makes it possible for a "Literal" statement to be, in fact, either true, untrue, or partially true. For example, we may state, expecting it to be taken literally, "Today it rained in Arizona", when it did not, in fact, rain. That is, we may falsify, using literal language, as well as use it to tell truth.

On the other hand, language which is "symbolic", not "literal", may describe great truths, such as do some allegories, metaphors, poetry and parables. Or it too can be used to mislead.

Example: Believing that the world was created in six days results from "Literal" reading of the Bible. About the creation of the world, the "actual words in ordinary meaning" include the word "day", six "days" of creation.

This belief, however, requires a mental activity more than "Literalism". "Day", according to Webster's, can have any one of fourteen more or less literal meanings. One is: "A period of time;" Sometimes what a reader supposes to be taking a verse "Literally" is really taking a personally preferred meaning and ignoring many other "Literal" alternatives listed in dictionaries. Of course, we are aware that, basically, always, "meanings of words are not in the words (or in dictionaries) but in our minds".

Interpretive: A dictionary definition is "explanatory". Thesaurus synonyms are "decoding", "clarifying", "understanding", and "translating". The book uses "interpretive" in these senses, with amending suggested by the contexts.

Example: If we take an "interpret by reason" approach, the word "day" in the scriptural verses cannot be the "ordinary meaning" of 12 hours or 24 hours or merely a thousand years. What length of time does it mean? We **interpret** by further reading, observation and reason.

Skeptical: "Doubting the fundamental doctrines of religion" is the closest dictionary definition for "skeptical".

Example: On the age of the earth, a skeptic does not take ancient scriptures seriously as divine sources of guidance, nor need take them either literally or interpretively, because these are only meaningful choices for "believers".

To understand more fully how this book has defined "Literal", "Interpretive", and "Skeptical" by their context in the questions and answers, one may see their uses on Tables from 23 on in Appendix A.

Preface

When we are acquainted with young people who are troubled by science and religion, who are questioning religion because of science, or science because of religion, we want to understand them and the issues. We should feel, as did Alfred North Whitehead, that "The distress of sensitive minds (over the relations of science and religion) . . . must command our sincerest sympathy."[1] And we might consider what a former chief of secondary education for California, Aubrey A. Douglass, wrote about the adjustment problem of the adolescent:

> This often leads him to a state of mental turmoil that is not lessened when the teachings of science begin in his mind to conflict with a religious creed. Left to himself, he may not be able to resolve the conflict, and he may wash his hands of the whole matter and assume an attitude of indifference that augers ill for the future.[2]

We have known alert young people who were seriously concerned by their attempts to reconcile some religious teaching with their scientific reasoning. Some of them learned limiting literal views when young, and learned them as if they were vital to the truth of their religion, which they were not necessarily. Later, upon learning some science, they were not prepared to consider religious interpretations which provided alternatives which would be even more true, because they fit both religion and science. So some seemed slow to resolve the conflicts in their minds.

Problems of young people concerned me. Could such divisive stress be prevented? We asked why some have little trouble about science and religion. Why had it not bothered me much? Was it because most of my church teachers imparted what I have called the "Interpretive" viewpoint, which was compatible with science? I concluded that my views came from a combination of their instruction with the example that my father set of a deeply moral and essentially religious man with a reasoning approach to life.

When I was a church education teacher I wanted to help young people resolve conflicts without dulling their enthusiasm for either scientific or religious truth. I believed that personal harmony between science and religion could help produce personalities that are also harmonious---integrated, purposeful, and productive. So when Utah's high standing in scientist production came to my attention, it appeared that much help to young people could be found in the backgrounds and beliefs of those scientists. Can scientific minds harmonize religion and science? What religion with what science? How? These questions led to this book.

In 1990 the newest edition of American Men and Women of Science was published, with 120,000 biographies. This volume opened the way to my present (1992) study of scientists of Utah origin. It facilitated a fascinating comparison of their religion-science beliefs today with those of two generations ago, (the 1949 volume), a study made in 1955.

The original basis for this book was a doctoral dissertation directed by a University of Utah graduate committee and completed in 1956. My reasoning for having it accepted was as follows. Since I was a Church education administrator, since one curriculum concern in this role is science and religion, a dissertation on Utah scientists was justified in my case.

Later one member of the dissertation committee said that if the study concluded that Mormonism and science could be harmonized, he would not sign it. But it did find that to be true; nevertheless, he was convinced and did sign it. This book contains all of the facts which were in the approved dissertation. With the chapters, the Appendices and Tables give the whole picture.

By digging in the tables and pondering afresh, a reader can discover facts and implications that go well beyond this book. While I am not aware of any that contradict the general conclusions I have drawn, there is material for some additional ideas. While this book should settle some questions, it will stimulate other questions, which will become departure points for more research and more answers.

The heart of the book is in Chapters IV and V, testing the claim to a scientific religion. Scientific religion? To some this would seem an oxymoron. But please read on. Can scientific minds harmonize science and religious doctrine? I have presented evidence and a conclusion. The other chapters are only preface and postlude to this theme.

I write with some caution, yet with the conviction that this is a distinctive contribution to the subject, a more scientific, at least more quantitative, approach to some issues than has previously been available. I am only too aware, nevertheless, that there are approaches that would be more precisely scientific. But I do not believe they have yet been used. Hoping that others will go further, I submit this step forward toward understanding the issues. Nevertheless, I am confident that the answers presented, the conclusions reached, are reliable as far as they go.

I believe that the reporting of facts is accurate and that the conclusions I have given for each chapter are general truths. Yet it is improbable that I have expressed matters clearly enough to avoid all misinterpretation or confusion. It does not appear that even the scriptures manage that, human language as it is and human beings as they are. So I welcome feedback of any kind from anyone.

An immediate reason for publishing this book is that I think its data and findings should be available to students of the subject. When the dissertation was completed in 1956, it was available at the libraries of the University of Utah, Brigham Young University and from University Microfilms. It is available now only at University of Utah and Utah State University. The 1992 Encyclopedia of Mormonism published by MacMillan was unaware of it as a reference for science and Mormonism. I saw that it needed to be in published book form. The Improvement Era published findings. The Proceedings of the Hawaii Academy of Science also published some in 1958.

My friend, Dr. Kenneth T. Slack, who was the superb librarian of the Hawaii Campus-B.Y.U. when I was there, and later Director of Libraries of Marshall University, had a broader perspective and encouraged me to publish a book from the dissertation. I am taking his advice, 28 years late! This does not so much reflect on Dr. Slack's persuasiveness as it does on my priorities.

I am doing it now because I have more time and discovered that the 1990 edition of American Men of Women of Science is available on "Dialog" as a CD-ROM data base. This made an up-to-date follow-up study feasible, even with 120,000 biographies to search.

So I have replicated the 1955 study based on the 1990 biographies. In the generation from 1938 to 1960 the number of scientists in the United States more than doubled, but Utah still remained far beyond the second place state in population-related scientist production. Will Utah have retained its lead in 1990 after another generation and another doubling of scientists? Will its scientists state they harmonize science and their religions? What are their views now on issues like the age of the earth and evolution? I was motivated to do this 1992 research to provide up-to-date answers.

The earlier study was valuable for showing whether, at one period, a religion and science were harmonized by scientific minds. Has science changed in the two generations to disrupt the chances for harmony? Have scriptures that touch on science changed since the 1955 study? (Not that I have heard.) But have the emphases and interpretations of the religion's teaching organizations changed to make science more, or less, acceptable? There was a challenge for a new study. Why should I go after this information and publish it? Perhaps because, like the proverbial mountain, it is there!

Acknowledgements

The names of the hundreds of Utah scientists whose responses supplied the wealth of information for this study could well deserve to be here. I feel obligated to them and will show this gratitude at least by struggling to accurately write and publish their views. Many of them asked that I send them the results of the study, which I have done.

For the 1992 study I credit Dr. Bruce D. Merrill, Director of the Center for Media Research of the Walter Cronkite School of Journalism at Arizona State University, for advice and assistance on the representativeness of the returns. Of course, I bear the responsibility for any shortcomings in this book.

In the early phases of the 1955 study, many educational and religious leaders encouraged me. (The positions named here were, of course, those they held then.) They were Dr. William E. Berrett, Vice-president of Brigham Young University; Dr. Don Orton, Dean, College of Education; Dr. Henry Eyring, Dean of the Graduate College; Dr. Paul C. Fawley, Chair, Department of Educational Administration, University of Utah; and President (then) Marion D. Hanks, now emeritus, of the Seven Presidents of the Seventy of the Church of Jesus Christ of Latter-day Saints.

My loving gratitude to my supportive and patient soul-mate, Helen, for preparing tables, typing manuscripts and reading copy for the 1955 work, and, for the current book, editing, fine ideas, and encouraging companionship. Conversations with my science-educator son, William R., the finest science philosopher I know personally, provided precious insights and paternal pride. I am grateful to him and to my English teacher daughter, Cynthia Rieben, for professional proofreading. And love and admiration also go to my grandson, David Ludeman, who at age fourteen typed the entire 1955 manuscript and sixty-one tables into the PC-XT with "awesome" accuracy.

R.T.W.

Introduction

You are interested in religion, science, or their interactions. As Chapter I shows, you are in wise company. They are concerns for human welfare. The conflict between the Roman Catholic form of Christianity and science contains some lessons for religious leaders and thinkers. Chapter II addresses this. Chapter III examines the claim that Roman Catholicism supports science well.

Now some evangelical churches in America, with their literalistic Bible base are rejecting legitimate science by supporting Special Creation "science". Mainline churches have little contest with science, while Liberal churches have a notable harmony with it. Jewish and Unitarian church cultures have high per membership numbers of scientists. The Unitarian is a church which tends to attract scientists from some other faiths.

About which churches support science, the production of scientists by each state is revealing. At the low end of the scale there are mostly the states of the "Bible Belt". They are the fundamentalist, evangelical, and literalistic emphasis. Their production, per million white population, is only about one-fourth that of the high end, which consists of Northern states. Then the very top is an astonishing revelation. As one goes up the scale of production, each state is just a few percentage points above the next lower state. But from the second highest state to the top state is a jump of 21 percent.

That any state was so far ahead of the second place is unusual. That any state has maintained such a lead over fifty years, while several states have moved back and forth for other top places, adds to the wonder. And that the top state is one in which a scriptures revering, authoritative, and missionary minded church is the dominant cultural force is most remarkable. That state is Utah. The details are in Chapter IV.

When Utah's lead in scientist production first became known, over fifty years ago, I was curious about why. What is the status of education in Utah? What are the cultural differences, the socioeconomic factors? What are the religions of Utah-born scientists? Were they active in their religions? Did they believe their churches contributed to scientific achievement? Were they "believing" members? Did they believe they harmonized their religion and science, or otherwise? What did they think about salient issues such as the age of the earth and evolution?

My interest led to a doctoral dissertation for the University of Utah. It found impressive answers. These are in Chapters V and VI. But would the answers of Utah scientists fifty years ago be quite different from those of today? In 1991 I surveyed the 1990 edition of American Men and Women of Science and sent questionnaires to graduates of Utah Universities. These contained most of the identical questions from my 1955 dissertation survey.

What such scientists believe now about religion and science makes these data timely. The comparisons between then and now are placed alongside the earlier data in the tables of the Appendix as bold type and in Chapter VIII. The results are surprising.

For a quick general picture of the results on Utah scientists you may go directly to the summaries on pages 19, 44, and 60. From there you may go into the chapters for related background and more detail. The major summary is Chapter VIII, and whatever else one reads, this is most recommended. The Appendix has all the tables. There are gems and nuggets of insight to be mined from this mountain of information.

Saints and Scientists, 1992, is unique. It is the most comprehensive, objective and data-based look at a state's production of scientists in relation to religion. We found no similar such work currently in Dissertation Abstracts, Books in Print, Forthcoming Books or in periodical journals. It is thus, I believe, the broadest data-based and most reliable reference on the subject to date. The University of Utah graduate committee for the dissertation judged that the conclusions of the 1949 AMS study were reliable. The current survey was of 415 of the 1,954 scientist graduates of Utah universities listed in AMWS, 1990, a representative sample. Statistical consultant on the study was Dr. Bruce D. Merrill, Director of the Media Research Center of the Walter Cronkite School of Communication, of Arizona State. The author is Professor Emeritus of the University, once Department Chair in the Division of Policy and Leadership, and a social scientist.

This is not necessarily the end of such studies. One important feature of scientific method is that results are to be made public, can be scrutinized by anyone, and can be tested by replication. The author has on file for other researchers to use all of the documentation which went into this study, including the questionnaires completed by the scientists and their addresses. The letter sent with the questionnaires and the questionnaire used are in the appendices of this book. The tables with all of the data are also in the appendix.

The statistics may be used to support some current opinion and refute others. One may respond, "These are **mere** statistics." But are not statistics, as counts of true instances, among the best representations of "things as they are", i.e., "truth"? When derived honestly and carefully, are they not likely far closer to truth than most **mere** opinion? The figures in this book are accurate as far as support of any of the conclusions in the book are concerned, and they will support many additional conclusions which the reader may form from this quest.

CHAPTER I

SCIENCE-RELIGION CONFLICT IS SERIOUS

> The effort of Christianity to survive Copernicus and Darwin is the basic drama of the last three hundred years.[1] Will Durant.

Harmonizing of science and religion is important to those concerned with human welfare. Truth, reasoned reality, is sometimes set against mankind's faiths and fears. Issues have existed since humanity has had souls for faith or minds for reason. Must they be set against each other? Must one win? Could they not flourish together?

Between Christianity, in the form generally known, and science the controversy has been sharp and dangerous to scientists and other truth seekers. On March 5, 1616, the Holy Office of the Inquisition of the Roman Catholic Church, pronounced that it was "false" and "erroneous" to believe that the earth is not the center of the universe or that it has a daily rotation. It then condemned the astronomer-thinker Galileo for writing otherwise.[2] The great church of the time officially affirmed to be false that which was, in fact, true. This issue, whether the earth rotates on its axis and has an orbit around the sun, is settled. But other issues were far from settled, and controversy not only persists but causes problems in our times, particularly about evolution of living creatures.

Alfred North Whitehead, a noted modern philosopher, wrote about science and religion: "The future course of history depends upon the decisions of this generation as to the relations between them . . . We are involved with nothing less than the future course of history."

Why are the relations between them so important? Because of the standing of each, and because the existence of conflicts between them diminish the potential effectiveness of one, the other, or both for humanity's welfare.

THE IMPORTANCE OF RELIGION

Let us look briefly at the importance of religion. I do not expect readers of this book to need much persuasion on this point. But they may be surprised to learn that some writers noted for apparently antireligious points of view, believe that some religion is supremely important to humanity. We call them to the bar of truth as what lawyers call "adverse witnesses." These are ones we would expect to be prejudiced against religion, or neutral. Each has been critical of specific religions and each has a following of persons seldom found in Sunday Schools.

RELIGION LOSS: LOGIC OF TERROR

The most notorious, likely, was the Nineteenth Century German philosopher, Frederic Nietzsche. Some people believe he was a precursor of Nazism. However, he lamented the collapse of religious belief in Europe. Because some intelligent people were "seeing through" the European religions, he feared that Western culture would undergo a period of "rupture, destruction, downfall, revolution, a stupendous logic of terror". His philosophical writings were bold attempts to give the world his new "religion": Devotion to our descendants being better than we are.[4]

Though no saint, he was a prophet. He predicted that something like Nazism or Stalinist Communism would result if people lost religious faith. It did indeed. But now is there enough beneficent religious influence to help inspire the current "democratic, civil rights, free market" nations?

From the history of religion we need not suppose that just any religion inspires peace and decency or progress. Historically, some religions, particularly fundamentalist and authoritarian, have been the inspiration of much violent mistreatment of human beings. Today's violence hot-spots are fired by some religious zealots--Moslem, Hebrew, and Christian. The term "religion" may cover many worships. The need for religion is the need for the best in religions, according to those who testify.

OTHER UNEXPECTED WITNESSES FOR RELIGION

Another unexpected witness for the importance of religion, George Bernard Shaw, the sometimes irreverent Irish playwright and critic, said, "I have lived to see modern Germany discard 'Hail Mary' and substitute 'Heil Hitler' and for the life of me cannot bring myself to regard the change as an improvement."[5] Shaw gives a specific insight into how unbelief hurts society. "Many people still believe quite seriously in hell; and though a considerable number of influential persons scoff at it, the results are not reassuring: those who no longer fear anything beyond the grave are sometimes dangerously unscrupulous on this side of it."[6] Shaw lectures more on the irreligious. "Their children have neither the old Mosaic discipline nor any new faith. Moral anarchy becomes rampant. Unscrupulous imperialism, unscrupulous nationalism, unscrupulous individualism, unscrupulous corybantics and anacreontics have culminated in monstrous world wars and smash-and-grab revolutions to settle questions that could and should be settled reasonably.[7] . . . "Christendom is supplanted by Scoundreldom"[8], and concludes by affirming his belief "that society cannot be held together without religion."[9]

Another adverse witness was the American socialist, Upton Sinclair, writer of a book critical of denominations. In the conclusion to The Profits of Religion, he says, "Do I mean that I expect to see the Church---all churches---perish and pass away? I do not, for I believe that the Church answers one of the fundamental needs of man. It is a statement which many revolutionists would resent, yet it is a fact, nevertheless, that we need a new religion, need it just as badly as any of the rest of our pitifully groping race . . . much in the old moral codes is based upon facts which will not change as long as man is what he is."[10]

For now, one last witness will suffice. John W. Draper wrote The History of the Conflict Between Religion and Science. It condemns the Roman religion for its conflicts with science, but regarding religion he said, "The tranquillity of society depends so much on the stability of its religious convictions, that no one can be justified in wantonly disturbing them."[11]

Religion seems of supreme importance. We may want an awareness of our relation to our Creator. We seek a vision of what God had in mind by placing us on earth. We need hope that the struggle is worthwhile. We can use divine commandments for conduct to help us live happily, at peace with ourselves and with other men. We need a society bound in unity of faith and fraternity as sons of God.

Humanity, as God's children, cries out for its freedom to develop, and for its fellows' help and respect. But humans, if viewed as creatures of evolutionary accident instead of intelligent creation, may be seen as having neither origin nor destination different from the lower animals. We can expect a consistent disrespect when it suits the proclivities for plunder or passion of irreligious exploiters.

THE IMPORTANCE OF SCIENCE

About the importance of science, in our age we are all witnesses. Almost all see its obvious products, providing more food with less acreage and work force, saving lives by miracle medicines and machines, spanning the earth and space with wonders of transportation and communication (creating new heavens and a new earth), warning us of the damages we are doing to the atmosphere and earth, and showing promise of even greater blessings, if we do not first use it to annihilate ourselves in war.

Let me bring two witnesses from the realm of religion to testify to the importance of science. A notable theologian, Joseph Fielding Smith, once President of the Church of Jesus Christ of Latter-day Saints, affirmed, **"Science has rendered incalculable service."**[12]

So unanimous is the respect for science today that a leading Catholic theologian, writing in a book officially approved by his church, generously praised science. The Reverend Martin J. Scott, in Things Catholics Are Asked About, declared of science, **"It is man's greatest natural achievement and the promise of his greatest earthly advancement."**[13]

My survey of the books by men of religion commenting on science at a large state university library turned up not one religious writer who had anything but praise for the general importance of science to people.

Religion! Its supreme importance to man trumpeted not only by ministers and church members but even by independent critics!

Science! Its astonishing accomplishments universally applauded, even by the church that once persecuted scientists for telling the truth!

EFFECTS OF SCIENCE-RELIGION CONFLICT

"We have here the two strongest general forces (apart from the mere impulse of the various senses) which influence men," said Alfred North Whitehead, adding ominously, "and they seem to be set one against the other---the force of our religious intuitions, and the forces of our impulse to accurate observation and logical deduction." He advises us that "The distress of sensitive minds, and the zeal for truth, and the sense of the importance of the issues, must command our sincerest sympathy."[14]

Perhaps no one knows more keenly about the religion-science battle than one who has had it fought in his own mind. How did the bright and erudite Catholic feel in centuries past, to take one instance, when he had been taught by his Church as doctrine, as it had been taught for centuries, and affirmed by high and most solemn councils, that the earth does not revolve, and that it does not orbit the sun, when he learned from scientists that his Pope, councils, priests and their official books were dead wrong? Disillusionment, sadness, and various degrees of alienation from Catholicism were consequences.

The Catholic guardians of the faith correctly thought that if the science of Copernicus and Galileo was believed among the masses, then parts of the supposedly inerrant Bible, such as Joshua 10:14, which says that "the sun stood still", would be seen as error. And if the "Word of God" were mistaken, could it be the word of God? What other mistakes might it contain, if we only knew? Is it then, after all, not a divine guide? And is the Church that has mistakenly proclaimed it inerrant herself an unreliable guide? The Church, by this view, is too wondrous, too important, to be so undone. Better, instead, to try to undo the truth which threatens it.

In every age some religious leaders lower the standards of truth--as established by honest, intelligent, and disciplined minds--to assert what they consider to be an overriding, practical, perhaps humane, or comforting "truth" of their religion. In other words, they feel that the merits of the faith as an end justify the means, suppressing truth.

So the science-Catholicism conflict caused some bright, educated, sensitive people, if they were also bold, to leave the Church. Some who were not so bold stayed in, with wounded faith, their joy of life impaired, drawing some comfort still from the familiar rituals, while in doubt about her reliability. Some who were not so bright, but perhaps happier, just forgot what little insight from reason they might have had and avoided the conflict.

In the choices offered by the Reformation, some disillusioned formed or joined other churches. This jarred not only Catholicism. The Bible, which had become the Protestant authority, could not be viewed through the eyes of science as literally true. Untold numbers slid to indifference, skepticism, and materialism. Historic conflicts between the religious and science, with dire results predicted by Neitzsche and Shaw, have taken their toll in too many sad ways to mention here.

An alert youngster of today can find fundamentalist Protestant church teachings, which he has grown to love and believe, an unnerving contrast to what he learns about science in good schools. For example, the keenest fellow cryptographer in my World War II Signal Corps center told me he was an atheist. When I asked how he got that way, he told of being taught in youth as a Baptist that the King James Version of the Bible was all literal revelation from God. He said he later discovered by himself that it contains internal contradictions that preclude its having all come forth from a deity who is at once intelligent, honest, and possessed of complete influence upon the literary production of the Bible writers. So he dropped Christianity in its theological entirety, God and all, in what I tried to show him, with some success, was a non-sequitur. Had he been familiar with a religion that only believes the Bible "as far as it is translated correctly", his reaction might have been more temperate upon finding some errors.

If we are to obtain the blessings of religion along with keen appreciation and support of science, we might well devote ourselves to ways of viewing religion and science that are compatible. Harmonizing religion and science, if it can be done, is helpful to our welfare.

As our adverse witness, George Bernard Shaw, said, "science and religion at loggerheads are reflected politically in suicidal world war."[15] (He meant World War II.) His observation might apply to any future inhuman slaughters as well. But not all the materialists or atheists are Communists or foreigners. Some are competitive "survival of the fattest" capitalists and politicians at home. The science-religion contest is within our borders, too, and always has been. The good of our own people and of the world are in the balance.

We should have profound concern to preserve and promote true Christianity of the essential type that undergirds our free and humane way of life. Can the respect of person for person, necessary to the individual freedom and rights of all, finally flourish without widespread conviction that there is a God who is the concerned Father of each and all? Can this conviction be widespread without effective religious teaching? Can religious teaching be effective if it is not believed? And will it be believed by alert and honest people if it is inharmonious with science--an openly honest, a highly disciplined, and an impressively successful method of finding and knowing truth?

CHAPTER II

A REVIEW OF THE CONTEST BETWEEN SCIENCE AND RELIGION

Many debates between theologians and scientists in the past may seem one-sided from the vantage point of modern learning. In their times they were vital controversies. Will some of ours seem as foolish, looking back some day? Or looking clearly today?

Andrew D. White, first president of Cornell University, wrote an important study of the conflicts between science and theology. He showed that in the medieval and renaissance periods there were grave disputes over such matters as whether the earth is round or not, whether there were remote parts of earth populated by humans, whether the sun goes around the earth or vice versa, whether comets and meteors are supernatural agents or natural events, whether storms are the immediate result of supernatural intervention on earth or of natural forces, whether disease is a visitation for wickedness, and whether God condemns medical study of the human body by dissection.[1]

Draper and White each also dwelt on points that are still active questions, as noted later in this chapter. Draper discussed the nature of the soul, the age of earth, the flood, the antiquity of man, the criterion of truth, and the role of law in the universe.[2] White dealt with the conflict over evolution of the species, the age of the earth, the flood, and man's antiquity.[3] Lane, a more recent writer, identified six major conflicts in the history of science and religion as the shape of the earth, the heliocentric theory, Newton's law of gravitation, the antiquity of the earth, the antiquity of man, and evolution. In his book, however, he only dealt with the problems of evolution and of geologic time, considering the others to be already completely resolved against the early church views.[4]

SOME CONSEQUENCES OF THE CONFLICTS

The well known case of Galileo highlighted some consequences. For breaking a previous pledge, which Roman Catholic Church leaders coerced him into making, not to teach that the earth moves around the sun, he was threatened with torture, forced to recant humiliatingly, and imprisoned.[5]

The outcome of this controversy embarrassed the Church. For example, she had to cope with such questions as, "Were Popes Paul V and Urban VIII infallible, when they condemned Galileo for holding true scientific theory?"[6] and "does not the Galileo case prove your Church's enmity to science, and did not his condemnation hinder the progress of scientific research?" Conway in answering stated, "Pope Paul V and Urban VIII together with the Cardinals of the Index (1616), who rendered their judgements in the Popes' names were mistaken about the truth of the Copernican theory." He also said, "It retarded for a time the special researches that were one day to make the Copernican theory morally certain."

Why did theologians get into such an awkward spot over a question that seems so religiously insignificant today? It was because they believed that they were defending the truth of the Bible and therefore the ideological structure of Christianity. The Scriptures say in Joshua 10:13 "And the sun stood still . . . So the sun stood still in the midst of heaven, and hasten not to go down about a whole day." Interpreting this literally, the theologians had concluded that the Bible says that the sun moves in relation to the earth, ordinarily. Therefore, they rejected the theory that it is the earth that moves; they declared it to be against the revelations of God.[8]

But the Copernican theory gathered so much evidence from mathematical reasoning and observation that even the church leaders finally accepted it. Did they then say, "Since the supposedly inspired scriptures are proven wrong, we must admit that they are not the Word of God, and that, therefore, Christianity is false"? No. They said, as they now do, "In that case, the Cardinals would allow us to interpret the words of Joshua X. as metaphorical expressions."[9]

The question arises why the theologians did not admit this possible interpretation in the first place, sparing Galileo, the others it retarded from making scientific researches, and the Church itself the resulting embarrassment? Apparently they had to learn by experience the disadvantages of reliance on strictly literal interpretations of scripture when confronted by scientific theory.

Whatever caused this mistake, it was not the only instance of conflict between theologians and scientists that tarnished the truth of that church. There is the list as delineated by White.

Draper summarized well the points at issue between theologians and scientists in medieval times and their outcomes, demanding:

> When a science is thus commanded to surrender her intellectual convictions, may she not ask the ecclesiastic to remember the past? The contest respecting the figure of the earth, and the location of heaven and hell, ended adversely to him. He affirmed that the sky is a firmament, the floor of heaven, through which repeatedly persons have been seen to ascend. With the globular form demonstrated beyond any possibility of contradiction by astronomical facts, and by the voyage of Magellan's ship, he then maintained that it is the central body of the universe, all others being in subordination to it, and it the grand object of God's regard. Forced from this position, he next affirmed that it is motionless, the sun and the stars actually revolving, as they apparently do, around it. The invention of the telescope proved that here again he was in error. Then he maintained that all motions show God's intervention, though the <u>Principia</u> of Newton demonstrated that they are due to irresistible law.

Draper made a pointed challenge:

> Is it at all surprising that the number of those who hold the opinions of the Church in light esteem should so rapidly increase? How can that be received as a trustworthy guide in the invisible, which falls into so many errors in the visible? How can that give confidence in the moral, the spiritual, which has so signally failed in the physical?[10]

A grave aspect of the theology-science controversy was the danger that when theologians allow themselves to proclaim something as if official doctrine that turns out to be untrue, the religion that they were supposed to be defending becomes, instead, discredited.

MAJOR POINTS OF CONTEST IN RECENT TIMES

Alfred North Whitehead moved from the past to more recent conflicts stating, "In the seventeenth century the doctrine of the motion of the earth was condemned by a Catholic tribunal. A hundred years ago the extension of time demanded by geological science distressed religious people, Protestant and Catholic. And today the doctrine of evolution is an equal stumbling block." He thus identified the two major recent areas of misunderstanding, the antiquity of the earth and the theory of evolution.[11]

Literature on the subject from Protestant, Catholic, and Mormon sources showed general agreement which matters were at issue.

SCHOLARLY PROTESTANT VIEWS

H. H. Lane, once a Professor of Zoology at University of Kansas, son of a minister, and thirty years a very active member of an evangelical Protestant body, dealt with the antiquity of the earth, of man, and the doctrine of evolution in his work.[12]

Other Protestants who have written books of some prominence in the area are J. Arthur Thomson, Late Professor of Natural History, University of Aberdeen, and lecturer at Union Theological Seminary[13]; Alexander Winchell [14]; W. A. Whitehouse, reader in Divinity, University of Durham[15]; C. E. dem Sajous, Professor of Endocrinology, University of Pennsylvania[16]; and James Y. Simpson, Professor of Natural Science, New College, Edinburgh, and lecturer at Union Theological Seminary.[17] Each reconciled religion with evolution and the age of the earth.

There was another Protestant viewpoint typified by Harmony of Science and Scripture by Harry Rimmer. He tried to show that science has in some respects substantiated the Bible. He introduced subject matter that was not dealt with by the modernists cited above, such as the flood of Noah, and Jonah and the Whale.[18]

The Catholic writer Conway took up the questions of the antiquity of man, the universality of the flood, the miracle of Joshua, Jonah, and evolution.[19] Jesuit author Scott wrestled with the problems of evolution and Darwinism.[20]

The writings and speeches of leading Latter-day Saints recognized similar issues. Brigham Young accepted an "aged" earth.[21] Dr. James E. Talmage wrote favoring evolution and the "aged" earth.[22] Dr. John A. Widtsoe discussed the flood, Joshua and the sun, interpreting with the spirit of truth, affirmed the great age of the earth, and acknowledged the God-directed evolution.[23] Joseph Fielding Smith worked at greater length on evolution, the antiquity of man on the earth, the age of the earth, and the flood, all viewed by him with historically perilous literalism. [24]

SOME CAUSES OF THE CONFLICTS

White criticized Draper for regarding "the struggle as one between Science and Religion," and said "I believed then and am convinced now, that it was a struggle between Science and Dogmatic theology."[25] It may bring out the true nature of the conflict even better to speak of it as between theologians and scientists, not between abstract systems of knowledge.

Draper's text placed his views closer to White's and highlighted that the conflict was not between science and all religion or religions. He exempted the Greek Orthodox Church from putting itself in opposition to the advancement of knowledge.[26] Furthermore, while he recognized that some Protestants, past and present (1896), had also opposed science, he believed that there was no irreconcilable gulf between Protestantism and science. He observed that the doctrine of the right of individual interpretation favored science.[27] He noted the scientific advances of Moslems at one period. His book, therefore, was a history of the conflict between Roman Catholic theologians and science. The major cause of conflict in the past, as seen by Draper, was "a power which kept Europe in a stagnant condition for many centuries, ferociously suppressing by the stake and the sword every attempt at progress."[28]

END OF WORLD BELIEVED AT HAND

Simpson cited a pathetic cause of ecclesiastical indifference, if not antagonism, to science. He said, "To those under a firm but mistaken impression that the end of the world and the last Judgment were imminent, it seemed sheer waste of time to occupy themselves with the attempts of the human mind to understand that world."[29] But this cause later lost significance as the obvious continuance of the world exposed the theological mistake. (This "end of the world" idea also came as A.D. 1000 approached and is seen in some Christians as A.D. 2000 looms.)

White cited the cause of conflict in the noted case of Galileo. He wrote:

> Herein was one of the greatest pieces of ill fortune that has ever befallen the older Church. Had Pope Urban been broad-minded and tolerant like Benedict XIV, or had he been taught moderation by adversity like Pius VII, or had he possessed the large scholarly qualities of Leo XIII, now reigning, the vast scandal of the Galileo case would never have burdened the Church.[30]

Such a statement showed that a major cause of a conflict was the lack of broad important qualities of one Pope, instead of the Church as a whole.

LEADERS PUT CHURCH IN UNTENABLE POSITION

White showed that individual ecclesiastics continued to put their church in an untenable position in another instance:

> Even after the beginning of the 18th century--long after the demonstrations of Sir Isaac Newton--Bousset, the great Bishop of Meaux, the foremost theologian that France has ever produced, declared it (the Copernican theory) contrary to scriptures.[31]

Lane showed that another element in the papal mistake in the Galileo case and on the Copernican theory was that at the time there were rival scientific theories and that the papacy backed the wrong one.[32] The significant question is: Why did it back any? It now knows that it didn't have to back either then.

Fortunately, the Catholic Church has apparently learned the lesson. Conway stated:

> The Galileo case was providential, because it taught churchmen the folly of too hasty a resort to ecclesiastical censures. The theologians of the day who urged the Holy See to condemn Galileo, were led by a high motive--to defend, as they thought, a truth of divine revelation. They were right in holding

> that as a general law Scriptural texts are to be interpreted in their literal sense; they were wrong in forgetting the wise teaching of both St. Augustine and St. Thomas, that in describing the phenomena of nature, the Bible speaks according to appearances.[33]

While some older issues seemed to have been resolved, there were other underlying causes of conflict that remained. Simpson mentioned "the absolute and unquestioned authority of the Old Testament scriptures in relation to all questions of cosmology, geography, anthropology, and history. . . . This rigidity of attitude was the main element provoking the inevitable struggle during the succeeding centuries."[34]

White observed that some conflicts came from attempts to interpret scriptures literally.[35] Crowther quoted a letter which Galileo wrote to a duchess, which stated that "the Grand Duchess had spoken well when she said the Holy Scriptures could not err . . . that the decrees therein contained are absolutely inviolable . . . Though Scripture cannot err, its expounders and interpreters are liable to err in many ways. The most grave errors arise from literal interpretation. If this is accepted, God would have . . . forgetfulness and lack of foresight."[36]

These were some kinds of mistakes theologians have made. But as Whitehead warned, these ideas will be "in a wrong perspective if we think that in these controversies religion was always wrong, and that science was always right. The true facts of the case are very much complex, and refuse to be summarized in these simple terms." He further explained, "science is even more changeable than theology. No man of science could subscribe without qualification to Galileo's beliefs, or to Newton's beliefs, or to all his own scientific beliefs of ten years ago."[37] Whitehead was one of the great objective philosophers of our time.

George Bernard Shaw was a similar pen. He wrote:

> Both our science and our religion are gravely wrong; but they are not all wrong; and it is our urgent business to purge them of their errors and get them both as right as possible. If we could get them entirely right the contradictions between them would disappear; we should have a religious science and a scientific religion in a single synthesis.[38]

On this broad cause of conflict there was impressive unanimity; from Whitehead to Shaw and then to the Catholic, Conway, who agreed in these words:

> The opposition between science and faith, that we hear about so much today, is only apparent. It originates either in the errors of scientists who put forth unprovable hypotheses as undoubted facts, or in the mistakes of theologians who teach their private false opinions as Gospel truths.[39]

A Latter-day Saint writer, John Henry Evans, said:

> If the Mormon prophet (Joseph Smith) were living today, he would no doubt say that

> the conflict between religion and science is not conflict between the truth in science, but rather a clash between the teachings of science and the unwarranted dogmas of men. Man-made religion had been placed in juxtaposition with man-made science. If the truth in religion and the truth in science were placed side by side, there would be no disharmony at all.[40]

So while Whitehead warned not to let the "mistakes" of one side blind us to the "mistakes" of the other, and while Shaw declared both religion and science partly wrong, the Catholic and the Latter-day Saint agreed that true religion and true science harmonized. Some also implied that if science did not conform, science was wrongfully causing the conflict. For example, President Joseph F. Smith, once head of the Mormon Church stated the issue this way: "so-called 'science' has changed from age to age in its deductions . . . views as to the lesser (science) should conform to the positive statements of the greater (the Church.)"[41]

President Brigham Young viewed the cause of conflict from slightly different angle, and maintained in a sermon that it sometimes arose because "religious teachers of the people advanced many ideas and notions for truth which are in opposition to and contradict facts demonstrated by science, and which are generally understood." Here it was the religious teachers, not the scientists, who were warned to conform to truth.[42]

A Nobel prize winning scientist, the late Dr. Robert Millikan, added an idea, namely, that science was sometimes misrepresented, a cause that he did not limit to scientists themselves. He said:

> The responsibility (for the conflict) is a divided one, for science is just as often misrepresented as is religion by men of little vision, of no appreciation of its limitations, and of imperfect comprehension of the real role that it plays in human life--by men who lose sight of spiritual values and therefore, exert an influence upon youth that is unsettling, irreligious, and sometimes immoral.[43]

There was a last question on the causes of conflict. Have there been cases where mistaken scientists criticized religion concerning a scientific matter on which the scientists were later proven wrong? We did not find any such instance from any of the writers cited in this study, except one by George Bernard Shaw. He believed certain scientists were guilty of teachings that were damaging nonsense. He commented:

> When I was young, and Darwinism in its first vogue, scientists were fond of saying that all the books in the British Museum library could have been written by Natural Selection without human consciousness, and would have been word for word the same. This sample of the blazing nonsense of which secularists and scientists are capable is not now even amusing.[44]

Shaw rejecting the theory of creation by chance of atheist Natural Selectionists doesn't necessarily establish that they were wrong. However, the work of Professor

Charles Eugene Guye,[45] apparently mathematically showed the extreme improbability of their being correct. It appeared that this was an instance of some scientists being mistaken and injuring faith by their mistake. Even so, no evidence appeared of their persecuting religion by coercion as theologians had sometimes done to scientists.

RECENT EFFORTS TO RESOLVE SOME ISSUES BY THEOLOGIANS AND SCIENTISTS

Theologians with their positions questioned by science might have reacted by condemning the works of science. But research showed no present mainline faith wanted the position of officially attacking science.

In the face of past persecution of scientists, Conway quoted the Vatican Council as follows: "The Church, therefore, far from hindering the pursuit of the arts and sciences, fosters and promotes them in many ways . . . Nor does she prevent sciences, each in its own sphere, from making use of their own principles and methods."[46] Walsh added "As a matter of history, the Popes were as liberal patrons of science as of art."[47] The Jesuit Priest Scott seemed more enthusiastic about science and said, "It is man's greatest natural achievement and the promise of his greatest earthly advancement."[48]

As for the Protestants, all their authorities quoted above--Lane, Thomson, Winchell, Whitehouse, Sajous, and Rimmer--praised science with little or no qualification.

MORMON LEADERS PRO-SCIENCE

For the Latter-day Saints, President Brigham Young not only praised science but put his powerful influence behind its promotion in Utah. He affirmed its value in several sermons and said specifically, "We want every branch of science taught in this place that is taught in the world."[49]

Dr. John A. Widtsoe, who was a member of the Quorum of the Twelve, and himself a scientist, affirmed that, "The Church . . . looks with full favor upon the attempts of men to search out the facts and laws of nature. It believes that men of science, seekers after truth, are often assisted by the Spirit of the Lord in such researches." He added, "the vast body of scientific facts has been so carefully garnered that it may in the main be accepted without question."[50] (It may be significant that in the governing body of the Latter-day Saints Church there have also been two other recognized men of science, Dr. James E. Talmage and Dr. Joseph R. Merrill.)

President Joseph Fielding Smith stated:

> **Science has rendered incalculable service to society; her achievements are innumerable--and the hypotheses of scientists should be carefully examined and their argument fairly weighed.**[51]

By thus at least verbally accepting science, the theologians of these faiths have believed it worthwhile to show that their systems were not contradicted by science, when any doubt arose. (Except Smith who readily rejected science when it did not accord with his view of scriptures.)

When, for example, the scriptures seemed to say there was in Noah's day a universal flood that covered all the high hills and mountains, and scientists found evidence for such a universal flood lacking, what did theologians say?

Rimmer quoted Professor Leonard Wooley to the effect that evidences of a flood of "unexampled magnitude" have been found in the Mesopotamian Valley. It only seemed universal from the point of view of the Genesis writer.[52]

Conway said, "Catholics today do not believe in the geographical universality of the deluge, although they believe that it destroyed the whole human race."[53] Elsewhere he cited "the wise teaching of both St. Augustine and St. Thomas, that in describing the phenomena of nature, the Bible speaks according to appearances."[54] Catholics could apparently accept the explanation that the flood only appeared to be universal.

Dr. John A. Widtsoe explained, "The details in the story of the flood are undoubtedly drawn from the experiences of the writer."[55] He also quoted Professor Leonard Wooley regarding the evidence of great floods in Mesopotamia. But for some Latter-day Saints the flood had to be large enough to move Noah from one continent to another.[56] To some it also had to be universal enough that the whole earth was wet at once. "Though the whole of the earth was covered with water," he said, "the depth was immaterial."[57] This apparently avoided the main objections scientists made.

For Bible interpretation, Elder Widtsoe quoted President Brigham Young as follows: "Do you read the scriptures, my brethren and sisters, as though you were writing them a thousand, two thousand, five thousand years ago? Do you read them as though you stood in the place of the men who wrote them?" And Elder Widtsoe added, "This is our guide. The scriptures must be read intelligently."[58]

Yet, research revealed nothing that established this as an official Latter-day Saint Church pronouncement on the flood.

Another point of view that was current among Latter-day Saints to some extent was represented by President Joseph Fielding Smith. He held out for a universal flood and maintained that the mountains were not as high in the days of Noah. President Smith said:

> We know from the dynamic force of water a flood of such proportions could not occur without making great changes in the surface of the earth.[59] He added, ". . . so that many of the great geological conditions ascribed by geologists to time millions of years ago could have taken place suddenly, and evidently did."[60]

He was apparently arguing that some great geologic formations that were obviously once under water but are now high and dry were laid down by the flood of Noah and not gradually in the seas of millions of years ago. As with Dr. Widtsoe's works, this, too, was not the official position of the Church. This study did not reveal the existence of any such official church position on these matters of science and religion. It is just as well, because as we shall see in Chapter VI, Mormon geologists who are very strong believers and active in the Church see this "taken place suddenly" as unbelievable.

AGE OF THE EARTH CONTROVERSY

Another issue that existed in the earlier history and has persisted into the present concerns the age of the earth. A very literal interpretation of Genesis 1 showed that the Lord made the earth in six days. Scientific evidence did not support such a view. What explanations did the theologians give?

The Protestant group who were quoted in this study paid comparatively little attention to the question of the age of the earth, and seemed for the most part to consider it settled by the explanation that the "days" were obviously not meant by the writer of Genesis to mean anything but "indefinite periods of time." They accepted the great antiquity of the earth. Lane objected to the attempts by some to correlate the six "days" with the geologic periods. He pointed out that geologists do not discern six periods and that the order of appearance of plants and animals in Genesis does not accord with geology. So to Lane this part of Genesis is to be interpreted figuratively.[61]

Two questions put to Conway were: "Is the history of creation in the first chapters of Genesis scientific history? Are Catholics bound to believe that the world was created in six days of twenty-four hours each?" He replied, "No, we answer to both questions. A careful examination of the account of creation in Genesis shows that it is given in an almost poetical form, expressed in popular, not scientific, language,"[62] He listed five explanations that have been made by scholars, and said that Catholics may adopt any these theories that do not deny the historicity of the first three chapters of Genesis.[63]

Conway then quoted from St. Augustine what he called "some very sensible words of advice, when discussing this very question," as follows:

> In things that are obscure and remote from sight, if we read anything even in Scriptures which, with safety to our faith, can bear different meanings, let us not by precipitate assertion so throw ourselves into any one interpretation, as to be ruined in case a fuller investigation of the truth should overthrow our view. This would be to fight, not for the meaning of Holy Scripture, but for our own meaning.[64]

FACTS OF GEOLOGISTS TO STAND

President Brigham Young suggested to the Latter-day Saints that he did not oppose the explanations of the geologists that the earth existed for "thousands and millions" of years and continued, "In these respects we differ from the Christian world, for our religion will not clash with or contradict the facts of science in any particular." Then he added, "How long it (the earth) has been organized is not for me to say. . . ."[65]

Dr. James E. Talmage, an Apostle of the Latter-day Saints Church, approved in one of his early works (1888) a statement by Professor Winchell to the effect that fossil footprints "have been preserved in all their perfection for thousands of ages."[66]

Later in a tabernacle address (1931) Talmage said:

> Any questions when that beginning was are largely futile because unanswerable. . . . Years are as inadequate in any attempted survey of the stages of earth development as are miles to the astronomer who would span the distances of interstellar space. He speaks in terms of light years.[67]

Neither President Young nor Dr. Talmage in references cited went on to reconcile their views with Genesis. It was possible that they did not consider this imperative, for two reasons. One was that the Latter-day Saint Church, while it revered the Bible, was not committed to its inerrancy. President J. Reuben Clark in a recent book quoted Joseph Smith, Jr. as having said:

> I believe the Bible as it read when it came from the pen of the original writers.

> Ignorant translators, careless transcribers, or designing and corrupt priests have committed many errors.[68]

The second reason was that the Latter-day Saints have their own accounts of the creation in The Pearl of Great Price. In one account the word "day" was not used at all but was replaced by the word "time." Therefore, Latter-day Saints did not need to be committed to creation in twenty-four hour "days."[69]

Dr. Widtsoe noted that there were "at least three prevailing answers among faithful Bible-believing Latter-day Saints" to the question "how old is the earth?"[70]

The first group subscribed to literal Genesis and the "Book of Moses" in the Pearl of Great Price. The second held that each day of creation was really one thousand years, since the Apostle Peter said (in a far distant part of the Bible and a totally different context), "one day is with the Lord as a thousand years."[71]

The third group "believe that the creation of the earth extended over immensely long periods of time." Widtsoe subscribed to the latter, agreeing with President Brigham Young and Dr. Talmage, He said, "Recent discoveries in the field of radioactivity have furnished a 'time-clock' which compels the belief that the earth is very old, far beyond the former, accepted beliefs."[72] He concluded that "every person must decide for himself, on the basis of the evidence produced, which of these three opinions as to the age of the earth, before Adam, seems most reasonable to him."[73]

President Joseph Fielding Smith in his chapter "The Earth's Temporal Existence" championed the second position, that each day of creation was a thousand years.[74] President Smith's conclusion was, quoted by his son-in-law, Elder Bruce McConkie, "We can hardly be justified in trying to harmonize the days of creation with the extended periods of millions of years according to the reckoning of the so called scientists."[75]

Chapter VI of this book goes into the views of many "Strong" Believer Mormon scientists, among others of Elder McConkie's "so called scientists", on the age of the earth.

MAIN QUESTION TODAY IS EVOLUTION

The question today, however, as Whitehead remarked, was the issue of evolution and the origin of man.[76] All the Protestants quoted previously dealt at length with the theory of evolution. None of them denied evolution as a fact. Lane titled his third chapter "The Fact of Evolution." He said, "Evolution is the only satisfactory answer to the question raised by these phenomena."[77] He said further that the evidence for man having evolved was the same type as for the other species. Lane, also being an active lay member in an evangelical Protestant body, was a Professor of Zoology.

The Protestant writers quoted above affirmed that upward evolution from simpler to more complex forms of living things was the process which scientific research showed was the one God used to produce man's mortal body.[78]

In harmonizing Christianity and evolution, the Jesuit priest Martin J. Scott[79] essentially agreed with the Protestant writers as summarized above. Still, he did not go as far as to say that evolution is a fact. Yet he did not reject it as a working theory. Like the Protestants and Shaw he did bluntly and explicitly reject evolution by chance "Darwinism." He quoted a list of noted (and non-Catholic) scientists who have rejected "Darwinism." After the list he commented, "But all these men are upholders of evolution as a scientific theory." He explained that "Darwinism is not evolution." Then he clearly stated the Christian position:

> If materialistic evolution were true, man would be merely a resultant of material forces,

> obliged to act on material impulses, and consequently actuated by forces over which he had no control, thus making him a sort of animal automaton, without any moral responsibility. . . . No soul, no conscience, no judgment, no hereafter! . . . . Christianity is true. Darwinism is false.[80]

Conway, answering the question "may a Catholic believe in evolution?" said, "As the Church has made no pronouncement upon evolution, Catholics are perfectly free to accept evolution."[81] He added, "It is good to remember that evolution is not a proved fact, despite the assertions of many pseudoscientists."[82] Conway called attention to a Catholic position that "The Bible is not a textbook of science, and therefore, cannot be rightly quoted either for or against evolution." Further on he said, "Evolution is not set at variance with the theistic or Christian theory of life."[83] And he made this explanation:

> Man is composed of body and soul. His soul cannot owe its origin to evolution, for it is a simple, spiritual being . . . It can therefore come into existence only by way of creation. His body may have been evolved from an existing animal organism . . . [84]

Conway concluded by saying, "While not intrinsically impossible, this theory, although never condemned by any of the Roman Congregations, seems contrary to the general mind of the Church."[85] Note that he did not give any approval at all to "Darwinian" evolution.

Talmage, after he discussed evolution as shown by geology, said, "In due course came the crowning work of this creative sequence, the advent of man!"[86] Talmage left the way open for belief in evolution.

Dealing with the question, "To what extent should the doctrine of evolution be accepted?", Widtsoe said, "The answer to the above question depends on the meaning assigned to the word evolution."[87] If it is not interpreted as meaning "origination by chance" or meaning that God had only one method of operation in creation, then he said, "The law of evolution or change may be accepted fully."[88] Widtsoe said of Latter-day Saints, "They do not deny that an evolutionary process, a reflection of the gospel law of progression may be one of the methods of the Lord's labor in the universe." He cautioned, however, that "The theory of evolution does not explain the eternal man."[89] That is, he seemed to leave the way open to explain the creation of species, or even man's mortal body, by evolution, but not his eternal soul. Emphatically setting apart the evolution that might be acceptable from that which could not be, he said, "Any theory that leaves out God as a personal, purposeful Being, and accepts chance as a first cause, cannot be accepted by Latter-day Saints."[90]

ALL EVOLUTION DEPLORED BY MORMON ELDER

Elder Joseph Fielding Smith wrote against "evolution." He said that the teachings of "organic evolutionists have gained ascendancy in the scientific world."[91] He called theirs the "most pernicious doctrine ever entering the mind of man: the theory that man evolved from lower forms of life."[92] He said it proclaims no judgments after death--encourages gratification of every urge, makes "mercy a fallacy . . . and "denies his divine origin as a child of God."[93] He disliked "scientific theories which deny that man is the offspring of God and that when we pray to him as our father our words are meaningless and that man is the offspring of some worm."

His views were summarized in a chapter subheading of a compilation of his works by his son-in-law which reads, "Evolution and Religion Cannot Be Harmonized."[94]

Elder McConkie wrote that President Smith also distinguished between the "God-directed" and the "chance produced" ideas and left little doubt about his position, stating:

> It is true that the school of evolutionists is divided into the two great classes, the Theistic and the Atheistic branches. But the Theistic evolutionist is a weak-kneed and unbelieving religionist, who is constantly apologizing for the miracles of the scriptures, and who does not believe in the divine mission of Jesus Christ.
>
> Again I repeat, no man can consistently accept the doctrine of the evolutionist and also believe in the divine mission of our redeemer. The two thoughts are in absolute conflict.[95]

Since both President Smith and Elder McConkie were members of the Quorum of the Twelve Apostles of the Latter-day Saint Church, their opinions no doubt guided some Mormons, although not writing officially for the Church.

Chapter VI shows that a majority of Mormon scientists who are "Strong" or "Very Strong" Believers in Christ as Savior and Joseph Smith, Jr. as Prophet also believe that evolution was probably God's method of creating the species. How many Mormon scientists Elder McConkie surveyed, and by what methods, to arrive at his negative labelling of many scientist believers in the quotation above, is not stated in his book.

As found by our survey of Utah scientists through the reliable methods the present book describes, there are several hundred Mormon scientists with very strong testimonies who embody refutations of the notion that "The two thoughts are in absolute conflict".

So, to the ranks of notable Roman Catholic prelates in history who, as we have seen in this Chapter, made pontifical pronouncements which were untrue when dealing with science, Mormonism contributed two of its own who took untenable positions on the age of the earth and evolution.

Theirs differed from some Catholic mistakes in that they did not have any genuine stamp of Church doctrine. (They were evidence of freedom of expression in Mormondom.) But they were not given <u>ex cathedra</u>, to use a Catholic term for an idea of "official and binding" which can also be usefully applied to teachings from Mormon sources.

At any rate, Mormonism still had some scientifically sound statements (also not at present official doctrine) from President Brigham Young and Elders Widtsoe, Talmage, and Merrill of the Twelve. It also has many living scientist High Priests, Bishops, and local Presidents who represent a Mormon tradition of careful regard for truth, even as careful as scientific method. Chapters following will examine facts about Mormonism and scientists more fully.

SUMMARY

This chapter reviewed briefly the contest between theologians and scientists in the past. Causes were analyzed. The chapter concluded with a review of recent efforts to resolve some issues between scientists and theologians.

A. The major points of contest between theologians and scientists in medieval and renaissance times, absurd as they seem now, were the following:

1. Is the earth round or flat?
2. Are there antipodes and are they populated?
3. Does the sun go around the earth or vice versa?
4. Are comets supernatural agents or natural events?
5. Are storms natural forces or supernatural interventions?
6. Is disease a visitation for religious wickedness?
7. Is dissection of the human body disapproved by God?
8. What is the nature of the soul and mind of man?
9. Is the earth thousands, or billions, of years old?
10. What was the flood of Noah?
11. How long has man in his present form been on earth?
12. How can we find truth? Are authority and Spirit supreme?
13. How does law (Newtonian, etc.) in the universe relate to God?

B. Some important consequences of the early debates were:

1. That the Church was embarrassed by mistaken interpretations of Scriptures by her leaders.
2. That the Church learned some disadvantages of reliance on literal interpretation of Scriptures when confronted by science.

C. Major points of contest in recent times were as follows:

1. The antiquity of the earth.
2. The evolution of the species.

Some minor points of contest recently were these:

1. The nature of the flood of Noah.
2. The miracles of Joshua and Jonah.
3. The meaning of the confusion of tongues at Babel.

D. Some causes of the conflicts were as follows:

1. Certain theologians were contending with some scientists; the contests were not between religion and science, per se.
2. The past conflicts were mainly between Roman Catholic theologians and scientists. More recently two Mormon theologians came to share this questionable distinction.
3. Literal interpretations of the Bible caused some ecclesiastics to attach their theology to erroneous theories.
4. Both scientists and theologians have at times been in error, but mostly the former.

5. Instances of scientists criticizing religion on an issue where some scientists were later shown to be wrong are scarce but not totally lacking.

6. Instances of scientists persecuting theologians were apparently nonexistent.

7. There were several instances of theologians persecuting scientists where the theologians were later proved to be wrong.

E. Research on recent efforts to resolve some issues between theologians and scientists showed the following:

1. No present major faith was found officially attacking the value of science; all appeared to praise it.

2. Most writers who harmonize religion and science do so by interpreting the Bible with reason, not as infallible nor always meant to be taken literally. This was true of Protestants, Catholics, and Latter-day Saints.

3. This study did not discover any official Latter-day Saint Church position on the issues of the age of the earth, evolution, or the flood.

Members were free to choose and believe as they deemed best, as long as "God's hand" was acknowledged.

CHAPTER III

THE SEARCH FOR A SCIENCE SUPPORTIVE RELIGION: A LOOK AT CATHOLICISM

We have seen the vital nature of controversy between religion and science. We followed this with a review of the history of the conflict. We saw the high value of a science supportive religion, if there were one. Let us look first at the Christian church of history.

After what we have seen of the religion-science controversy, the following by an official Catholic writer, Martin J. Scott, may seem incredible, for a start into the subject: "For the past two thousand years the Catholic Church has been the best supporter of science..... there is no truer friend of true science than Catholic Church."[1]

This is a quite different picture than one gets from Albert Einstein, who wrote, "the churches have always fought against science and have persecuted its supporters".[2] Is Scott just rationalizing as an apologist of the Catholic Church? Or was Einstein carelessly making a statement out of his field? Are the scholars White, Draper, and Simpson only special pleaders in their books on the controversy of the Catholic Church with science, or are they right that Catholicism has been an enemy of science?

ARE QUOTES ENOUGH?: THEY CAN BE PRO OR CON

Along with George Bernard Shaw, the Irish intellect, we are, say, seeking a scientific religion. Is Catholicism that? Trying to answer this question with quotations pro and con, judging from the contradictory statements we have here from Scott and Einstein, will not get us enough closer to the truth!

If even the Catholic Church can deny that it has been an enemy of science, if even she can claim to be its "best supporter", then we might well wonder if there is any church that cannot field a claim to being "scientific".

When Shaw asserts that our religion is "gravely wrong" and needs to be purged of its errors, he not only explicitly included in the term "our religion" the Church of England but also the Roman Catholic. Again we are involved with opinions, and against Shaw, to pick one of his contemporaries in literature, we could cite G. K. Chesterton, a fine writer and able Catholic defender. How, then, can we settle this issue?

We shall not settle it, of course, regarding Catholicism in this book. The purpose of introducing the question at all is to illustrate the difficulty of getting at such problems through appeals to partisan opinion, to mere claims, even if the partisans are highly intelligent men.

But if we cannot work fruitfully on such problems by quoting intellectuals, how can we identify a science supportive religion? The essence of this book, contained in Chapters IV and V, is a quantitative method coupled with questions that have to do with production and reality rather than with image building. Let us start by applying the approach of scholarly study to the Catholic claim as a supporter of science.

THE MOST ENLIGHTENED CATHOLICISM: AMERICAN?

Let us assume that the Roman Catholic Church in America today represents that institution in its most enlightened time and place (which it may or may not be). Then one of the questions we would ask is this: What are the facts about Catholic support of science in America today? Now we are probing for something that may reveal more than the opinions of partisans. We may not only get facts but get them in some meaningful quantities as well. What we are proposing is that we get a little scientific about finding out who's scientific.

Raising exactly the question we suggest is Catholic scientist Julian Pleasants of Notre Dame. "What", he asks, "is the actual relationship between American Catholics and natural science? Is it a happy marriage, a divorce, or a simple case of nonsupport?"

Professor Pleasants has sought the facts in his own institution, and he writes that the statistics indicate "nonsupport". Roman Catholic colleges, he finds, turn out relatively few scientists and spend less than their share on scientific research: They apply for far less than their share of government money earmarked for science; fellowship funds go begging for applicants from Catholic schools.

The cause of this, says this Catholic (and now we are somewhat back to opinions, but at least, being a Catholic with this type of testimony, he is an "adverse witness" and hence more credible than, say, Martin J. Scott, the Jesuit propagandist), the cause of this "nonsupport" is that "prevailing Catholic philosophy is almost sheer formalism, obedience to certain arbitrary prescriptions for the sake of an arbitrary reward......Where the formulas do not apply, the matter is of no real significance, Nothing new need be added. Formalism does not forbid creative activity -- it just takes the heart out of it."[3]

Another Catholic Professor of Notre Dame, J.A. Reyniers, gives us this picture:

> On the basis of productive scholarship we have no prominent universities. Among the schools which have reached the university status, we are at the bottom of the list of published research, just as our medical schools are at the bottom of medical ratings lists. The over-all picture is still blacker....There is only one-fourth as much productive scholarship coming from Catholics as our numbers warrant.... Neither in its quantity nor its quality is there the slightest room for complacency about Catholic scholarship.[4]

Not only Catholics have documented the above. Dr. Kenneth Hardy, in a Science article "Social Origins of American Scientists and Scholars", concluded, "Roman Catholics are extremely low producers of scientists and scholars, but fundamentalistic and traditional Protestant faiths are also low producers."[5]

MORMON CHURCH 25 FIVE TIMES MORE PRODUCTIVE OF EMINENT SCIENTISTS THAN CATHOLIC CHURCH

The following are not known to be Catholics, but the facts to which they refer could be verified by any other investigators as can most facts of science.

Dr. Harvey C. Lehman of Ohio University and Dr. Paul A. Witty of Northwestern Univ. made a study of scientific eminence and church membership. They reported that, "Among 1,189 outstanding scientists, three only report membership in the Catholic Church." (Four were members of the Mormon Church which had only about one twenty-fifth as many members in the United States as the Catholic Church.)

Lehman and Witty wrote, "The conspicuous dearth of scientists among Catholics suggest that the tenets of that church are not consonant with scientific endeavor.... Noticeable indeed is the close relationship between the liberality of the church and number of scientists which it shelters."[5] Knapp and Goodrich made a study of the undergraduate college origins of American scientists. They observed:

> Finally, we may note that this list does not include any institutions controlled by the Roman Catholic Church, though a variety of private institutions

> of Protestant affiliation as well as a number of state-supported institutions appear. A closer examination of the Catholic institutions reveals that, without exception, they lie among the least productive 10 per cent of all institutions and constitute a singularly unproductive sample.[6]

The list of which Knapp and Goodrich speak, of colleges most productive of scientists, did include the Utah State Agricultural College and the Brigham Young University, universities mainly attended by Mormons. The University of Utah, with less Mormon percentage, was less so.

We are not likely to conclude, from what we now know, that Catholicism is the science-harmony religion for which we may search. Nevertheless, we should keep in mind that the Catholic Church has changed materially in doctrine and rituals over centuries, and its present views in America, as we have sampled in the writings of Bertrand Conway, do not seem to throw it in any fixed contradiction with science, from her viewpoint.

CATHOLIC DOCTRINE NOT NOW ANTI-SCIENCE?

Although the Vatican Council (Sess. 111) has pronounced that the books of the Bible are "revelation without error" and "have God for their author, and as such were delivered to the Church herself", official Catholic writers are now permitted to say that "the sacred writers generally speak of scientific matters in more or less figurative language".

They now write, "We must remember that the Bible on its material side is a human document handed down to us in a human way. Therefore, we naturally expect find in each succeeding copy or version material variations, additions, omissions, and other errors with which critical scholarship has to grapple."[7]

Were I Catholic, I truly do not suppose that I would "naturally" expect to find "material variations, etc., and other errors" in books I had accepted on an authoritative Council's word as "revelation without error", having "God for their author, and as such ... delivered to the Church herself." But that is a contradiction I may leave gratefully to people who are of that faith to resolve. But if they have enough faith, by the ways of many great religions, they may not feel need to be guided by requirements of reason.

At last being free to interpret the language of the Bible figuratively, or stating that their doctrine is compatible with believing the text has suffered in translation and can be erroneous as they have it, contradictory as this is with earlier Catholic dogma, allows the Catholic now to develop a harmony with science that is somewhat satisfactory. There have been eminent Catholic scientists, even though the general Catholic picture from studies in modern America shows nonsupport of science. We have not found in Catholicism a notably scientific religion.

CHAPTER IV

TESTING THE CLAIM TO A SCIENCE SUPPORTIVE RELIGION

Sounding like the prominent Catholics writing of their church, Brigham Young, second president of The Church of Jesus Christ of Latter-day Saints, said of Mormonism, "Our religion will not clash with or contradict the facts of science in any particular."

With such a belief, President Young urged an assembly of Latter-day Saints, "It is your duty to study to know everything upon the face of the earth in addition to reading those books (the Scriptures)." Referring to his colonies in the West he declared, "We want every branch of science taught in this place that is taught in the world."[1]

In Chapter III we saw how hollow were the Catholic claims of support for science when we proceeded to look beyond the words of its propagandists to the insignificant numbers of scientists it produced, even in the United States.

Albert Einstein said, "The churches have always fought against science and have persecuted its supporters."[2] He certainly included the Roman Catholic Church. Was he indicating that Brigham Young must have been wrong? Did Einstein think this applied to the Mormon church? Likely he was speaking of churches before Mormonism existed, churches Mormonism was created to remedy.

Learned attacks on theologies, religions, or churches were almost always aimed at the established institutions of Europe and were not, of course, intended as views of Mormonism, which did not then exist. The original Gospel had not yet been restored.

Some writers highly critical of the great churches, but also aware of Mormonism, were, in fact, complimentary to Mormonism. Leo Tolstoy, the great Russian novelist, who wrote critically of the Russian Orthodox Church, was reported to have said of Mormonism, "If the people will follow its teachings, nothing can stop their progress; it will be limitless."[3] A Soviet journalist, Boris Polevoi, speaking in Utah during the Nixon detente period, said, "The Russian people know of the heroic Mormon Church, particularly through Tolstoy, as the great American religion". And George Bernard Shaw, who was critical of the Anglican and Roman Church, saw Mormonism as one of the hopeful parts of American history, "the most amazing episode in the Anglo-Saxon settlement of the world."[4]

Still it was possible for Joseph A., a Utah Mormon, a lawyer in Washington, D. C., to say to me of Mormonism, before he knew the facts of this chapter, "It casts a pall of intellectual darkness over the state of Utah." (He later retracted this idea.)

The Mormons have had better known and more published detractors, sounding like the historian Samuel Smucker, who wrote a comprehensive book on Mormonism up to 1858, and stated as his conclusion, far from the support of learning professed by Brigham Young, "In proportion as intelligence and knowledge crowd around her (Utah's) borders, it (Mormonism) will eventually languish and die."[5] Today trying to picture "intelligence and knowledge" crowding in from her bordering states, is amusing.

How, then, are we to decide whether Mormonism, in fact, was a religion supportive of, and harmonious with, science, as Brigham Young stated? Several noted Mormon scientists have written persuasive volumes dealing with science-religion issues, the most influential of which is probably Evidences and Reconciliations by Dr. John A. Widtsoe.[6] A person wanting a Mormon understanding of science and religion from a Church Apostle who was also a scientist would do well to read this book. A comprehensive more recent book by a noted Mormon scientist is Creation, by Zoologist Frank B. Salisbury.[7] A still more recent (1991) book Joseph Smith and the Creation is by the highly respected emeritus Chair of the Geology Department of the University of Utah, William Lee Stokes,[8] a strong believing and active Mormon who affirms that Mormonism has promoted science and is harmonious with it. Dr. Stokes has also written three other excellent books on science and Mormonism, stating their harmony. All of the above books rely on quotations from scriptures, from a few Mormon authorities, and some fine reasoning and science expertise to support the Mormon harmony with science hypothesis. But they are not based on studies of large numbers of Utah scientists, let alone statistically reliable studies.

A MORE RELIABLE WAY TO TEST HARMONY

What would happen if the harmony of Mormonism with science were subjected to quantitative tests, that is, scientific tests, instead of "quotation" methods? What if we start asking how many scientists, relatively, Mormondom produces? How many Mormon scientists are "Believers"? What are the solid facts? Do Mormon claims to support of science prove any better than Catholic in such things as vocational choice and universities producing scientists?

Mormons can name several outstanding men of science and technology who were Mormon "Believers", men such as Dr. Harvey Fletcher, the father of stereophonic sound, Philo Farnsworth, the inventor of television, Dr. James Chipman Fletcher, twice head of the National Aeronatics and Space Administration, or Dr. Henry Eyring, a world leader in theoretical chemistry.[9]

But what are the facts about the hundreds of Utah scientists? What kinds of Mormons are they? Do they think Mormonism and science can be harmonized? The notion of Mormon harmony with science could rise or fall with the true answers to these questions.

THE METHOD OF A NEW APPROACH

To put the harmony of Mormonism and science to a hard test under conditions of critical examination, I proposed a hypothesis for graduate research at a state university, as follows: Scientific minds can harmonize science with the Latter-day Saint religion. The committee of graduate school professors approved the study and judged the results. You may take assurance from this that the methods of the study were appropriate to test the hypothesis, that the data were reliable, and that the conclusions were valid. Details on the methods of the study and the nature of the questionnaires sent are in Appendix B. This chapter and the next two will present the findings and conclusions of the research.[10]

We tabulated the 50,000 scientists listed in the 1949 edition of American Men of Science by state of birth. Then questionnaires judged valid for the purposes of this type of study were sent to all scientists born in the state of Utah. The facts in this chapter and in the next two are tabulations of the results from these questionnaires. You could turn to Appendix C and read the questionnaire before continuing in the chapters.

THE STATES AS SCIENTIST PRODUCERS

The biographies of scientists nominated by scientific societies, industries, universities, and previously recognized scientists are contained in American Men and Women of Science.

These volumes, issued periodically, are standard reference books found in most public libraries. The recent volumes are also computer accessible through the DIALOG network on line, which made the current reference to 120,000 scientists feasible.

Tremendously important to the welfare of society is the production of such men and women of accomplishment as scientists. Our incomes, the quantity and quality of the food we eat, the potential of the medical profession to understand illness and guide prevention and healing, the excellence of our means of communication and transportation, the ability of the nation to defend itself and aid other nations, and the answers to our questing minds about many puzzles of the heavens, earth and its creatures are powerfully affected by how large a part of our population devotes itself to science.

States may pride themselves on production of goods, but the most valuable contribution to a nation that a state can make is the production of men and women who are productive themselves and who can educate others to be productive. Among the most important of these, without doubt, are the men and women of science.

There are people in the general population, of course, who have stereotypical views of a scientist: The odd genius, the atheist, and the laboratory denizen uncaring about people. Those harboring such inaccurate impressions are not likely readers of this book, but we would like to include a statement about scientists from a book published by the Mormon church's Deseret Book Company. Its author is a Very Strong Belief Mormon and one of the scientists surveyed in this study. In his book Creation, Dr. Frank Salisbury wrote the following:

> ....of the perhaps hundreds of scientists with whom I am personally acquainted throughout the world, I don't know a single one whom I would consider an evil person. Most of these people know nothing about the restored gospel, nor do they live its tenets in every respect. Most do not live the Word of Wisdom, and only a few attend church or take part in any of the rituals connected with religion. Of those whom I know personally, all seem to be fundamentally good persons. Typically, they exhibit an exemplary love for their families, and they are clearly on the side of human justice and world brotherhood. Often, after a few hours spent working or communicating socially with these persons, I have felt a thrill of brotherhood quite comparable to that experienced with my fellow members of the Church.[10]

In production rates of scientists how do the states compare? Three significant studies of scientists by states of birth, were made from various volumes of American Men of Science, covering an entire generation. The first was by Dr. Edward L. Thorndike of Columbia University using the 1938 volume. The results were astonishing to many. This was not only because of which state was highest but because of how far it was ahead of any other state. The top state was Utah. It was 32 percent beyond the second place state. It was 100% beyond the average state in production of scientists per million white population.[12] Please note that scientist production rates throughout this book are in proportion to white population. States with high populations, such as New York, produce far more actual numbers of scientists than do states with small population. Small population, however, is clearly not why some states are high in relative scientist production. For example, New York was near the top even on a per capita basis, while the low population state of Maine was near the bottom, in spite of being a Northern state.

CONSECUTIVE STUDIES ON UTAH'S LEAD

In Dr. Thorndike's study there were about 28,000 scientists listed. In 11 more years the number went to 50,000. As the number of scientists doubled, what happened

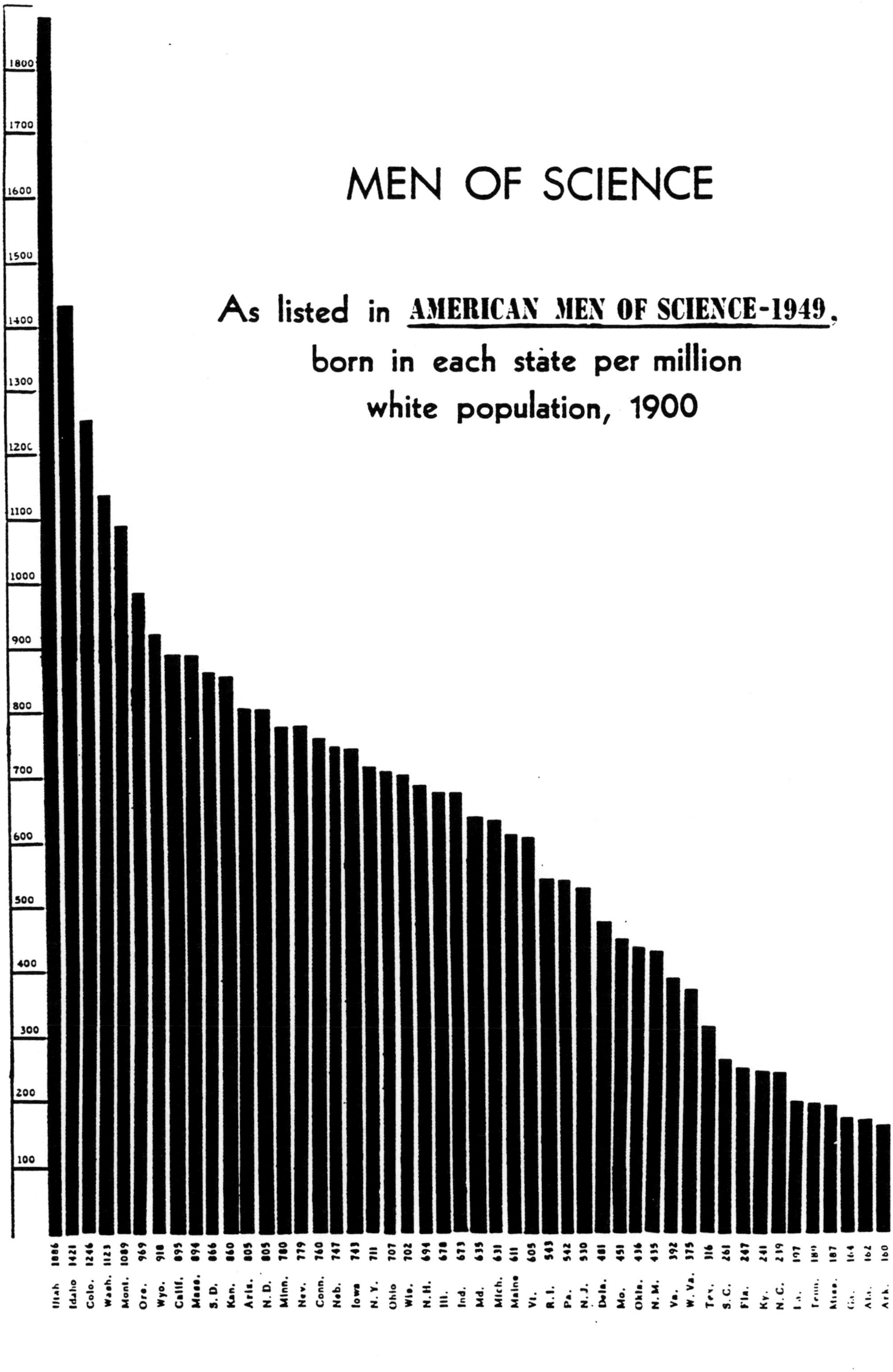
MEN OF SCIENCE
As listed in AMERICAN MEN OF SCIENCE-1949, born in each state per million white population, 1900
1800
1700
1600
1500
1400
1300
1200
1100
1000
900
800
700
600
500
400
300
200
100
1886 Utah
1421 Idaho
1246 Colo.
1123 Wash.
1089 Mont.
969 Ore.
918 Wyo.
895 Calif.
894 Mass.
866 S.D.
860 Kan.
805 Ariz.
805 N.D.
780 Minn.
779 Nev.
760 Conn.
747 Neb.
743 Iowa
711 N.Y.
707 Ohio
702 Wis.
694 N.H.
678 Ill.
673 Ind.
635 Md.
631 Mich.
611 Maine
605 Vt.
543 R.I.
542 Pa.
530 N.J.
481 Dela.
451 Mo.
436 Okla.
435 N.M.
392 Va.
375 W. Va.
316 Tex.
261 S.C.
247 Fla.
241 Ky.
219 N.C.
197
Tenn.
187 Miss.
162
160 Ark.

IOWA'S CONTRIBUTION TO AMERICAN MEN OF SCIENCE, SEVENTH EDITION

H. E. ZABEL

The latest directory has appeared during the war when many fields of science are marking time and when we have adopted a policy of interrupting the production of scientists. It thus becomes a landmark and an analysis of the data it presents has special significance.

In this directory Iowa has not only maintained her position among the leading states in production of scientists but has slightly improved this relative standing.

NATIVE SCIENTISTS

Iowa has 258 new native son scientists but has lost 76—56 by death. This makes a net gain of 182 for a total of 1292. In the previous edition, six states had more native scientists than Iowa, Indiana surpassing Iowa by a margin of 4. Now Iowa has surpassed Indiana for sixth position by the same margin.

We may follow a method suggested by Dr. E. L. Thorndike (Science July 1940) for computing the number of scientists per million of population. We then use the 1900 census and find Iowa has 580. Only three states outrank Iowa: Utah 1065, Colorado 657, Vermont 589. On this basis, from 1938 to 1944, Iowa has increased her number of scientists per million of population from 538 to 580. She has passed Connecticut and Massachusetts since the appearance of the 6th edition.

The total number of names in the present edition is 34,114, an increase of 23.2%. Iowa's increase over her very high previous total is 16.4%.

ALUMNI

A better showing is made by the increase of alumni of Iowa colleges, where the total stands at 1064, an increase of 208. This is an increase of 24.3%, slightly above the rate for the entire United States: 23.5%. Only seven states have a larger increase of alumni: Illinois 491, Ohio 460, California 451, Pennsylvania 434, New York 386, Massachusetts 332, and Wisconsin 219.

In figure 2, we have the states arranged according to the totals of their alumni scientists. The entire graph for each state indicates these totals. The shaded part of each graph indicates the amount of the increase since 1938. The rate of increase of Iowa is slightly above the average. Especially large rates of increase will be noted for Illinois, Ohio, California, Minnesota, Texas, and Washington.

Iowa is in ninth position in the total number of alumni scientists to the productivity rate of all the states? Was Utah's earlier lead a fluke? Was it going to hold up?

I made the tabulation of the 1949 volume after the number of total scientists had doubled to 50,000. Utah was still in first place; its lead over the second place state was 32 percent. But the second place state was no longer Colorado. Utah had increased its lead over Colorado to 51.3 percent. The second place state had become the state with the second highest Mormon population, Idaho.

Then in the next decade, bringing the span of these studies to cover a generation, the number of scientists in American Men of Science, 1962 edition, had grown to almost another doubling. What happened to ranks by state then? The study of that edition was by Dr. H. E. Zabel of Minnesota. Utah was still the highest, but its lead over the second place state, still Idaho, had increased from 32 percent to 44 percent![13] Since most of Utah's population has been Mormon, and since the role of the Mormon Church was the major sociological distinction from other states, the facts above are prima facie evidence of Mormon support of science.

FACTORS IN UTAH'S SCIENTIST PRODUCTIVITY

The only reasonable contest to such a conclusion would be to show that Utah had factors that, except for the Mormon influence, would have made it even farther ahead of all other states. Where are any such factors? The modest incomes of its people (they were just above the Southern states in per capita income, and they--the Southern--are the lowest states in per capita white production of scientists) seem to work against such production in other states. Affluent states were usually the higher.

Talk of special factors in its lead other than some Mormon influences are untenable on their face, although perhaps not impossible. Included in Mormon influence would be the possibility that the converts to Mormonism who came to Utah from Northeastern United States, Canada, Great Britain, Germany, and Scandinavia (where most of them were from during the early populating of Utah) were, as to scientist potential, genetically superior.

I know of no study establishing any such genetic superiority, except in a circular way by citing Utah's productivity of doctorates in other than science. (See Hardy study cited in Chapter VIII). Certainly there are a number of other states whose populations are of similar national origins, who are far below Utah in scientist production. So did the Church convert superior individuals from the regions mentioned above? The only data which indicate this, as far as I know (and I have been alert about this), is Utah's scientist lead itself and top productivity index for other doctorates.[14] But here we get into circular reasoning, so the answer is, "Very unlikely."

Dr. Thorndike, in a letter to Gerald L. Ericksen, a former Mormon Army chaplain, wrote:

> Possibly the selection of its population by endurance of tribulation and devotion to an ideal had a good deal to do with it. A Mormon student of psychology was of the opinion that plural marriages of the older generation gave an opportunity for the abler men to produce a larger proportion of children and there may be something to that.[15]

Utah produced under some conditions which were probably handicaps. A study by Cattell (the AMS publisher) showed that cities produce more scientists in proportion to their population than do rural areas. The same research revealed that 43% of scientists in the nation came from homes of business and professional people. Since this is out of proportion to the percentage of this class in the total population, it is evident that such homes, either by heredity, home environment, greater educational opportunity, or a combination of factors, produce far more scientists than homes of other vocational classes.

But only 27% of Mormon scientists in 1949 had parents of college education or any professional vocation, in contrast to 50% of the non-Mormon ones of Utah, and the majority came from farm homes. The Cattell survey reported that in the nation as a whole farm homes were among the least conducive to scientific achievement.

Utah's advantage was not in amount spent per pupil and teacher. Colorado was approximately 20% ahead of Utah education in these measures. Mormon Church influence on both teachers and students probably compensated for some disadvantages.

Mormon influence had to outweigh deficits in Utah. It is on the conservative side to postulate that at least Utah's lead in scientist production over Colorado and, later, Idaho was caused by the Mormon Church.

A useful question is what Mormon influences produced such a phenomenal lead in scientists? Was it connected to Mormon harmony with science or not? This was the idea I tested by getting more facts. Let us pursue this intriguing quest.

For many years Utah's educational system was judged by several studies to be among the nation's best, at least along some lines. But what accounted for this standing in education? Ray L. DeBoer (a Presbyterian) designed a doctoral study at Denver University to study this matter. His conclusion was this:

> In the absence of good evidence which would suggest more important causative agents, this study holds that the operation of Mormon educational philosophy in Utah in the past and today is the chief cause for Utah's high level of educational achievement.

We asked, "And did Mormon philosophy also cause Utah's high level of production of scientists? Does Mormon doctrine, in fact, harmonize with science?" Chapters V and VI attempted to answer these questions.

CHURCHES OF UTAH SCIENTISTS

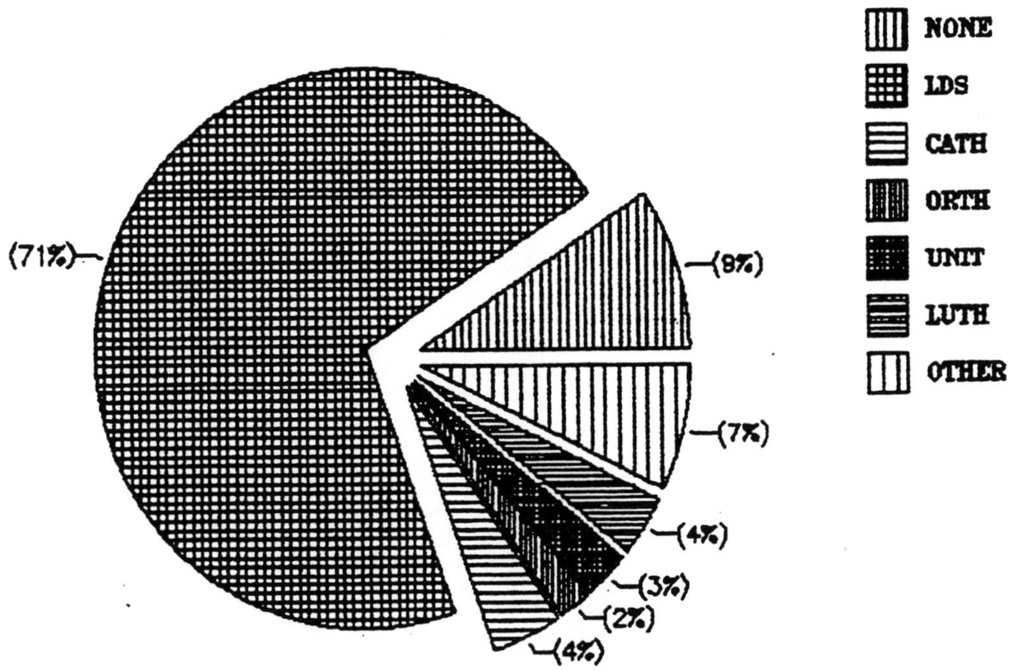

***Utah university graduates in 1990 AMWS.**

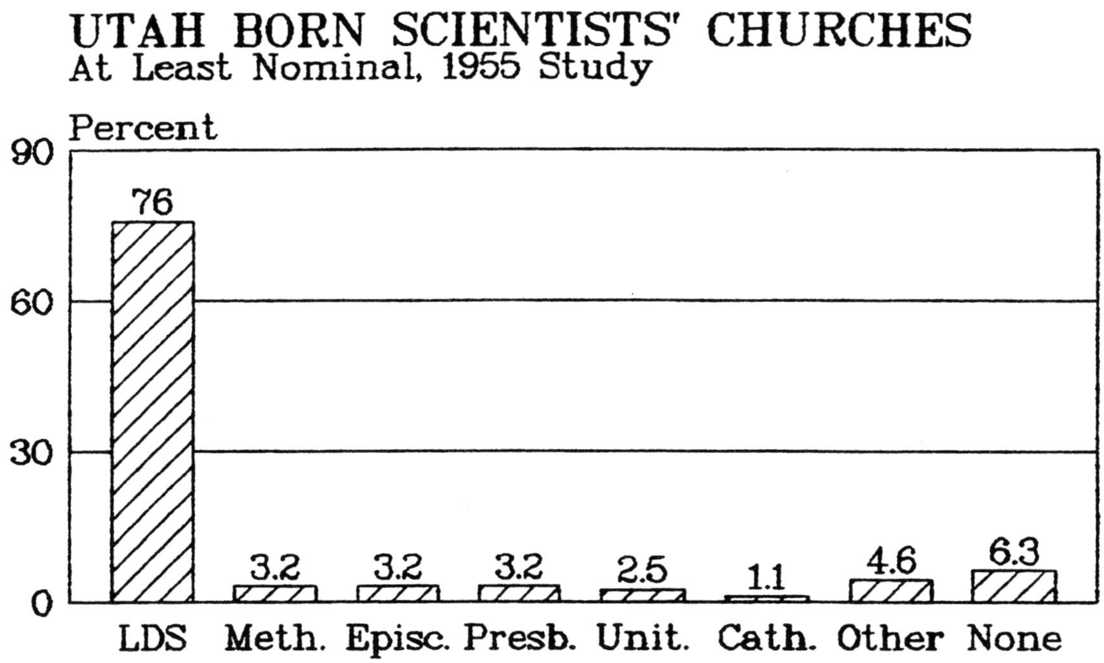

The 76 percent LDS figure for 1955 and the 71 percent for 1992 are not strictly comparable, because the 1955 percent is of a population born in Utah, while the 1992 percent is of scientists who were Utah university graduates. Of course, relatively more non-Mormons come to Utah and attend universities than are born in Utah. This accounts for a large part of the higher figure of non-Mormons, 29 percent, in the 1992 study than shown for the 1955, which was 24 percent.

A different population basis was used because the 1990 American Men and Women of Science could be sorted by computer on-line by universities of undergraduate degrees but not on a basis of state of birth. In 1949 I obtained the states of birth by searching biographies by hand. I was not about to do that for the 120,000 in 1990.

However, we know the states of birth of the 1990 group because the questionnaire asked for that information. The percent of the scientists of the survey born in Utah was forty-eight. Nine percent of those born in Utah were non-Mormon, 91 percent Mormon. Thirty-eight percent of Mormon graduates of Utah universities were born other than in Utah, mostly in Idaho, but a few in California, followed by a scattering in several other states.

CHAPTER V

MORE TESTS OF THE SCIENCE-MORMONISM HARMONY HYPOTHESIS

Impressive as was Utah's scientist production, it ought not be the sole test of Latter-day Saint religion-science harmony. What if the non-Mormons in Utah were outproducing the Mormons in scientists? Or even if the scientists born in Utah were mostly Mormons, what if they did not attend church much nor were active in it? What if they did not now believe in the important doctrines of the Church? What if they did not think the Church had much to do with the production of scientists? Perhaps they themselves did not harmonize Latter-day Saint doctrine with science. Or perhaps they were antagonistic to the church.

There may turn out to be many believing Mormon scientists, but what if they were mostly in fields of science that have little to do with the running controversies between science and religion? Or what would it augur for the future of the Latter-Saint Church and science if the older scientists were believers, but the younger ones were departing from the faith?

To add up the evidence for or against the proposition that the scientific mind can harmonize Mormon doctrine and science, we searched for answers to these questions. The answers were found in the responses to the questionnaires which were sent to all Utah born scientists. (A copy is Appendix C.) Answers are in this chapter.

UTAH BORN SCIENTISTS WERE MOSTLY MORMONS

The biographical questionnaire for Who's Who inquired as to the religion of the scientists included, but only 25 percent of them listed any such affiliation. (American Men of Science did not request religious affiliation for biographical data.) In contrast, more than twice this percentage of people in the general population of the United States give religious affiliation for the census. What of scientists born in Utah?

Church membership of Utah-born scientists is in Appendix A, Table 1. They were 75.9% L.D.S., at least nominally. Later tables will show whether they were Mormons in more than name only. Episcopalians, Methodists, and Presbyterians had equal numbers, tying for second place with 3.2 percent each. The Catholic Church, consistent with the findings in chapter II, produced only 1.1 percent of Utah's scientists in this survey, although it was the second largest denomination in Utah.

If the Latter-day Saint population produced more than its proportional share of scientists, the role of Latter-day Saint Church influence would be confirmed by one additional test. The census year nearest the median year of birth of these Utah men of science was 1900. The white population of Utah was then 276,749. The closest year to this in which the census reported Latter-day Saint numbers in Utah was 1906, when it showed 151,032. Thus the Latter-day Saint population in the period when the scientists were born was about 54.6 percent of the total Utah population at that period.

This 54.6 percent of Utah's population produced 75.9 percent of the Utah born scientists. That is, it produced 36.6 percent more than its per capita share. That this 36.6 percent was similar to the figure of Utah's 32 percent lead over the second place state in production of scientists may be just interesting coincidence. But that the Mormons clearly outproduced the non-Mormons tends to confirm that the Church influence had much to do with Utah's lead.

From here on, the figures believed to be most pertinent to the hypothesis, that is, important to the study, are included in the text, with an occasional chart to highlight the most important. (There is a reference to which Table contains them. But the text gives the real picture. One need not struggle with the tables. They are there, as Appendix A, only as a reference for any readers whose curiosity can overcome the tedium.) Bold number percents are on some tables. These are the figures from the 1992 study on the same questionnaire item and category of answer. But the important figures are also in the text of Chapter VIII and its clear charts.

WERE THE MORMON SCIENTISTS "BELIEVERS"?

It was the members of the Latter-day Saint Church who produced Utah's lead in scientists. But were the scientists devoted members? One measure of devoutness in Christianity is the degree of conviction that Jesus is a divine person of the Godhead. Table 2 shows how the scientists stood on this. Among Latter-day Saint scientists 76.2 percent believed this doctrine, a "Very Strong" conviction with 43.5 percent of them, while only 11.7 percent had "No Such Conviction."

Comparisons on this Table between the various churches other than Latter-day Saint were of limited reliability because of the small numbers of scientists represented in each faith, only 9 in those with the most to 3 in that with the least, compared to the 214 Latter-day Saints. The three Catholics among the 282 Utah Scientists showed the highest percentage of "Strong" or "Very Strong" faith in Christ, 100 percent. Next came the Latter-day Saints with their 76.2 percent of 214, followed by Episcopalians with 44.4 percent "believers." Lowest were the Unitarians with 71.4 percent in the "No Such Conviction" column regarding Christ's divinity.

DEFINITIONS OF RELIGIOUS CATEGORIES IN THE TABLES

A group of scientists were labelled in most of the tables and comments that follow as "Other Churches' Believers". By definition, these were the Utah scientists who were members of other churches than Latter-day Saint and who possessed a conviction regarding the divinity of Jesus of either "Fair", "Strong", or "Very Strong". This is an important definition in the coming presentations.

Of the 68 non-Mormon scientists in this study, 32% were "Other Churches' Believers", that is believers in Jesus as divine. Of the 214 Mormon scientists, however, 76.2% were "Believers" in Jesus as a divine person of the Godhead.

Other Churches' Believers divided about equally between "Fair", "Strong", and "Very Strong" convictions on this.

The Mormon scientists, however, had only 11.2% "Fair", 21.5% "Strong", and 43.5% "Very Strong" belief in Jesus.

The Mormon Church brought more than twice the percentages of Utah scientists "to Jesus" than did other churches. (Table 1 and Table 2) See Chapter VIII for comparisons to the 1992 study. The picture has changed.

Devoutness of belief for Latter-day Saints also included a conviction that God still may speak to man , that there are modern "prophets", and that Joseph Smith, Jr. was inspired by God in the formation of The Church of Jesus Christ of Latter-day Saints.

Latter-day Saint scientists had 73.8 percent who could be called "Believers" by the test of this basic Latter-day Saint tenet, counting those who classed their convictions that Joseph Smith was a prophet as "Fair", who were 14 percent, "Strong", who were 22.9 percent, or "Very Strong", who were 36.9 percent. (Table 3)

(Twelve percent Other Churches' Believers indicated that they had a "Fair" conviction that Joseph Smith was inspired by God in the formation of the Latter-day Saint Church.)

Those who called their conviction "Weak" were listed with those who said "No Such Conviction" opposite the category in the tables called "Nominal L.D.S.", meaning Mormons in name only.

The way the Latter-day Saint scientists divided on this question about Joseph Smith was by definition in the text and discussions that follow, "Nominal L.D.S.", "L.D.S. Fair Believers", and "L.D.S. Strong Believers". It is important to remember this because these terms are found in much of the book from here on, both in this chapter and in the next two.

The overwhelming percent of convictions among Latter-day Saints' tended to support the hypothesis of Science-Mormon religion harmony. See Chapter VIII for results of our 1992 survey of current (1990) Mormon scientists. It supports the hypothesis even more decidedly.

A belief which can distinguish devout Mormons from others was that the Latter-day Saint Church was the only authoritative church of Jesus Christ on the earth today. Statements of conviction on this were sought as a double-check upon those stated in the previous questionnaire item. This posed a somewhat more severe test of devotion to Latter-day Saint belief, and 12 percent less Latter-day Saint scientists met this test of "orthodoxy" than met the one regarding the inspiration of Joseph Smith. Even so, a large number, 61.7 percent of L.D.S. scientists, held this conviction, half of whom, 32.7 percent, were in the "Very Strong" category. (Table 4)

The steadfast orthodoxy of large percentages of Latter-day Saint scientists on these two convictions above showed that they had found ways to harmonize Latter-day Saint doctrine and their sciences, thus supporting the hypothesis.

A MEANING OF MORMON SCIENTISTS' BELIEF

The claims of Joseph Smith to divine revelation strike many intelligent people as astonishing, if not incredible. So the present fact that about two-thirds of 214 scientists (in the 1955 study--20% more in the 1992) believe his claims may be, for some people, one of those awkward, tension producing wonders which challenge development of new insights. When we are aware that most of these scientists have Ph. D.'s from the graduate colleges of the leading universities of America, then the most valuable meaning of these facts may be: Doubts about the supernatural origins of Mormonism can be overridden in minds of this competence by some means. As means, Mormon scientists refer to evidence, reason, and faith through the "Holy Spirit".

HISTORY DOES NOT COMPEL BELIEF

However, while the facts clearly show strong belief, it was still true in 1955 that about one fourth of the Latter-day Saint "born" scientists did not "believe". Assuming--if we could--that they, too, were well acquainted with the full story of Joseph Smith's life and the early history of Mormonism, it was evident that these were not so overwhelmingly clear in their implications as to compel belief. There was still a choice, but in view of the three-fourths of the scientists who did believe, the least that can be concluded was that the facts of Mormonism's supernatural origins, in the larger religious contexts, were such as to permit belief in them by scientific minds which chose to do so. **The results of the 1992 study are in Chapter VIII and support even more the hypothesis that scientific minds can harmonize science and Mormonism.**

DID THE SCIENTISTS BELIEVE THEY SHOULD "COMPARTMENTALIZE"?

I already have assumed that a high percentage of scientists believing in the important doctrines means that they could harmonize such doctrines with science. But in this study I tried to assume as little as possible and, instead, check with the facts from the scientists themselves.

Instead of harmonizing science and religion, a choice was "compartmentalizing", that is, putting science and religion into such different categories in the mind as not to face any necessity for harmonizing them. As one scientist said, "My scientific vocation has nothing to do with faith. I see no need to mix the two."(Table 5)

Only 16 percent of the Other Churches' Believers, the Utah scientists who believe in a church other than Mormon, say "No" to "compartmentalization", and as many as 20 percent state "yes" to the proposition that the fields of religion and science were so far removed from each other that no attempt was logically necessary to harmonize them. Most of the Other Churches' group answered "Partially".

This was a different point of view than that held by any of the L.D.S. groups. Among L.D.S. "Strong Believers" the "No" answers rang out with 86.8 percent and only 3.1 percent "Yes" to justify "compartmentalization". L.D.S. "Fair Believers" went as high as 76.7 percent "No" answers. These "No's", remember, were in comparison to only 16 percent "No" among the scientist believers of other denominations.

Latter-day Saint scientists were far more inclined to think of religion as claiming objective truths which require harmonizing with science than was true of scientist believers of the other churches. This required that Mormonism might have been put to a more stringent test by its scientific minds than non-Mormons required of their faith. Many Latter-day Saints believed their faith must, and does, face the facts, all of which tend to support the hypothesis of Latter-day Saint Religion-Science harmony.(Table 6)

DID SCIENTISTS BELIEVE THAT THEIR CHURCH DOCTRINE AND SCIENCE COULD BE HARMONIZED?

Ninety percent of the Latter-day Saint scientists who were "Strong Believers" answered "Yes" to this question and another 8.5 percent said they could "Partially". Among the L.D.S. "Fair" Believers, the percent of "Yes" dropped to 53.3 percent and "Partially" rose to 43.3 percent. And among the Nominal L.D.S., only 14.5 percent said "Yes" and 41 percent "Partially" with the "No" answers up to 34.5 percent.

Harmonizing of religion with science was important among Latter-day Saint scientists. Those who believed most in the Church believed most that Mormon doctrine and science could be harmonized. Those who were only Nominal L.D.S. had only one-sixth as many affirmative answers. (Table 6)

DID THE SCIENTISTS THEMSELVES BELIEVE THAT THEY LOGICALLY HARMONIZE RELIGION WITH SCIENCE?

This question was related, and cross-checking, to that above on Table 6 and the answers were almost identical. The only differences were that the scientists seemed a little more sure about whether they themselves actually harmonized doctrine and science than about whether they believed it could be harmonized. That is, less of them checked "Partially", "No Opinion", or gave no answer.

Although large majorities, thus, believed in the harmony of their religion and science, there were still many scientists, running about 33 percent of the total in all but the L.D.S. "Strong" Believer group, who stated that they only "Partially" harmonize. Something had yet to be achieved toward full harmony, in the opinions of about one-third of the scientists. Even so, the results from this question tended to uphold the hypothesis. (Table 7) See also Chapter VIII.

WAS UTAH'S SCIENTIST LEAD ATTRIBUTABLE TO MORMON INFLUENCE?

Why was Utah 32 percent ahead of the second place state, Idaho, in per capita production of scientists? This was a question of too large a scope to be finally answered here by much more than the opinions of the scientists themselves. There were no doubt many complex causes for Utah's total scientist output. However, these scientists, born in Utah and most of them reared there, have the background for relatively enlightened opinions on the question.

Larger percentages of the Other Churches' Believers gave either no answer (13%) or made comments (also 13%) than did the other groups. Forty-eight percent of the Other Church "Believers" said "No", and 26 percent said "Yes". On this question the "Yes" answers came in far greater percentages from Latter-day Saints. A majority of the merely Nominal L.D.S. even answered "Yes", with the L.D.S. "Strong Believers" going as high as 89.8 percent and the L.D.S. "Fair Believers" in between at 76.7 percent. (Table 8)

We can only guess at the reasons for the disparity between the opinions of the Latter-day Saints and those of the non-Mormons. From the fact of religious allegiance the Latter-day Saints may be swayed to have given credit to the Mormon Church and the non-members to withhold credit from it. Or perhaps there may some combination of these two explanations. The answers to this question weigh in favor of the harmony hypothesis.

The questionnaire incited comments from the individual scientists on this question. All in all, 5 percent commented, and their comments covered a large range of possible reactions. Here are typical comments from those who did believe that Utah's lead in scientist production was attributable to L.D.S. influence:

SOME COMMENTS BY SCIENTISTS

A non-Mormon scientist wrote, "I feel this church, more than others, has emphasized general education." Another wrote, "In part probably through their emphasis on education and, in part, due to the excellent orientation toward work and life in general."

The Latter-day Saint Church was credited by two scientists with (1) "Giving a purpose, other than monetary, to improvement". (2) "Desire to be of service to one's fellow men."

One scientist was impressed that "Parents of Latter-day Saint youths often make sacrifices they can ill afford to see that their children obtain an education that will qualify them for greater service to mankind, and that will give them greater joy in that service."

"One of the fundamentals of the Church," another commented, "was to provide each member with a job or responsibility or part in the Church's activities. It teaches reliability and honesty and resourcefulness."

Specific doctrines of the Latter-day Saint Church were mentioned by several Mormon scientists as beneficially influencing scientist production.

"1. Mormon doctrine of eternal progress. 2. Encouragement of the church to pursue all lines of truth---i.e., scientific knowledge. 3. Word of Wisdom---abstinence from alcohol and tobacco."

"A Mormon scripture says 'Whatever principle of intelligence we attain unto in this life, it will rise with us in the resurrection. And if a person gains more knowledge and intelligence in this life through his diligence and obedience than another, he will have so much the advantage in the world to come."

On the other side of the issue, however, were some comments taken from the questionnaires of those who did not attribute Utah's lead to Church influence.

"Small land holdings and lack of other resources forced me into additional schooling and training."

"Germany probably produces more scientists per capita than even Utah. I have never heard of this production rate being attributed to Martin Luther. And then there was the USSR!" (Has this respondent interpreted our hypothesis to mean that Mormonism was <u>necessary</u> for production of scientists? And, at that, did he have evidence that Germany and the former U.S.S.R. produce more scientists per white population than Utah?)

"Utah seems to produce scientists in spite of the L.D.S. influence. The presence of many people from Northern European countries where education was held in high regard was a more important factor."

"Any small isolated and closely knit group, especially if it considers itself persecuted or benighted may produce an unusually strong motivation among its members. Consider the Jews." And, "In general, people of higher native intelligence, who question what they receive and seek a reasonable answer, were converted to the L.D.S. Church."

"This was an empirical problem, and one would have to explore many possibilities before giving an answer." (A wise comment, no doubt.)

DID THEY BELIEVE THEIR OWN CHURCH CONTRIBUTED SIGNIFICANTLY TO THEIR ACHIEVEMENT?

While one might not know what influence a church had on others, one might have a much clearer view of what it did for oneself. Did the scientists think their church helped them achieve in science?

Among the Latter-day Saints, the "Yes" answers were related to the strength of their belief in the Church. "Strong" Believers gave credit to the Church with 85 percent "Yes", "Fair" Believers with 56.7 percent, and Nominal L.D.S. only 27.3 percent.

A far smaller percentage of Other Churches' Believers stated that their churches contributed to their achievements--only 44 percent. Mormons were evidently more impressed that their church promotes scientific achievement than were other scientists about their churches and science.

Judging by the opinions of the men of science regarding their own lives, the Latter-day Saint Church contributed significantly to scientific achievement in a large number of cases. The facts from this question seemed to indicate that the doctrines of the Mormon Church foster science. (Table 9)

DID THE UTAH SCIENTISTS ATTEND CHURCH REGULARLY UNTIL 18 YEARS OF AGE?

How much a church affected one's life should relate to exposure to it. So we wanted to know whether the scientists were regular attenders at church during their early years.

Among the Latter-day Saints, those who turned out to be "Believers" were regular attenders, 88.4 percent of the "Strong" and 83.3 percent of the "Fair". Twice as many Nominal L.D.S. group said they did not attend regularly, 30.9 percent compared to only 13.3 percent of the "Fair" and 11.6 percent of the "Strong". Apparently some Latter-day Saints can have a strong testimony without regular attendance in youth, and that with regular attendance some can still resist belief. But these were evidently the less likely cases. There was clearly ample exposure to Church influence among the Latter-day Saints who became scientists. (Table 10)

Church attendance in youth was far less a factor in the lives of the Other Churches' Believers. Only 52 percent of them had attended regularly in comparison to the above 80 percent for "Believing" Mormons.

WERE THEY ACTIVE IN THEIR CHURCH DURING COLLEGE AGE?

Activity in a church brings more involvement than mere attendance. (We love whom we serve.) What were the young people who became scientists doing for their churches in their college years? For the Other Churches' Believers, 68 percent were doing nothing, as were 67.3 percent of the Nominal Mormons. The relationship between activity in these years and later "Belief" was unquestionable and striking, more than twice as many, 60 percent more, Believers had been so active as were others. And the L.D.S. "Strong" group was 73.6 percent active.

Only 28 percent of Other Churches' Believers were active, probably because their churches give no such opportunities for office holding by young people as does the L.D.S. Church's unique lay religious leadership. (Table 11)

(Of course, this does not settle the question of whether they were active because believing or believing because of active, or what combination.)

Ample exposure to the church to know its doctrines and feel its influence was present, particularly among the Latter-day Saints. Since the attitudes of these scientists came out so favorably to the church, with more than two-thirds of the Latter-day Saints coming as "Believers" in the divine inspiration of Joseph Smith, these facts also tend to support the hypothesis that Mormon doctrine and science can be harmonized by scientific minds. (Table 12)

ACTIVITY AS A SHOWING OF ALLEGIANCE

This question served as a check on whether we had correctly categorized Latter-day Saints as "Nominal" or "Strong". This becomes a matter not of mere verbal statement of belief but of dedicated service, since offices in the Mormon Church at the congregation (Ward) and diocesan (Stake) levels are unpaid.

Seventy-seven percent of the L.D.S. "Strong Believers" proved their belief by service in Church positions, 32.6 percent as Stake leaders. On the other hand, we have correctly classified the "Nominal", because only 5.5 percent hold any Church office at all!

Among non-Mormon "Believers", only 16 percent held offices in their churches, probably because their churches, with a paid ministry, do not have as many jobs to be filled by lay members. (Table 13)

SCIENTISTS' ATTITUDES TOWARD THE LATTER-DAY SAINT CHURCH AS AN INSTITUTION FOR PROMOTING HUMAN WELFARE

Belief in the supernatural elements of a church is different from observing its practical fruits and judging them. It may be assumed that scientists would not favor an institution for human welfare if they had judged it to be a significant deterrent to science. If an institution appeared to scientists to be antagonistic to science, one might expect them to respond with antagonism to that institution.

Besides whether the scientists believe in the doctrines of the Church, attend it, or were active in it, we wanted to know their attitude toward it.

Overwhelmingly favorable response to the Latter-day Saint Church as an institution for promoting human welfare came from the Utah scientists, 88.3 percent favorable! Even the least favorable group, the Other Churches' Believers, had less than one out of twenty with an antagonistic attitude. However, unusually large percentages, for this study, of non-L.D.S. were in the "No Opinion" or "No Answer" columns, a total of 12 percent. Twenty-four percent were "Indifferent", but by a majority of 56 percent of the Other Churches' Believers were favorably disposed toward the Latter-day Saint Church.

Attitudes among the Latter-day Saints ran from 87.3 percent favorable among the "Nominal L.D.S." to 100 percent favorable among both "Fair" Believers and "Strong" Believers. If belief were based only on the test set up by Jesus, "By their fruits ye shall know them," (Matt. 7:20) there might be almost no Latter-day Saint nonbelievers. The antagonism to the Church among the merely Nominal L.D.S. was only 1.8 percent. Ninety eight percent of the Mormon scientists, believers or not, like the Church.

The large percentages favorable to the Latter-day Saint Church may show that many Utah scientists see support of their science's viewpoints in L.D.S. doctrine and/or practice. The facts of this part of the research support the hypothesis of harmony between the L.D.S. Church and science.(Table 14)

WERE THE LATTER-DAY SAINT SCIENTISTS IN FIELDS OF SCIENCE WHERE THE CONFLICTS EXIST?

Also related to this question was whether the Latter-day Saint scientists in certain fields of science were less inclined to be "Believers" than those in other fields. Most of the data of this chapter regarding harmony of Latter-day Saint doctrine and science would be of less weight for "harmony" if the Latter-day Saint scientists were not in fields where the controversies discussed in Chapter II have existed. They would also be of less weight for "harmony" if the Latter-day Saints who have no belief were the ones in the fields of science most exposed to controversy with religion.

As we saw in Chapter II, the main issues between science and religion in the past which are still with us concern the age of the earth and the theory of evolution. The age of the earth was evidenced in the fields of geology and biology, primarily. The theory of evolution finds evidence in geology but most of it comes from the biological sciences.

Perhaps the fields of science should not have much to do with what one believes on issues such as these. One might suppose that any well-educated person, to the degree implied by a Ph. D., would be well versed in the facts underlying estimates of the earth's age and supporting the theory of evolution. But in Chapter VI we will encounter ample evidence that the fields of science did make some difference in the beliefs of scientists on some of these science-religion questions.

Whatever the implications, the physical sciences have drawn the largest percentages of Utah scientists, 53.3 percent. Other Churches' Believers showed the largest percentage of physical scientists of the religious categories, followed by the L.D.S. "Strong", 52.7 percent.

These were larger percentages than found among the whole group of <u>American Men of Science</u>, in which only 44.2 percent were in the physical sciences.

LESS BELIEVING CATEGORIES TEND NOT TO BE IN PHYSICAL SCIENCES

There is some tendency for the less believing categories, "Nominal L.D.S." (41.8 percent) and L.D.S. "Fair"(46.7 percent) to be less in the physical sciences and more in the biological sciences, where, for example, the "Nominal L.D.S." had 34.5 percent compared to the L.D.S. "Strong", 25.6 percent.

In social sciences, where only 7.1 percent of Utah scientists were listed (<u>American Men of Science</u> contained about 7 percent social scientists) the "Nominal L.D.S. had 10.9 percent social scientists (mostly psychologists), while L.D.S. "Strong" had 7 percent (also mostly psychologists).

The breakdown on the above chart leaves us some questions, because a field like physical sciences contains both geology, which has much to do with the controversies, and chemistry, which has less. It will answer some questions if we arrange the data so that it shows the various degrees of Latter-day Saint belief by field of science. (Table 15)

DID MORMONS WITH THE STRONG BELIEFS TEND TO BE IN CERTAIN SCIENTIFIC FIELDS?

There were some tendencies, but apparently there were numbers of believers and unbelievers in all of the fields. It can be seen from Table 15 that the percent of Mormon

"Very Strong" Believers drops from a high of 51.8 among agricultural scientists to 36.3 percent among biologists, down to 20 percent among geologists and 19 percent among social scientists. Geology, however, also shows the highest percent of those with "Strong" testimonies among the Latter-day Saints. Geology also shows the lowest percent, 6.8, of those with "No Such Convictions", which is, no testimonies.

If we scrutinize the data of Table 16 with care, we may detect a small depressing effect upon testimonies from specialization in Biology, which was a field right in the midst of the evolution and age of the earth controversy. This suggests that it may be a little less simple to harmonize Latter-day Saint doctrine with biology than with other fields of science, probably because of the theory of evolution.

A most obvious fact was that a notably large percent, 43.6, of the Latter-day Saint men listed in the social sciences were only "Nominal" members. But only 15 of the 214 Latter-day Saint scientists were in the social sciences, the same percentage, 7, as found in the whole group of American Men of Science. The editors have been conservative about listing social scientists as men of science. A study among much larger numbers of Latter-day Saint social scientists would be necessary to give reliable data. Nevertheless, the figures may cause some doubt whether Latter-day Saint doctrine and the recent state of psychology as a field of science were as compatible as was Mormonism with other fields.

But, overall, the facts show that the Latter-day Saint scientists were distributed throughout the fields of science very nearly like the whole of American scientists, that they have not been notably in fields removed from the controversies, and that Latter-day Saint scientists who were "Believers" were in a strong majority, except psychologists, despite fields.

DID THE SCIENTISTS FIND CHANGES OF SCIENCE-RELIGION BELIEFS EMOTIONALLY TROUBLING?

Counselors and others who are aware of the problems of adolescence can testify that some young people become emotionally upset when they encounter theories and ideas which threaten deeply held religious convictions. To what extent did this occur among Utah scientists? Was it more, or less, true of Mormon scientists than of others? Did the amount of troubling show any relationship to whether the scientist was later a "Strong Believer" or otherwise?

About 30 percent of all Utah scientists say that they were somewhat emotionally troubled during changes of science-religion belief. The only significant variation from this 30 percent was among the L.D.S. "Fair Believers", among whom it went as high as 56.7 percent.

Only very small percentages said that they were intensely troubled, the low being L.D.S. "Fair Believers" with 3.3 percent and the high being Other Churches' Believers with 12 percent intensely troubled, according to their statements of their own recollections.

The largest percentages of "No" troubling were the "Nominal L.D.S.", 54.5, and the L.D.S. "Strong Believers" with 45 percent. It appears that decisiveness, which results in the person being either not active and nonbelieving in the Church (only Nominal), or else in his being a "Strong Believer", was associated with lesser emotional troubling over the questions of science and religion. Those with "Fair" degree of conviction about the Church had the largest percentage troubled. We have little basis for deciding whether they were troubled because of having only "Fair" testimonies or had only "Fair" testimonies because they were troubled about the conflicts between science and religion.

While the meaning of "Somewhat troubled" was vague, it probably suggests the existence of a problem, the problem of whether important religious doctrines learned in youth by these scientists were harmonious with science. It appears that one-third of the

Utah scientists, including the Latter-day Saints, had some difficulty harmonizing their religion and science as they matured. (Table 17)

Other Churches' Believers did not have significantly more nor less emotional problems over science and religion than the Latter-day Saints as revealed by "Somewhat" and "No" answers. However, from about twice to three times the percentages of Other Churches' Believers were "Intensely" troubled over science and religion as any L.D.S. category. This may indicate that it was generally less difficult for Latter-day Saints to harmonize their religion and science than for Other Churches' Believers to do so with their religions.

Such large percentages of all groups gave no answer to this question, as one can see from Table 17, that the true picture may not appear. Caution should govern any attempt to draw conclusions from this data, but one may say that there was apparently room for improvement in the ease with which church doctrines, Latter-day Saint or otherwise, can be harmonized with science.

WERE YOUNGER SCIENTISTS LESS LIKELY TO BE BELIEVERS THAN OLDER ONES?

The effectiveness with which Latter-day Saint doctrine was being harmonized with recent trends in science, if judged by whether the younger Latter-day Saint scientists were more, or less, likely to be "Believers," was a matter related to the hypothesis.

The data showed no trend for the older scientists to be more devoted to the Latter-day Saint Church than the younger ones. Larger percents of the "Believing" categories ("Fair" and "Strong") were found in the columns of least time in science than the percents of the Nominal L.D.S. found there.

In the cumulative percents of each "number of years in science" column, the higher percents for the least number of years were always in the "Fair" and "Strong" category. For example, 70 percent of the L.D.S. "Strong" groups have under thirty years in science, while only 56 percent of the nominal L.D.S. group have under thirty years. Also, 17 percent of the L.D.S. "Strong" group have under twenty years experience while only 10 percent of the Nominal L.D.S. have under twenty years. However, only 5 percent of the L.D.S. "Strong" group have over forty-five years in science compared to 7 percent of the Nominal L.D.S. group. (Table 18)

It appears that the more recent crop of Latter-day Saint scientists was, if anything, slightly more likely to be "Believers" than was the older crop. This in turn seemed to suggest that Latter-day Saint doctrine was standing up to comparatively recent trends in science, judging by the adherence of scientists, or Mormonism had done a better job of indoctrinating the younger group. Chapter VIII reveals that the next generations of Mormon scientists were much stronger believers than the older.

SUMMARY: TESTED SCIENCE-HARMONY RELIGION

The hypothesis was: Latter-day Saint doctrine and science can be harmonized by scientific minds. The tests and findings about Latter-day Saint scientists were as follows:

How strongly were they exposed to Church influences? Huge majorities (76.3 to 88.4 percent) attended Church meetings regularly in youth. Furthermore, large majorities (60 to 73.6 percent) of those who became "Believers" were active in college years as officers, teachers, or missionaries. Only 32.7 percent of those who became Nominal L.D.S. were so active in college years as officers, teachers, or missionaries. Evidence showed strong exposure to Latter-day Saint influence.

Fully aware of the Church influence, what effect did they see it having regarding science? Majorities, ranging from 56.4 percent of the Nominal L.D.S. to 89.8 percent of the "Strong Believers", believed that Utah's notable production of men of science was attributable to Latter-day Saint Church influence. Also, sizeable percentages, from 27.3

percent of the Nominal L.D.S. to 85.3 percent of the "Strong Believers", believed that their Church contributed significantly to their own professional achievements. A much smaller percentage of Other Churches' Believers thought that their churches did so.

What were the opinions of the scientist themselves on whether their religion and sciences can be harmonized? First, did they believe that science and religion were so far removed from each other in domain that no harmonizing was called for? They did not. Against such an idea was 86.8 percent of L.D.S. "Strong Believers" down to 43.6 percent of Nominal L.D.S. Significantly, only 16 percent of "Believers" in Other Churches said "No" to "compartmentalization." This shows that Mormons had more expectation that religion and science should face each other on the same grounds, with a necessity for compatibility, than did Other Churches' Believers.

After the Mormons agreed almost unanimously that attempts at harmonizing must be faced, did they think that harmony could be achieved? The L.D.S. "Strong Believers" did think their religion could be harmonized with science, 89.9 percent. But this was in contrast to the Nominal L.D.S., only 14 percent of whom said "Yes", although 41 percent of them said "Partially". Almost exactly similar percentages by categories as the above said they believed that they themselves harmonized their church doctrine and science in their own philosophy of life.

What kinds of "Believers" were Mormon scientists? About three-fourths, 76.2 percent, of Mormon scientists believed in the divinity of Christ and nearly the same, 73.8 percent, believed in the divine inspiration of Joseph Smith. Mormons stated strong belief in the divinity of Christ more than did the Other Churches' Believers. Since we could expect scientists to be more cautious and thorough in arriving at beliefs, it was impressive that about 75% of the Latter-day Saint scientists affirmed "testimonies".

Were the Latter-day Saints in fields of scientific study removed from the classic controversies between science and religion? No, they were divided among fields much as scientists as a whole in America. The field of science was not strongly related to degree of religious conviction, except the few psychologists who seemed to have been less religious.

Was the harmonizing of religion and science an emotionally troubling experience? This might be expected if it was difficult to harmonize a religion one cares for deeply with a science to which one also wishes to be dedicated. From twice to three times as many Other Churches' Believers said they were "Intensely Troubled" as did any category of the Latter-day Saints. Apparently Mormonism was not as difficult to harmonize with sciences as were other religions, or else the Latter-day Saints were somehow better prepared for the task. However, while only 6.7 percent of the Latter-day Saints found the science-religion adjustment process "Intensely Troubling", not all harmonizing was simple for all Mormons. Something remained to be desired in harmonizing Mormon doctrine and science.

Granted all the evidence of scientists harmonizing Mormon doctrine and science, what trend was seen in younger scientists compared to older ones? The facts of the 1949 study show that the newer generation of Mormon scientists was slightly more apt to be believing than was the older one. The 1992 study shows the new generations much more "believing".

The climactic evidence of Mormon harmony with science, however, the prima facie evidence, which our tests above tended only to confirm, was that the state of Utah outproduces all other states by far, in proportion to white population, in scientists. If each state increased its scientist production only to the rate represented by Utah's lead over the second place state, the number of American scientists would be increased 42 percent. And if all states produced up to Utah's total rate, our scientist supply would be doubled!

HARMONIZE RELIGION & SCIENCE?
LDS Strong Believer Scientists, 1955

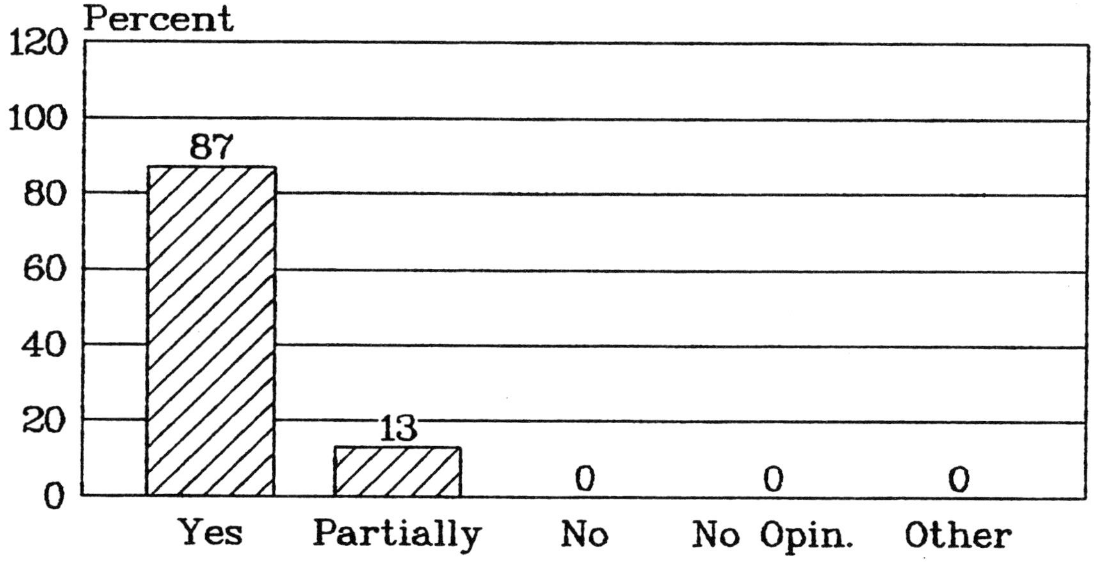

HARMONIZE RELIGION & SCIENCE?
LDS Strong Believer Scientists, 1992

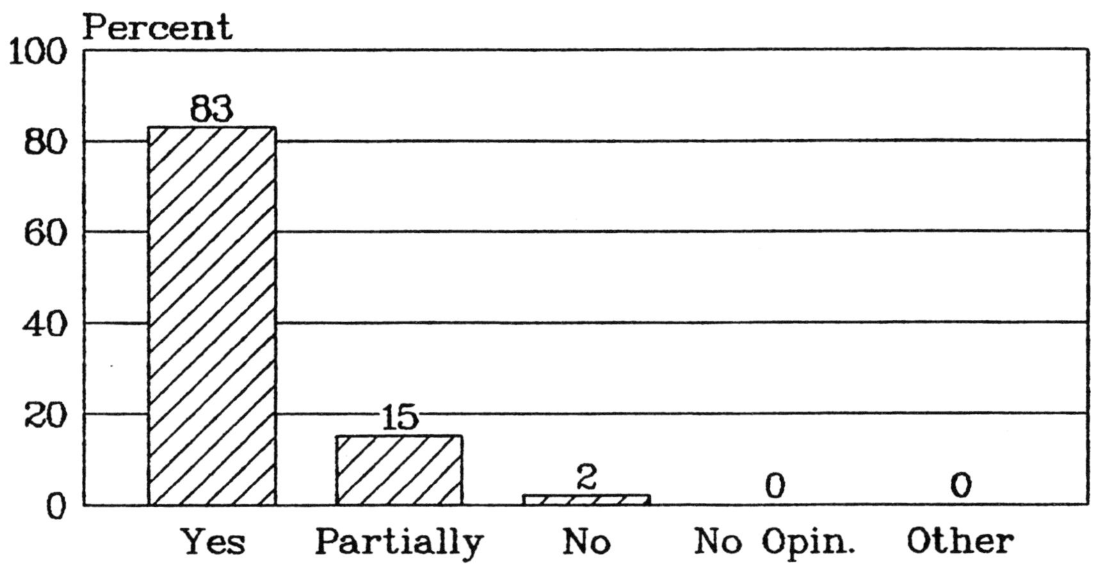

The hypothesis of the research, by the facts of this chapter, was probably substantiated: Scientific minds can harmonize science and the Mormon religion. The claim of Brigham Young that "Our religion will not clash with or contradict the facts of science in any particular," was genuine. When he said "We want every branch of science taught in this place that was taught in the world," he apparently meant it, and the Mormons put his declaration into effect. Mormonism has, in reality, a distinctive status in the world as a science supporting religion.

CHAPTER VI

SCIENTISTS' BELIEFS ON MAJOR CONTROVERSIES

We know what a few theologians believe about the earth's age and evolution, men such as Conway for Catholicism and McConkie for Mormonism. We have also seen opinions of several scientists who were published on the issue, Mormons such as Apostles Widtsoe, Talmage, Dr. Salisbury, Dr. Stokes, and some Protestants. But until this research, the hundreds of Utah scientists, some at least as eminent as those who were more widely quoted, have not had their beliefs either noted or quoted. And while truth is not necessarily established by counting noses, not even the curious but careful ones of scientists, we suppose we will be closer to truth by counting most of them instead of a few.

In counting, we produce statistics. "Dry" and "cold" as they may seem to some, readers of a book like this visualize, for each unit "1", a real person, for each percent, a group of real people. This book has much humanity in it, representing conversations with hundreds of most interesting and accomplished individuals.

As I affixed the name and address labels while sending the questionnaires, and as I read their responses, I was aware of their distinctiveness and talents and related them to well educated and dedicated men and women I have known personally. Some of them, it turned out, I had known well. One was the biology professor colleague of mine at the B.Y.U.-Hawaii Campus, long ago. For another, I put a brief note with the questionnaire, asking, "Are you the 'Chuck' I knew who lived on 16th East?" On his response he wrote, "I am that Chuck, Dick, and am glad to hear from you." We had been in a Boy Scout troop together. Another scientist wrote recalling teachers and pals we had in Junior High school. I put notes in the envelopes of a few cousins of mine. Hearing from me was not that much of an event for them, it seems; I had no responses! But this was also human.

Numbers of the scientists wrote comments on the questionnaires, and some page long letters to me, all of which were helpful, some especially friendly, wishing me well in this study. One electro-chemist, not aware that he was relating to an interest of mine (except that it ought to interest many) sent in his return a copy of a recent scientific publication of his, verifying that a palladium-heavy water process, was "cold fusion". Under most rigorously controlled conditions, they produced the necessary helium.

More could be said. Anyway, these great folks are represented by statistics in this book, but they are not "mere" statistics, as you can feel and understand. Let us go to "interview" our hundreds of scientists by reading the Tables of their views. The Tables are available as Appendix A. This chapter will present the important findings from the Tables. The number of the table will accompany the findings which are taken from that table. The data given in the chapters was all that was essential to answer the questions posed for the study, or likely to interest the reader. But if a reader wants more, the tables are available.

The percents and tables referred to in this chapter contain the results of the 1955 study. Where applicable, results of the 1992 study are on the same tables in bold numbers for comparison to the 1955. Results of the 1992 study are not significantly different except on the degrees of religious conviction and beliefs on evolution. Chapter VIII makes these comparisons in greater detail.

THE AGE OF THE EARTH

The Utah scientists emphatically do not believe that the earth was created in a few thousand years, or anything short of millions. Only 7.2 percent believed in a young earth. Among L.D.S. Strong Believers, belief in a young earth was 12.6 percent, but with only 2.4 percent Positive agreement.

Huge percentages of all categories disagreed with the belief of the earth's age as only thousands of years. Among L.D.S. Strong Believers, 84.5 percent disagreed with that belief. Fair Believers disagreed in slightly larger numbers, 86.6 percent and Nominal L.D.S. in still larger, up to 94.6 percent.

The number of periods in creation is encountered early in the Bible, Genesis I. If we take literal views, a day means 24 hours, (or does it mean about 12 hours, namely, the opposite of night?) not just an undefined period. If we also believed in strictly literal views, we will conclude that the earth was created in less than a week.

As children we first learn to read literally and narrowly. Each word is to mean one specific and concrete thing. Sunday School stories are simple, not wanting to distract young minds, we suppose, from the larger moral of the story. They do not deal with such subtle questions as various usages of the word "day". As our minds develop, we may add to earlier simple ideas elaborations and distinctions to correspond to the complexities of reality. Yet there is a tendency for early patterns to persist, and many otherwise competent people apparently do not overcome the semantic naivety of their childhood, do not become skilled in reading. (This is a matter of mere literacy, not a special possession of the "learned".)

Utah scientists who were Other Churches' Believers had almost twice as many agreeing with the young earth idea as did any category of the Mormons. That is, more of them took the Bible in the limited literal sense than did the Mormon scientists. We might say that the Mormons were better at outgrowing their childhood naivety which favored limited understanding of Genesis. (Tables 19 & 20.)

The Seminary teachers were not as much exposed to the facts of science, yet even they mustered only 34.6 percent agreement for the quick creation of the literalists, with only 9.6 percent positive agreement. A relatively large percentage of Seminary teachers, 19.2, checked No opinion. They were apparently less sure on this issue than the scientists, who had only small percentages, four and under, in the No Opinion column. (Table 56) (Information on 1955 Seminary teacher study: Appendix A, after Table 19.)

Only one in twenty scientists amended the questionnaire on this item. Some typical comments were: "add 'undefined period of long duration'", "religion merely states that the earth and inhabitants were formed by God. It does not explain how." "Do you mean its entire life to present?" "Six periods of time not specified."

SCIENTISTS' BELIEFS ON THE AGE OF THE EARTH BY FIELDS OF SCIENCE.

There were only five of the Utah scientists who expressed Positive belief that the earth was created in a relatively short period, which is, in some thousands of years. Who were they? By religion they were three Mormons, one Presbyterian, and one Unitarian. **Only three of the 214 Mormon scientists Positively hold the young earth belief**.

By fields of science one was a petroleum engineer, one a biochemist, and one an explosives expert. Not one was in the major fields which have the main evidence about the age of the earth--geology, biology, or paleontology. It is uninformed for the religiously literal minded to try to support their traditional ideas on the age of the earth by quoting scientists. From among the Utah group, they would be quoting an almost nonexistent minority, and even those few are speaking outside their fields of science. (Table 21)

Saying that they Tentatively believed in a young earth are a slightly larger group, 15. Their fields of science? Again, not one in the fields with the evidence about the age of the earth. Only one lone Mormon "Literal" comes close to being in a field knowledgeable about earth's age, a metallurgist-explosives expert.

DID THE EARTH TAKE HUNDREDS OF MILLIONS OF YEARS TO CREATE?

When the age of the earth question was put in its contrary, namely, "The earth took at least hundreds of millions of years to create", the responses were consistent with the answers to the question about a young earth. Almost all agreed that it took at least hundreds of millions of years to create. Again, the Other Churches' Believers were more Literal minded than the Mormons. Only 9.3 percent of the Mormon Strong Believers disagreed, although most of their agreement, 42.1 percent, was Tentative.

The Seminary teachers divided about evenly on this, and definitely had larger percentages in disagreement with the aged earth idea. (Table 22)

THE INTERPRETIVE VIEWPOINT

Agreement that the earth took at least hundreds of millions of years to create was what we have labeled as Interpretive. It meant the forming of beliefs with an awareness of the alternative legitimate meanings for the words of scriptures which allow, and sometimes require, interpretation to convey meaning from the original writer to the modern reader in ways consistent with other sources of truth. It is a viewpoint compatible with the basic Latter-day Saint conviction that Joseph Smith was inspired by God in the formation of the Church and with a high degree of Church activity. However, it does not make up, as the Literal does not, an officially orthodox Latter-day Saint Church viewpoint.

AMENDMENTS ABOUT THE AGE OF THE EARTH

The amendments scientists made about the age of the earth help us to understand their thinking. One said, "Facts not available." Another commented, "billions of years." Another, "Change to a comparatively long period of time."

The great antiquity of the creation was known to some close associates of Joseph Smith. W. W. Phelps, one of the Prophet's secretaries, wrote to Joseph's brother William that "eternity, agreeably to the records found in the catacombs of old Egypt, has been going on in this system almost two thousand five hundred and fifty five million years." This letter was published in 1845. Phelps used this reference to let William know that Latter-day Saints could accept ideas which were being proposed by scientists then. Why did Mormon literalists like Elder McConkie not accept this information, from the Prophet's office?

Such a belief is not in accord with the quick creation of six 24 hour days or thousand year periods, which includes, seen Literal, not just the earth but also heaven, the firmament, the sun, moon, and stars. The latter three luminaries, by Literal readings, were created on the fourth day. How the few "thousand of years" literalists can believe that the sun, moon, and stars were created in a "thousand year" day, is as unfathomable as how the old Catholics believed the sun goes around the earth.

The belief in creation's grand antiquity expressed by W. W. Phelps is strikingly similar to that held by modern science, and, as we have seen, by almost all Latter-day Saint scientists.

DID MAN'S BODY EVOLVE FROM SIMPLER SPECIES?

This issue was a hotter controversy than the age of the earth. Common sense, and religion, told the masses of men for centuries that the sun moves in relation to the earth, obviously moving across the sky. The findings of astronomy and physics had to establish the truth not only against the opposition of the Catholic Church but also against the common observations of people. So it is with the theory of evolution. It is common observation that each species gives birth to its own kind. This is reinforced by Literal rendering of Genesis and the subsequent teachings of many churches. In the creation account of the Bible we read, "And God said, Let the earth bring forth the living creature after his kind, and cattle after their kind, and everything that creepeth upon the earth after his kind." The Book of Moses and Book of Abraham in the Latter-day Saint scriptures have accounts of the creation, and the words "after his kind" are found in all accounts.

Do the words "brought forth after his kind" mean: (1) All of the various kinds of plants and animals always have and always will give birth to exactly their own kind? This would be the narrowly Literal view. Or does it mean (2) The various kinds usually have and usually will bring forth their own kind, but there could be exceptions. Or (3) After God developed them by means not mentioned in the Bible, the various kinds then brought forth only their own kind? Or (4) Most kinds, after their initial creation, by whatever means, then usually bring forth their own kind? And is a "kind" a species, genus, or family, as Dr. Stokes asked? These are just a few possible variations which are still respectful of the wording in Genesis.

The Literal usages above with the words all, always, and exactly throw the scriptures into direct contradiction to the facts of nature and the theory of evolution. They do fit, like the early view of the sun moving around the earth, the common but limited observations of many "unlearned" people about reproduction.

The Literal beliefs do not, however, fit the less common observations, but nonetheless truthful, that some plants and some animal life have, if rarely, brought forth somewhat different forms from time to time through mutations.

Beliefs of Utah born scientists on the theory of evolution were obtained by five questionnaire statements to which they responded. Three were contrasting opinions about the creation of man and two were the main opposing views about the creation of other species. The three about man were that (1) his body did not evolve at all from simpler species, (2) God created man's body, probably by making changes from simpler to more complex forms over millions of years (that is, evolution was God's apparent method), or (3) man probably came about through chance and selection instead of by the intelligent goals of a creator.

Among L.D.S. Strong Believer scientists, only 11.6 percent Positively agreed with the non-evolutionary view of man's origin. Tentative agreement by the L.D.S. Strong Believers with the non-evolutionary belief was 20.9 percent. A larger group, 32.6 percent, disagreed Tentatively and 12 percent Positively.

The non-evolutionary view had almost no agreement from the L. D. S. Fair Believers or Nominal L.D.S. We can see that although there were more evolutionists than otherwise among L. D. S. Strong Believers, they still contain less evolutionists in their midst than do those of less religious conviction.

A mere 12 percent of Other Churches' Believers agreed with the non-evolutionary point of view. They were less inclined than L.D.S. believers to accept a special creation for man. Although the Other Churches' Believers were more Literal than the L. D. S. on the age of the earth, they were definitely less so on the evolution of man, contradictory as this may seem. (Table 23)

A majority, 67.3 percent of the L.D.S. Seminary Teacher group, agreed with the non-evolutionary statement regarding man. This may be an indication of how the educated, but non-scientist, body of the Mormon Church membership might react on the evolution issue.

When a positive statement of belief in evolution as God's process for creating the body of man was put to the scientists, L. D. S. Strong Believers were almost two to one in agreement against disagreement, but a sizable percentage, 15.5, said they had No opinion. No L. D. S. Fair Believers showed disagreement with the idea of evolution as God's process for creating man's mortal body. The Nominal L. D. S. decided almost evenly for and against this statement, with a large percentage stating they had No Opinion. It must not be supposed, however, that the percentage of Nominal L.D.S. opposed to the idea of evolution guided by God were against evolution. It was the idea that it was guided by God which they opposed, as Table 24 shows.

About twice the percentages of L.D.S. Strong Believer scientists compared to Seminary teachers believed in evolution of man directed by God. It apparently takes a certain exposure to science, or to some sciences, to produce such belief in evolution in Latter-day Saints, but it could be done.

There is a religious view of evolution and an irreligious view. The irreligious do not acknowledge the hand of God in the creation but suppose that everything, including man, is the product of chance. The group among the Utah scientists which holds this evolution by accident and selection most obviously is the Nominal L. D. S., with 67.2 percent agreeing with it. (Table 25)

Agreement with this statement was classified neither as Literal nor Interpretive but rather as Skeptical. We would have guessed that no category of Believers would agree with this agnostic evolution. This was almost the situation, except that 20 percent of the Other Churches' Believers showed agreement with the Skeptical view. How any believers in the divinity of Christ could accept, even tentatively, a belief that man probably came into existence by chance and natural selection instead of by intelligent design, I do not understand.

The small degree of agreement checked by some L. D. S. Fair Believers and even some L. D. S. Strong Believers with this Skeptical idea was understandable as more apparent than real, because these were mostly cases where the respondents had checked agreement on this and the preceding statement. Since these two statements are clearly exclusive, one saying God created man's mortal body and the other saying it is not known whether a God made man, this puzzle is largely explained by careless answering. One scientist in an amendment said that he did not think chance and selection and intelligent design were mutually exclusive. The bulk of answers, however, showed that most of the scientists did consider them exclusive.

When the theory of evolution was stated to apply to the species other than man, the answers of the scientists were about the same as when applied to humans. Those who believe in evolution believe in it for both people and other life. (Tables 26 & 27)

SCIENTISTS' COMMENTS ON EVOLUTION

About one in twenty of the scientists amended their answers to these statements about evolution by commenting, which gave added insight into their thinking.

A scientist with a non-evolution belief stated, "I think that man as we are today was created all at one time." Another said regarding evolution, "A theory with only fragmentary evidence of support. Certainly small changes are possible as affected by environment in plants and animals."

Some evolutionists explained, "The single cell at man's conception has man in it, so in all past." "Add 'most processes of warm blooded animals are related--organs, enzymes, glands, nerves, etc.'"

But most of the comments came from believers in both religion and evolution and helped to show how they arrive at their religion-science harmony on this question. "Delete 'is not biologically related' in that it has similar organs and parts." "No revelation as to how God created man." (The implication here was that if there is no revelation about how God made man, then when science purports to show how, there was no conflict with religion.) Another scientist simply said, "Religion does not explain 'how'."

GOD ESTABLISHED LAWS

One L. D. S. Strong Believer said that he thought God created man's mortal body not by making many small progressive changes, etc. but instead by establishing laws for making many small progressive changes, etc. Another L. D. S. Strong Believer added, after the word God, "working as a master geneticist, created man's mortal body by making many small progressive changes, etc." And a devout Latter-day Saint, in what may serve here as a final word from the Mormons, wrote, "Man was created (organized) by means of using a period of time not known for sure, and the method used--special creation or organic evolution--is not a matter of faith."

A non-L. D. S. scientist suggested, "Change to 'man's mortal body was created by some logical intelligence'." Then another amended, adding, "The species are biologically related and probably developed by controlled or designed phenomena!"

SCIENTISTS IN WHICH FIELDS TEND TO BELIEVE IN SPECIAL CREATION?

Some scientists specialize in studying living things, their development and their genesis. These are zoologists, botanists, and geneticists, mainly. Other scientists need comparatively little knowledge about living things to qualify for their fields, for example, physical chemists, astronomers, physicists, metallurgists, engineers, and mathematicians.

Do those who know the most about living things believe in the evolution of living things or not? Table 28 shows that Utah scientists who believed Positively in special creation instead of evolution are few, only 10 of the 282, and of that ten only one is a biological scientist! (Another is an agricultural scientist.) Those Utah scientists who Positively do not believe the theory of evolution of living things are almost all in fields apart from the study of living things.

While only 3.5 percent of Utah scientists Positively reject the theory of evolution, 14 percent Tentatively reject it. What fields of science do they know most about? One fifth of them are in sciences classified as biological. Even this fraction contains no zoologists or geneticists. One was in Medical Sciences. Another was in nutrition, one in plant pathology, and two in biology. Four of them did not clearly agree with distinct creation against evolution because they also contradictorily checked agreement with the evolutionary viewpoint.

But if we count all Utah born biological and agricultural scientists who expressed any agreement with special creation of living things, they are only one-fifth of the Utah scientists in those fields.

While the fields probably closest to the evidence about evolution--zoology and genetics--contain no scientist respondents who reject evolution, the broader category of life sciences obviously contains a minority of non-evolutionists. This may mean that the evidence for evolution is not as compelling, say, as is the evidence that the earth is hundreds of millions of years old, a proposition with which none of the Utah scientists in the relevant fields, such as geology, disagreed. (Table 29)

ABOUT NOAH AND THE FLOOD?

And the waters prevailed exceedingly upon the earth; and all the high hills that were under the whole heaven were covered. Fifteen cubic upward did the waters prevail: and the mountains were covered. (Genesis 7:19)

To take this to mean that the tops of all the mountains, and Ararat, were covered at least 15 cubic deep and the whole earth correspondingly takes an extremely Literal and narrow reading of Genesis. It hinges on inflexible rendition of two words, <u>all</u> and <u>whole</u>. It gives no recognition that it may only a report of the scene as it appeared to the local observer, rather than as if God Himself were the writer, which, if one wishes to be Literal, the Bible itself does not literally affirm!

Large percentages, 24, of the scientists checked No Opinion on this matter. The largest agreement among the Utah scientists with this Literal reading was among the Other Churches' Believers with 20 percent. As on the matter of the age of the earth, other churches seemed to produce more Literal belief than did the Latter-day Saints. However, the L. D. S. Strong Believers were not much less than those of other churches, with 16.3 percent Literalists on the flood. (Table 30)

There was strong agreement among Seminary teachers with the Literal view on the flood, 57.7 percent, far more rigid than the scientists.

Scientists, we suppose, would be more likely than others to have such questions come to mind as: Could such a catastrophic inundation occur without leaving telltale evidence in many parts of the earth? And, why has such evidence not been turned up by geologists? Is there enough water on and around the planet earth to cover the whole earth to such a depth? (The crest of Ararat is farther above sea level than the topmost of the highest peaks in the United States.) What evidence is there that it, or the other mountains of the earth, was lower, instead of even higher, in Noah's days?

One lone Utah scientist believed Positively in the Literal universality of the flood. He was an Other Churches' Believer. Many more Utah scientists believed Tentatively than Positively in the literal flood story, 8.5 percent of the 282.

Again it is revealing to ask about the fields of science of those who hold the Literal views. Are they in the fields which have the information about the subject at hand? Regarding the flood, are they geologists, anthropologists, or archaeologists? Not one of them! In the fields which would have such knowledge as is available about a universal flood, no Utah scientists, Latter-day Saint or otherwise, believed that there was one as the literalists interpret Genesis. The largest numbers of those who believed in a literal universal flood were in chemistry.

While among religions the Literalists seem by numbers to be Latter-day Saints, by percentage the picture is different. The four of other religions are 20 percent of the Other Churches' Believers, whereas the twenty Latter-day Saints are less than 10 percent of the total 214 Latter-day Saint Utah scientists of this study. (Table 31)

SCIENTISTS' COMMENTS ON THE FLOOD

We can understand the thinking of the some scientists by their amendments to the questionnaire items. One asked, "As we know it (the whole world or as the writer knew it?) In one form or another, this is the main question. As another put it, "This may have been the 'whole world' according to Noah's knowledge of it at the time. Could have been a small region actually. Different wording of the thought was, "I do not know if the ancients meant the whole earth or not. There was a tendency for the ancients to refer to the part of the earth with which they were familiar as the whole earth."

A view less accepting of the Bible account was that Archeology has shown the periodic occurrence of such floods in Mesopotamia but no tie to Noah. The legend of a great flood is found in many primitive societies other than Judean. These probably have foundation in local floods somewhere.

The scientists were also asked to react to the statement: The flood of Noah was a reality, but the details must be interpreted differently than given literally in Genesis. Responses to this statement served as a double check on the opinions on the previous table. And they did give about the same picture. The least Interpretive group, as indicated by disagreement, were the Other Churches' Believers, 20 percent of them disagreeing. This corresponds to the 20 of them who agreed with the Literal on the flood issue. (Table 32)

Only 12.4 percent of the L. D. S. Strong Believers disagreed with this Interpretive statement, none of them Positively, but 17 percent showed No Opinion. The Seminary teachers divided about half and half and thus were far less of the Interpretive view than the scientists.

Here was another statement on the flood to which the scientists were invited to respond: There was not necessarily any such flood as described in Genesis. We labeled those who reacted in agreement to this as Skeptical, although one can agree that there was not necessarily any such flood, and still qualify as a Believer in Christianity. Of the Other Churches' Believers, 20 percent so agreed. And even of the L. D. S. Strong Believers, 14.7 percent agreed. But none of the Seminary teachers agreed with what we have labeled a Skeptical belief. (Table 33)

The data from the questionnaires showed that there were only 5 Utah born scientists who were Literal believers in each of the three Literal beliefs analyzed for field and religion, young earth age, special creation of species, and literal flood story. These five very Literal scientists were as follows: 1 Congregationalist--Biological; 1 Latter-day Saint--Metallurgical; 1 Unitarian--Chemical; and 2 Latter-day Saint--Chemical.

Sixteen Utah scientists were Literal on two of the three Literal beliefs analyzed for field and religion. Seven of these agreed on the first two, two on the first and third, and seven on the second and third.

Evidently very few scientists indeed, of the 282, consistently held to a Literal point of view in the science-religion area, as revealed by answers on these items.

WHAT ROLE SHOULD SCIENTIFIC REASON PLAY IN RELIGIOUS CONVICTION?

Religion is a matter of faith, not reason. This is a retort often heard when reason seems to be upsetting someone's pet religious beliefs, even from people who are pleased to parade their own use of reason to upset someone else's religious beliefs, when reason seems useful to their purpose instead of seen as threatening.

Should use of scientific reason or logical thinking as a means to religious conviction have a minor role? Most of the L. D. S. Seminary teachers, and a larger percent of the L. D. S. scientists disagree, 57.7 percent of the teachers and 73.7 percent of the L. D. S. Strong Believer scientists.

The group with largest percentages agreeing to a minor role for reason is the Other Churches' Believers, with 32 percent agreement, twice as much agreement as shown by the L. D. S. Strong Believers. Again we found confirmation that the Latter-day Saint religion tends more than others to encourage scientific beliefs. (Table 34)

It is difficult to establish that the idea of a minor role for reason is Literal, in the sense that questions on the age of the earth, the special creation of the species, or the universal flood might be called either Literal or Interpretive. But we supposed from our observation that those who choose the rigidly literal interpretation of scriptures necessarily would believe in a minor role for reason in religion. And, as we are now seeing, there is such an association.

Should the scientific viewpoint and method be held in very high regard and given a major role in all convictions? This is the contrary of the viewpoint that in religious convictions it should have a minor role. The words "all convictions" pose a strong test for faith in science. But the results are about the mirror image for what we found on the previous Table. Most of the scientists agree with giving the scientific viewpoint and method a major role in all convictions. The Other Churches' Believers, confirming a tendency seen throughout these statistics, were the least Interpretive, here the most in disagreement, 52 percent. (Table 35) Figures on this from the 1992 study are in Chapter VIII and show a divergence from these toward less faith in science.

Among the Latter-day Saints, the Seminary teachers split about half and half, while the L. D. S. Strong Believers were 59.6 percent in agreement, 31 percent disagreement. Substantial percentages of the L. D. S. Strong Believers, 18.7 percent. These, however, included almost as many amendments, 17 percent as agreements.

Seminary teachers had 37.4 percent agreement, which was more than among any Utah scientist group. However, a slim majority of them disagreed with a primacy in conviction from supernatural and authoritative sources. (Table 36)

The other side of this coin was the statement that religious conviction should come primarily from logical thinking upon the facts of history, the existing world, the fruits of religion, and personal experience. This is a highly realistic and practical test of religion, and there was substantial agreement with it from all categories.

Seminary teachers agreed with these realistic tests as much as the L. D. S. Strong Believers, 67.4 percent to 65.9 percent. The balance was not in disagreement, since sizable percentages made amendments. Of the L. D. S. Strong Believers, only 14 percent disagreed, and of the Seminary teachers, only 23 percent. Obviously Mormons believe that their religion can and ought to stand up to realistic or practical tests of truth. Other Churches' Believers are less in agreement that religious conviction should come from the realist. (Table 37)

The amendments clarified some views, but did not alter the pictures given by the above figures as to such comments as these: "Religious convictions, if any, cannot be derived by scientific reasoning." "Is it assumed here that religious conviction is desirable or necessary?" "I do not believe it should come through any process."

Several on the religious side amended to include prayer as a major means to religious conviction. One said, "I believe a person must integrate sound reasoning with prayers to achieve conviction." As to science another said, "It should be used as a means of inquiry substantiated finally by prayer and religious experience." Still another would agree with a major role for scientific reason but not superseding the role of spiritual humility and atunement to the spirit of God." In addition to the realistic tests, a scientist said, "Religious conviction should come from answers to prayers, teaching from religious authorities, and careful study. And the inspiration of the Holy Ghost." One simply commented, "Faith is a gift of God."

Certain limitations of science were implied by some scientists as amendments to the statements of the questionnaire. One said Science has little to say about human values. Another said, "to the extent that it is knowledge and not theory." Another, "Providing we consider facts beyond the physical side." Science should play a major role, another points out, where there is scientific evidence that can be applied.

DO SCIENTISTS BELIEVE THAT GOD INTERVENES IN HUMAN AFFAIRS?

A major issue on which thinkers differ about religion is the role of Deity in events on this earth. Some, by an all inclusive view of the meaning of the verse, "Against none is the anger of the Lord kindled, save he that acknowledgeth not His hand in all things," feel that we must be ready to see the hand of God intervening in anything and everything, day-in and day-out.

The Seminary teachers agree a little less with this than do the L. D. S. Strong Believer scientists, 21.2 percent to 23 percent: **Strong majorities of both the scientists and Seminary teachers disagree that God constantly intervenes in human affairs**. (Table 38)

As with most of our statements on the questionnaires, this one was followed by another, having a contrasting viewpoint. This time it was stated: God does not commonly intercede in human affairs: Man's life on earth is largely shaped by man's own agency. Very large majorities in all categories agreed with this statement which stresses man's own agency. Again, Seminary teachers agree with this more than even the scientists, 76 percent of the Seminary teachers. Mormonism stresses man's own agency rather than God's intervention. The Mormon is not expected to acknowledge the hand of the Lord in **all** things literally, to the extent of saying it is certainly God's wish that a child be run over by a drugged driver. A leading religious educator of the Church,

Wm. E. Berrett, emphasized his rejection of any such stretch of belief in God's intervention. (Table 39) A third viewpoint on the role of Deity in human events is known as the Deist. Some Founding Fathers of our country held this belief. It may be stated: There is a God who is creator but he never intervenes on earth now. This was rejected by Utah scientists. Even the largest agreement, which came from L.D.S. Fair believers, was only 13 percent. (Table 40)

While we have labeled the Deist view as Skeptical, one deserving the label more is the statement: God is completely unknown to man. This was the agnostic view. It was held by almost no Utah scientists at all, only 8 percent of the total. The largest agreement was among Nominal L. D. S., 21.9 percent. Even among them, however, agnosticism was held by a weak minority. (Table 41)

Comments of the Utah scientists about God's intervention on earth were varied. Against intervention one said, "It is a poor parent that does this with his married children. God does not intercede, said another, as pertains to individuals.

One scientist would delete the word "commonly" and change to "occasionally" and add or influences the human mind. A biologist says, "Nature is one whole and there are not supernatural exceptions." An orthodox and literalist Catholic man of science states, "Intervene, yes, if you mean by intercede to upset the workings of nature like when the sun stood still."

A Mormon chemist said that he could not check any of the questions about intervention either agree or disagree, but he stated for himself, "A God can be or work through nature not above and beyond it. I do not believe in the latter. I do in the former." I understand him to believe in God as a part of nature working through it. Another Latter-day Saint, a Strong Believer biologist, said, "God intervenes only in the sense that he governs according to divine laws which we do not comprehend."

To the statement that man's agency largely shapes earth's affairs, a Latter-day Saint scientist added, that this occurs, in light of his knowledge including knowledge of God's laws as revealed from time to time by his prophets.

IS GOD OMNIPOTENT?

Most people assume that God has power to do anything he may wish, virtually by definition. He created everything. He can do anything. At least one scripture uses the words "Lord God omnipotent." (Revelations 19:6) Much orthodox theology and ritual emphasize the omnipotence of God. If one is a rigid literalist, omni means all--all!

Beyond the well known and sassy question, "Can God make a rock so big that He cannot lift it?", there are other considerations that lead some to see God as at least limited by what He has decided and what He has done. For example, if He has made man a free agent, do not the actions of men serve now as a limitation on His power? If He is a God of law and order, does He not operate in obedience to universal laws or his own laws? A classic dilemma posed by skeptics to trap believers has three prongs. Since God does not now eliminate evil, either He does not know about it (is not omniscient), does not care about it (is not all good), or cannot now eliminate it (lacks the power). But this need be no trap to Mormons nor others who do not believe they are committed to a creed of omnipotence for God.

One view is that man's power as a free agent is at least one limitation on God's power. Much smaller percentages of Other Churches' Believers, disagreed with absolute omnipotence than did L. D. S. Strong Believers. It is 16 percent to 34.1 percent. Nevertheless, L. D. S. Believers, both Seminary teachers and scientists, were about equally divided on this question. A large percentage of L. D. S. Strong Believers made amendments. There were noticeable percentages of both scientists, 12 percent, and teachers, 26.9 percent, who agreed with both the omnipotence of God and that He is now limited, a contradiction, I believe. (Table 42)

Thus the percentages of agreement and disagreement with the belief in a limited God were not a mirror image of agreement and disagreement on the belief in the omnipotent God.

Note that 73.1 percent of Seminary teachers agreed that God Himself is now limited while 60 percent of the Seminary teachers also agreed that God can and may do anything at all. Exclusive as these two statements logically seem to me, they did not seem so to some Seminary teachers and some scientists, although they did to most. Note also that while the L. D. S. Strong Believers were evenly divided on whether God can and may do anything at all, 65.9 percent of them agreed that God is limited against only 15.6 percent disagreeing that He is limited. (Table 43)

The most likely explanation, as far as I can see, for this discrepancy is that Mormonism retains enough of the literal all powerful reference to God that it remains impressed even on those who also believe the good Mormon doctrine of man's free agency. Some may simply not have thought of it as a limitation on God, or may not wish to see it worded that way.

Large percentages showed that they have No opinion on this issue. Care should be taken in reading the percentages to make allowance for those with No opinion.

Most of the amendments were made by L. D. S. Strong Believers. One said that television is a contradiction to logical facts known to man, to show, we suppose that man's logic is not a suitable test of what is possible. Another said that God must conform to laws, and a Latter-day Saint physicist worded the same idea this way, "Within the frame work of laws established before the material universe was established."

HOW PERFECT MUST SCRIPTURE BE?

For centuries it has been an article of faith in orthodox Christendom that scriptures of the Bible are "revelation without error and as such were delivered to the Church herself." The Infallibly guided Roman Catholic Church had herself decided what writings were inspired and what, therefore, should form the Holy Canon. It is little wonder that at the time of the Inquisition some most highly placed Catholic thinkers were afraid of the effect if the populace discovered that there were errors in the scriptures which had been pronounced inerrant by Catholic Councils.

Although the claim of Catholic writers that the Catholic Church made the Bible and preserved it through the ages can hardly be contested, being historically true, an ironic result of the Protestant Reformation was to cause an even greater worship of the Bible as the sole and completely authoritative Word of God. Having broken away from the authority of the organized Church of Rome and the papacy, the Protestants needed a new source of authority. They chose the Bible as their source. This perpetuated a narrow reverence for the Bible, relieved only by the Protestant right of the individual to interpret the Bible for himself, which the Catholic Church did not, and does not, grant. However, the interpretation encouraged upon Protestants for generations was one of rigid narrowness and literalness. As we have seen, it is narrow and literal interpretations of the Bible, with ignoring the possibility of mistranslation, which brought theologians into their classic and ill-fated conflicts with scientists.

We are interested to see how the scientists regard the scriptures. The eighth article of faith of the Latter-day Saint Church is, "We believe the Bible to be the Word of God, as far as it is translated correctly. We also believe the Book of Mormon to be the Word of God." We requested response to the statement: The Standard Works are the Word of God, entirely without error, except mistranslation in the Bible. For the Latter-day Saint the term Standard Works includes not only the Bible but the Book of Mormon, the Doctrine and Covenants, and the Pearl of Great Price, the latter three being, to them, modern revelations from God.

Very few of the scientists in any category agree with this statement of inerrancy. The highest percent, 14, is among the L. D. S. Strong Believers. Seminary teachers ran much higher agreement, 36.6 percent. But even they had a majority in disagreement. (Table 44)

Large percentages among Other Churches' Believers stated No Opinion or gave no answer, 36 percent. They knew they lacked basis for an opinion on the Standard Works.

Amendments were mostly by those who agreed generally with inerrancy but wanted to state some qualifications. Most were by Latter-day Saints, one of whom added, "if properly interpreted, and the written word must always be interpreted." A Latter-day Saint chemist said, "Any errors are man's. Hardly a scientific treatise is written without errata or error." An Other Churches' Believer wrote, "Change 'Standard works' to 'Bible' and insert 'without essential error'. A Mormon deleted "without error" and added, "some not well written but the thought only was given. Another said, "May have minor errors."

Another question about the scriptures was: The 'Standard Works' are all inspired by God but each may reflect some human error and limitation because they are in man's language. Among the Believing Latter-day Saints there was overwhelming agreement with this statement, 86.1 percent for L. D. S. Strong Believers, 76.6 percent among the Fair Believers, and 93.1 among the Seminary teachers. (Table 45)

Large percentages of Other Churches' Believers and Nominal L. D. S. checked No Opinion on this item. The Strong Believers made almost all of the amendments. The following cover the ideas expressed: "As far as major concepts and significant principles, there are no errors." And, "The Book of Mormon so states." Finally, "All who create are inspired."

EXISTENCE OF SOME ERROR IS TENABLE BELIEF

The Mormon viewpoint that all of the inspired scriptures may contain some human error is a truthful and tenable belief compared to the orthodox Christian view that scripture, as the Church herself has it, is revelation without error. It helps put the Mormon Church hand-in-hand with the truth-seeking approaches of science, making possible the avoidance of conflict with science.

A Skeptical statement on the questionnaire about the scriptures was worded: The Standard Works are nothing but the thoughts of men and thus may contain many errors. Only the Nominal L. D. S. agreed with this view in any sizable percentage, 56.4, with 16.4 having No opinion. Overwhelming percentages in all other groups disagreed with the Skeptical view. Large percentages of the Other Churches' Believers either checked No Opinion or gave no answer. (Table 46) Amendments on this item were negligible in number and meaning.

HOW DO SCIENTISTS REACT TO LITERAL AS COMPARED TO INTERPRETIVE APPROACH?

These two questionnaire items provided the only places where the scientists themselves could respond to whether they believe in Literal or Interpretive' reading. By the way in which they have answered other items, we have presumed to classify them as one or the other. What do they themselves say about whether the scriptures in the Standard Works must be literally interpreted without effort to stretch them to fit supposed facts or theories of science?

Except for the Seminary teachers, who divided about half and half, the large percentage of all categories disagreed with the necessity for literal interpretation. (Table 47) Amendments were made mostly by the L. D. S. Strong Believers. Delete ' literally, insert 'correctly'. Add 'in light of philosophical and historical knowledge of the language of the times', Add 'subject to considerable interpretation. They may be used to derive whatsoever benefit the individual may be able to gain." It says, 'Delete 'to stretch them'.

What if the statement is turned around to read: Interpretation of the words of scriptures should be as flexible as language permits to harmonize with logical thinking or scientific reasoning? Of the L. D. S. Strong Believers, 17.1 percent then disagree. Since 8.5 percent amended, there was, as with the previous statement of literalism, a desire to make the statement clearer by comments. Other Churches' Believers were less inclined toward the flexible point of view than the Latter-day Saints. The Seminary Teachers divided about evenly, with a leaning toward disagreement with flexible interpretation. (Table 48)

Amendments were again made mostly by L. D. S. Strong Believers. They said, "Delete 'logical thinking or scientific reasoning,' substitute 'established truths'. Add 'Should not be stretched to change meaning or import.' Delete 'or scientific reasoning'. Add 'in regard to the Bible'. Delete 'all' after 'flexible'."

THE SOURCES OF OFFICIAL CHURCH DOCTRINE

Latter-day Saints not only accept the Bible and other scriptures known as the Standard Works as the Word of God but also believe in continuing revelation of God's will to man. They believe in God as a presently living and caring Father in Heaven who can reveal to His prophets additional truths of consequence to the well-being and eternal progress of man.

Three types of viewpoint as to what makes up the Word of God were presented to the scientists and Seminary teachers for their reactions. It should not be supposed that there are only these three viewpoints on this matter, but we feel that these crystallized the main types of belief. The first statement was: Most conference statements by the President of the Latter-day Saint Church are the infallible word of God, official Latter-day Saint doctrine. We believe the answers here show an amount of faith by numerous Latter-day Saint scientists and teachers that runs over the boundaries of what Church belief requires, yet 34.9 percent of the L. D. S. Strong Believers and 34.3 percent of the Seminary teacher agreed with this strongly worded statement, the strongest word being "infallible." (Table 49)

No Believers in Other Churches and few Nominal or Fair Believers among the Mormons believed in this infallibility.

The amendments showed how some scientists interpreted the statement and helped clarify some positions. A Strong Believer L. D. S. pointed out that revelation doesn't have to come from a President, saying, "Joseph Smith wasn't President when God revealed Himself to him." He added, "when spoken as: 'thus sayeth the Lord'. Another Mormon Strong Believer said, "Delete 'infallible'." Still another said, "Infallible Word of God, no, but official L. D. S. doctrine, yes." Several made amendments saying, in effect, this same thing.

A second statement of source of doctrine was: The Word of God, official Latter-day Saint doctrine, is found only in the scriptures or in pronouncements given by the president of the Church explicitly as revelation. This was a more cautious approach to what forms doctrine. Seminary teachers agreed, 55.8 percent, Mormon Strong Believers, 48.9 percent. The larger percentages of the Seminary teachers agreeing probably shows that more of them are conversant with the actual stand of the Church, which I believe is reflected more in this conservative statement than in the one with the word "infallible". (Table 50)

Large percentages of Nominal Mormons, 29.1, and of Other Churches' Believers, checked No opinion on this, but it was interesting that 12 percent of Other Churches' Believers agreed. Perhaps they were answering what they thought the Mormon belief is, not what their own belief is. Or perhaps some non-Mormons do accept pronouncements given as revelation by the President of the Mormon Church as the Word of God.

Very few of the Utah scientists in any group agreed that: Nothing from scripture or Church authorities is revelation from God. Such agreement as there was came almost entirely from the Nominal Mormons, less from Other Churches' Believers, and none at all from Seminary teachers. Larger percentages of Nominal Mormons and Other Churches' Believers showed that they had No Opinion on this, or gave no answer. There were a very small number of amendments. This was, apparently, a very clear and definite statement as it stood. (Table 51)

SOME OPINIONS ON DIVINE AUTHORITY OF CHURCHES

The two concluding statements were short: (1) No church is divinely authorized, and (2) No church is the only divinely authorized one.

Among Mormon Strong Believers, 88.4 percent disagreed, with the first and almost as many disagreed with the second. Disagreement among Seminary teachers ran 100% on the first and 90.4 percent on the second. Such agreement as there was occurred in the ranks of the Nominal Mormons and the Other Churches' Believers. They agreed more strongly with, No church is the only divinely authorized one, which even picked up a little agreement from Mormon Strong Believers and Seminary teachers. Most Latter-day Saint scientists believe that there is an only divinely authorized Church.

WHAT KIND OF TEACHERS HELPED UTAH SCIENTISTS MOST TO HARMONIZE RELIGION AND SCIENCE?

The scientists were invited to name writers, teachers, or speakers whom they recall helping them most in the science-religion area. Unfortunately, almost one-half of all the scientists did not list anyone. Perhaps no one stood out in their minds. Perhaps they were too tired of the questionnaire by this time!

We classified, in the manner showed on the Table 54, the ones they named. There were (1) Latter-day Saint Church General Authorities holding views which we labeled as Interpretive; (2) Those tending toward what we labeled as Literal views; (3) Renown (not Latter-day Saint) scientists or philosophers; (4) Latter-day Saint writers we were unable to classify; (5) Scientists unknown to the author; and (6) Any other than the above.

MORMON SCIENTISTS HELPED MOST BY "INTERPRETIVE" CHURCH AUTHORITIES

The help Latter-day Saint scientists acknowledged from the Interpretive General Authorities ran several times as many as from the Literalist General Authorities or from any other group. One third of the Mormon Strong Believers recalled assistance from the Interpretive compared to only 7.8 percent from the Literal.

Among Seminary teachers, the recognition of the helping group ran 28.8 Interpretive compared to 21.2 percent Literal. The Nominal Mormons reflected more influence by Renown Scientists or philosophers (not L. D. S.) than by any group or Latter-day Saint writers. (Table 54) A study almost identical to the 1992 study, but with fewer questionnaire items, asked about authors of influence. Among the Mormons, only four mentioned any authors of Literal views.

HOW MUCH DID THE LATTER-DAY SAINT BELIEVER SCIENTISTS TEND TOWARD LITERAL OR INTERPRETIVE?

As we have gone through the scientists' reactions to statement after statement in this chapter, **it has been obvious that the Utah scientists, including the Latter-day Saint Believers, are heavily of the Interpretive viewpoint.** While roughly half the Seminary teachers are also of the Interpretive philosophy, we could see that they were decidedly less so than the scientists.

Largest percentages of the Latter-day Saint Believers hold from six to ten Interpretive beliefs out of the possible eleven. In fact, 60 percent did so. Half of the Latter-day Saint Believers held only three or fewer Literal beliefs, and one-fifth held only one.

The Mormon Believer scientists have obviously answered much more toward the Interpretive viewpoint, 74.2 percent against 8.1 percent of them who answered more toward the Literal. Seminary teachers divided about evenly. (Tables 55 & 56)

THE SCIENTISTS BELIEFS' IN SUMMARY

In the classic controversies over the age of the earth and the evolution of the species, the Mormon Strong Believers scientists were massively opposed to the Literal and sturdily of the Interpretive theological interpretations. Among Mormon Strong Believers, 84 percent disagreed with the idea that the earth was created in merely thousands of years.

Among those in the fields of science which have data on the age of the earth, i.e., geology, anthropology, physics, none agreed with the idea that the earth was created in merely thousands of years, solidly believing many millions of years.

Almost half, 49.6 percent, of the L. D. S. Strong Believers agreed that God created man's mortal body, probably by making many small progressive change from simple to more complex over millions of years. Only 26.4 percent of Mormon Strong Believers disagreed with such evolution for man, while 15.5 percent held no opinion.

Of scientists who checked Positive agreement with the non-evolution beliefs, only one was in the ones with the data, i.e., the biological sciences. All others were in fields which might not have made them so aware of the evidence supporting evolution.

Among those who checked Tentative instead of Positive agreement with the non-evolution views, there were eight in biological sciences, but this was only 10 percent of the biological scientists of the study. None of these eight were geneticists or zoologists. And half of the eight had contradicted their answer by showing agreement with evolution elsewhere in the science-religion beliefs section of the questionnaire.

Mormon Believer scientists were preponderantly of the Interpretive viewpoint throughout. On science-religion problems touching their own fields, Mormon Believer scientists were virtually 100 percent of Interpretive viewpoint.

The wisdom of the Latter-day Saint Church which gives its members freedom of choice between such views as we have labeled Literal and Interpretive has been largely responsible, we may conclude from this chapter, for some compatibility of science and the Church. We may also conclude that those who are scientific in their approach to truth will find in the Interpretive approach an aid to faith and understanding. To the considerable extent that the Church encourages the Interpretive approach, it displays a receptivity to new truth and promotes a synthesis of scientific and religious truth which holds for the Church and humanity some promise of future progress. Yet the 1992 study came up with surprises. See Chapter VIII.

CHAPTER VII

HOW TROUBLED WERE UTAH SCIENTISTS BY SCIENCE-RELIGION CONTROVERSY?

> The developing Genesis problems must have contributed much to the growing lack of faith in the scriptures as the word of God and consequently must share a certain responsibility for the problems of our disturbed generation. Dr. Frank B. Salisbury.[1]

There were questions other than those answered in the previous chapters for which I also hoped to find answers from the scientists, such as:

1. To what extent did the Utah scientists change from one viewpoint to another on science and religion as they matured?
2. From which viewpoint did they mostly change?
3. Were some of them emotionally troubled by those changes and to what extent?
4. And, what is more important, perhaps, would the amount of emotional troubling be related to the viewpoint from which they changed? Or to which they changed?

It is not surprising that overwhelming majorities of the scientists changed their opinions on some science-religion questions posed by Item 17 of the questionnaire and discussed in the previous chapter.

Eighty-three percent of the Nominal L.D.S. and 80 per cent of the L.D.S. Fair Believers had made some changes. Still a large, percent of the Strong Believers had changed, 68 percent. There is clearly a positive relationship between the strength of L.D.S. belief and lower percentage of change; the stronger the belief, the smaller percentage had changed their viewpoints on the science-religion question. To some extent, though not large, it appears as if it might be an advantage to the strength of Latter-day Saint religious conviction for fewer changes to be necessary. Or it may simply be that with initially strong conviction less change of view takes place. (Table 57)

Of those who stated ages when they made most of their changes (that is, omitting the "No Answer"), 52 percent stated ages that fell between 22-30; 11.4 percent from 18-22; 3.5 percent from 14-18; 2.7 percent before 14; 10.3 percent after 30, and 18.4 were continual. Clearly, two-thirds of the changes took place during high school, college, and post-graduate college years. The importance of these ages as times of transition and decision, well-known to educators, was reaffirmed by these data. (Table 58)

NUMEROUS SCIENTISTS CHANGED BELIEFS

Having found that large numbers of the scientists had changed some beliefs as they matured, we ask from which viewpoints did they mostly change? (We already know from Chapter VI where they changed to---preponderantly to the "Interpretive.") Evidently they have changed most from beliefs called "Literal" showing that these are the prevailing early views, as we might have guessed. A sizeable fraction, around one-third, however, have changed from at least one belief that we labeled "Interpretive." A smaller percentage, around 12, changed from some Skeptical beliefs. (Very few had ever held Skeptical beliefs to begin with, as we know from Chapter VI.)

On the strictly science-religion questions taken up in Chapter VI---such as the age of the earth, evolution, and the literal reality of the universal flood---almost all changes were from "Literal" to either "Interpretive" or "Skeptical", preponderantly to "Interpretive." Such changes from "Interpretive" back to "Literal" as occurred were on those beliefs that were more theological than scientific in nature, such as the beliefs about the basis of religious conviction. (Table 59)

I guessed that having to change from early "Literal" beliefs would tend to cause some loss of faith, so that more of those who became merely Nominal Mormons would have changed from "Literal" than would be the case for those who arrived instead at a Strong Believer position. I supposed that starting with "Interpretive" beliefs, thus not having to change, would be associated with later strong Mormon belief. The facts in Table 59 showed no clear indication of this. In fact, the beliefs from which the scientists changed have little relationship to whether they later became strong believers or not. (Table 60)

Now back to the question about emotional troubling over changes of science-religion beliefs. At least four facts are clear: (1) That very small percentages of the Utah scientists said they were "Intensely Troubled"; (2) That sizeable percentages said they were "Somewhat Troubled"; (3) That the percentages of "Troubled" among the Other Churches' Believers were comparable to those of the Mormons, although tending to be higher; and (4) That substantial percentages did not answer this question.

The least "Troubled" were the Nominal L.D.S., with 54 percent "Not Troubled", and the L.D.S. Strong Believers with 45 percent "Not Troubled." The most "Somewhat Troubled" were the L.D.S. Fair Believers with only 26.7 percent of them not so afflicted. It is possible that those arriving at the poles of either "unbelief" or "Strong Belief" were less troubled because they were less "on the fence" than Fair Believers. Or the implications may have been that those who became Fair Believers were subjected to stronger antagonistic forces of sciences versus religion in youth that troubled them emotionally and resulted in their not having either left the Church or having developed Strong belief.

We could be concerned about "emotional troubling" about science, since from one-third among the Nominal L.D.S. and L.D.S. Strong Believers to more than one-half among the L.D.S. Fair Believers had been "Troubled" either "Somewhat" or "Intensely." While the meaning of "Somewhat Troubled" was vague, it still suggests the existence of a problem. And 3.3 percent to 7.8 percent of Mormon scientists who were "Intensely Troubled", while a small group, were no doubt eleven unhappy young people for a while. For them and for anyone interested in helping, there were problems. (Table 61)

A HYPOTHESIS REFUTED BY THE DATA

A second hypothesis was also not upheld by the research. I had guessed that there would be a relationship between degree of emotional troubling and changes from the "Literal" beliefs. That is, I thought we would find more "troubling" associated with more changes from "Literal" beliefs and less "troubling" with fewer such changes. The facts do not support such a surmise. That is, the percentages of changes from "Literal" beliefs remain the same whether the scientists were "Not Troubled", "Somewhat", or "Intensely Troubled."

These data are congruent with what psychiatrists and clinical counselors have said about troubled emotions, namely, that the real causes may lie deeper than what the individual consciously supposes is troubling him, here deeper than any intellectual problems of science and religion.

SUMMARY

We found that very few scientists even thought that they have been "Intensely Troubled" by their changes in science-religion beliefs. Roughly one-third of the Utah scientists in the study thought that they had been "Somewhat Troubled." We may conclude that harmonizing of religion and science was difficult for this one third, if we assume that "difficulty" was the cause of the "Troubling." For both Latter-day Saints and

Other Churches' Believers there were some remaining "rough spots" in the road of science-religion harmony.

The interesting thing shown by this part of the study may be that there are almost twice as large percentage of "Somewhat Troubled" among the L.D.S. Fair Believers as among either the Nominal or Strong. What is the connection between this large percent of "troubling" and merely "Fair" degree of conviction on the salient doctrine of the Church? Does the relationship suggest any means of reducing the "emotional troubling"? The alternatives seemed: (1) that the scientist who is first "Somewhat Troubled" over religion and science is likely to have his subsequent capacity for Strong belief impaired, or (2) the one who first has only Fair degree of conviction subsequently finds science-religion problems more troubling (difficult to resolve).

If indecision over whether Mormonism can be harmonized with science was causing either a reduction of faith or emotional troubling, Chapter IV and V should help one in firming up a decision that they can be harmonized, and Chapter VI should help in finding the philosophical "key" to harmonizing, namely, the "Interpretive" viewpoint. To the young person who thinks he is "Troubled" by science and religion, this Chapter can give reassurance that he is not alone, that others of scientific mind have also been troubled, and that they have shown that one can live with, or resolve, such problems and take one's place as a religious scientist.

CHAPTER VIII

RELIGIOUS BELIEFS OF UTAH SCIENTISTS 1955-1992

We looked at science-religion beliefs of Utah born scientists who were listed in the 1949 edition of American Men of Science in Chapters V and VI. Now, surveying the Utah scientists in the 1990 edition, we asked, "Are the newer generations much the same in beliefs or much different?" And has Utah gone up or down in per capita production of scientists compared to other states?

As to the 120,000 American Men and Women of Science listed for 1990, we repeated the previous study, counting the states of birth of the total, divided into the 1940 census figures for white population of the states.[1] In 1990 Utah stood 21 percent above the second place state, which was Delaware. Many states have changed rank order over these 41 years, but Utah has held its lead.

Utah was previously 32 percent above the second place state, which was then Idaho (now sixth). Why is Utah's lead now less? It is an actual decline in per million white scientists produced, down from 1,886 in 1949 to 1,658 in 1990. Our study does not show why. It shows that now more Mormon scientists than before were born outside Utah and Idaho.

In Science, an article entitled "Social Origins of American Scientists and Scholars", Dr. Kenneth Hardy wrote, "the Mormon groups are less productive than formerly."[2] This reflected the same trend.

Perhaps Mormonism's influence is a little less supportive of science than in the past. As we will see later in this chapter, the Mormon scientists have, in science-religion beliefs, moved in the direction of those religions which have the lowest productivity rates, namely, Roman Catholic and southern Protestants. Or perhaps the support of science in other states has tended to catch up, relatively. Nevertheless, Utah's lead is still impressive and causes curiosity as to the reasons for this phenomenon.

UTAH ALSO TOP IN DOCTORATE PRODUCTION INDEX

Confirming and adding to the reasons given in Chapters IV and V of this book, Dr. Hardy's landmark Science article was subtitled "Scholarly doctorates come disproportionately from religious groups having certain beliefs and values". He wrote, "The most productive state is Utah, which is first in productivity for all fields combined in all time periods. It is first in biological and social sciences, second in education, third in physical sciences, and sixth in arts and professions. Compared to other states in its region, it is deviantly productive. This result seems clearly to be due to the influence of Mormon values."

"The common beliefs and value systems of high producers seem to include naturalism; intrinsic valuation of learning and the individual quest for truth; emphasis on human dignity, goodness, and competence; a life pathway of serious dedication, of service to humanity, of continual striving; humanistic egalitarianism; a pragmatic search for better ways of doing things unfettered by traditional restraints . . . " (The traditional restraints would perhaps include those of the religions benighted about science, such as those promoting the anti-science Special Creation notions, and discouraging use of reason as a means to truth.)

The influence of Mormonism, and the harmony of Mormonism and science, as shown in chapters V and VI of this book, were important formerly in the Utah scientist production picture, as our 1955 study revealed. The major question for this chapter, from the 1992 study, is, "Are the Mormon influence and harmony still in place?"

States of Birth of American Men and Women of Science, 17th Ed., 1990, in Relation to White Population, 1950

State	Scientists	Population	Per Capita
Utah	1123	677,000	1658
Delaware	375	274,000	1368
Indiana	4501	3,759,000	1197
Kansas	2151	1,829,000	1176
New York	15191	13,872,000	1095
North Dakota	542	608,000	1055
Idaho	590	581,000	1015
Nebraska	1219	1,301,000	936
Wyoming	165	284,000	933
South Dakota	556	629,000	883
Illinois	6748	8,046,000	838
Colorado	1088	1,297,000	838
Massachusetts	3811	4,612,000	826
Minnesota	2344	2,954,000	793
Iowa	2078	2,729,000	761
Wisconsin	2577	3,393,000	759
New Jersey	3372	4,512,000	747
Hawaii	278	382,000	727
Pennsylvania	7121	9,854,000	722
Connecticut	1398	1,952,000	716
New Hampshire	377	532,000	708
Nevada	103	150,000	686
Ohio	4968	2,600,000	668
Missouri	2385	3,656,000	652
Rhode Island	503	777,000	647
Louisiana	1151	1,797,000	640
Georgia	1491	2,381,000	626
Oklahoma	1254	2,033,000	616
Vermont	231	377,000	612
Maryland	1187	1,955,000	607
Washington	1393	2,316,000	601
Oregon	890	1,497,000	594
Montana	325	572,329	568
Mississippi	649	1,189,000	543
Michigan	3181	5,918,000	537
California	4935	9,915,000	497
Arizona	322	655,000	491
Texas	3281	6,727,000	487
West Virginia	844	1,890,000	446
New Mexico	281	630,000	446
Alaska	41	93,000	440
South Carolina	569	1,293,000	440
Arkansas	643	1,482,000	433
Maine	391	911,000	429
Alabama	920	2,080,000	422
North Carolina	1197	2,983,000	401
Kentucky	1091	2,742,000	397
Tennessee	1055	2,760,000	382
Florida	751	2,166,000	346
Virginia	1750	5,282,000	331

SCIENTISTS PER MILLION

1949 AMS, White Population

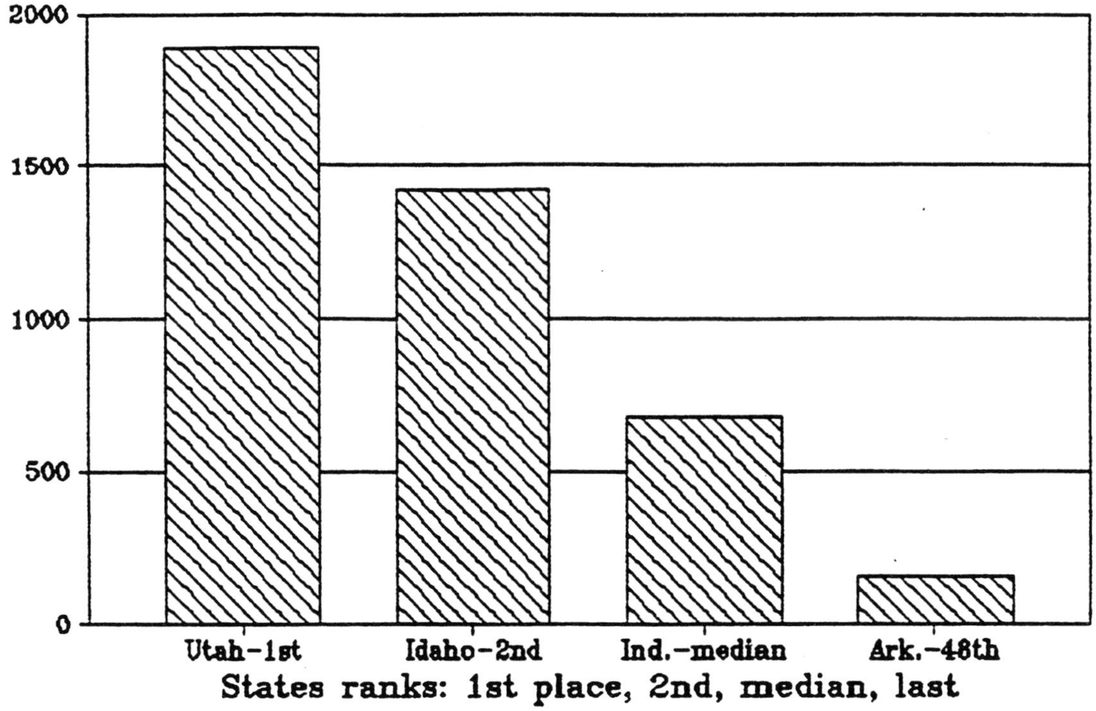

SCIENTISTS PER MILLION

1990 AMWS, White Population

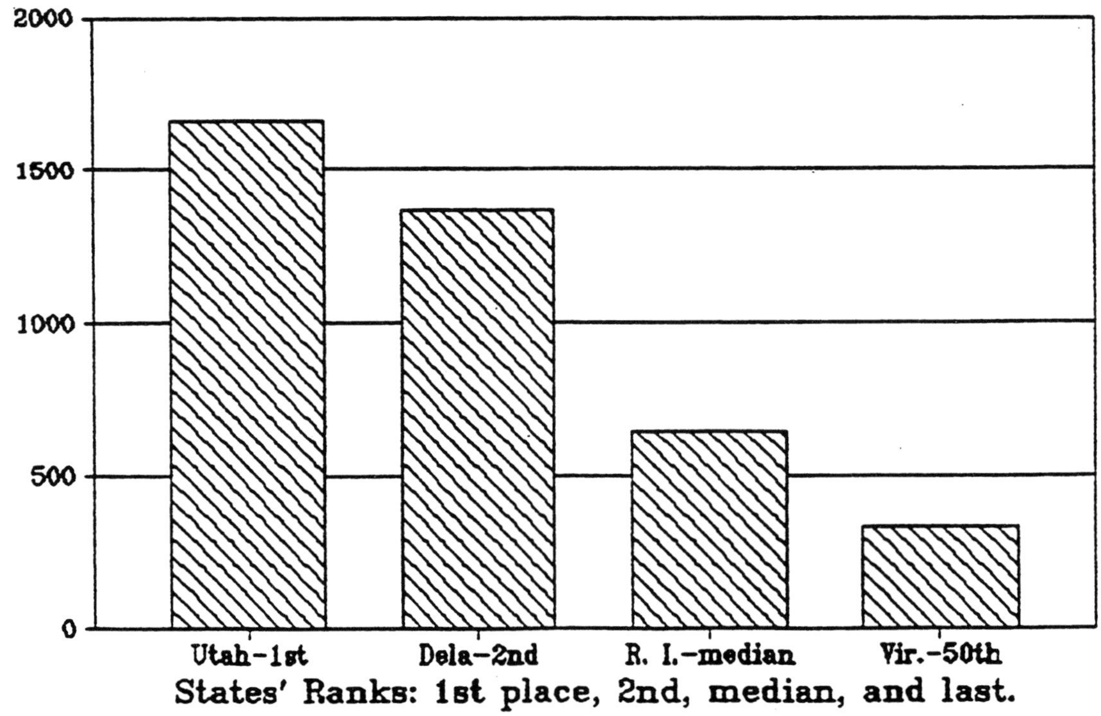

THE 1992 PICTURE OF UTAH SCIENTISTS

In 1992 we replicated the study reported in Chapters V and VI. This time it was based on graduates from Utah universities and listed in the 17th edition of American Men and Women of Science, 1990. (We omitted questionnaire items which were merely cross-checking, like opposites, and items that analysis showed irrelevant for the hypotheses.) The results now still uphold the hypothesis that scientific minds can harmonize Mormonism and science. They uphold it strongly more in one respect: In the percent of Mormon scientists identifying themselves as Very Strong Believers. In this there is a significant difference from 1955.

In all that follows, we are citing percentages of respondents, not of the total Utah scientist population. And we have confidence that the responses are sufficiently representative of the whole to justify the conclusions that we have reported. We have detailed our cross-checking tests in Appendix B, "Representativeness of the Studies".

DATA COMPARING 1955 TO 1992 HIGHLY RELIABLE

For comparisons with the earlier study, the data are particularly reliable, because we used the **same** wording in the questionnaire items in each, because the **same** researcher did the studies with the **same** methods, and because the percentage of response was nearly the **same**, namely, 63% 1955 to 65% in 1992.

HOW 1955 COMPARED TO 1992

We now go through the questionnaire items and state how the answers in 1992 compared to those of 1955.

First, in 1955 we did not ask whether the Utah scientists had changed denominations, but we did in 1992. Negligible numbers said they had changed. A few Mormon scientists were converts to the Church. A few had changed from Mormonism to something else, mostly Unitarianism.

MEANING OF THE TERM "STRONG MORMON"

We have often used the term "Strong Mormon" in what follows. This means Mormons who responded to the questionnaire that they have convictions that are either Strong or Very Strong that Joseph Smith was inspired by God in the formation of the Mormon Church.

Choices of None, Weak, or Fair were considered, for our tabulation purposes, as Mormon non-believers. There were negligible numbers who checked Weak or Fair in 1992.

(Mormon percents of conviction that Jesus is a member of the Godhead were virtually interchangable with those regarding Joseph Smith, although a little higher for Jesus as divine.)

The term "Other Churches' Believers" means members of churches other than Mormon who responded to the questionnaire that they have conviction of Strong or Very Strong that Jesus is a divine person of the Godhead. For our tabulations those choosing to respond None, Weak, or Fair were labeled non-believers. There were negligible numbers who chose Weak or Fair.

As we observe later, very large percentages of Mormon scientists, both in 1955 and 1992, were Strong Mormons by this definition. Believers said they were active in their Church. So did almost all Other Churches' Believers. But few of the latter were active between ages 18 and 24. Mormon Strong Believers were almost all active members between ages 18 and 24. (Table 11) From here on until otherwise noted there were **no certainly significant** changes from 1955.

WAS CHURCH THE CAUSE OF UTAH'S LEAD?

Did they believe that Utah's per capita lead in production of Men and Women of Science is somehow due to Mormon Church influence? In 1955 90% of Mormon Strong Believers did, but only 26% of non-Mormons, and 56% of Nominal Mormons. (Table 8) By 1992 86% of Strong Mormons, 45% of non-Mormons, and 40% of Nominal Mormons so believed.

Did they believe that their church contributed significantly to their professional achievements? Of Strong Mormons in 1955, 85% said "yes", of Other Churches Believers, 44% did. Of Mormons not in the Strong category, 56% said "Yes". (Table 9) In 1992, of Mormon Strong Believers 75% so believed, Other Churches Believers (speaking of their own churches) only 22%, and Nominal Mormons, 1%.

How did they view the Mormon Church as an institution for promoting human welfare? Almost all scientists in all categories responded, "Favorable"! All of Strong Mormons, as we would expect, did so view it. In 1955 56% of Other Churches' Believers and 87% of Nominal Mormons said "Favorable". In 1992 the non-Mormon "Favorable" had risen to 77%, the non-Strong Mormon, who were less in numbers, declined to 60% "favorable". Of Other Churches' Believers 22% were "Indifferent" as were 40% of the non-Strong Mormons. (Table 14) Almost none of the scientists checked "Antagonistic" toward the Church, only 4% at the most in any category, either year. By 1992 "Antagonism" was down to less than 1%, except non-Mormon non-Believers, who came in at 4%. (Table 14)

"BY THEIR FRUITS YE SHALL KNOW THEM."

By the pragmatic New Testament test of prophets, "By their fruits ye shall know them", the Mormon Church could, with reason, be known by many scientists as a church having true prophets.

One respondent, a Catholic scientist with Strong profession of belief in Christ, on the question about Joseph Smith's inspiration, wrote to us, "He certainly was farsighted and charismatic, and because of this the Mormons have been a blessed people."

NEED RELIGION BE HARMONIZED WITH SCIENCE?

Did they believe that the fields of science and religion are so far removed from each other that **no** attempt is logically necessary to harmonize them? In 1955 86% percent of Strong Mormons said, "No". Among non-Mormons the "No's" were only 16%. For nominal Mormons it was only 43% who said "No". For 1992 76% of Strong Mormons did not agree with the statement. Non-Mormons came in at 77% "No", with non-Strong Mormons at 20%. So scientists generally do not believe they needed to "compartmentalize" their religious beliefs, set them apart from scientific truth. This was specially true for the Believers, both Mormon and otherwise. Non-belief was strongly linked with the idea that science and religion are far removed from each other so that no attempt is logically necessary to harmonize them. (Table 5)

Some people might suppose that many scientists retain faith in religion and science by putting them in exclusive spheres, compartmentalizing. The responses of our scientists support the very opposite. It was mostly the Believers among the scientists who said they did not consider science and religion as so removed from each other as to need no attempt to harmonize. (Table 6)

DID UTAH SCIENTISTS BELIEVE THEY HARMONIZED?

Did they believe that they logically harmonize their church's doctrines and science in their own views of life? This was the question with most direct connections to the

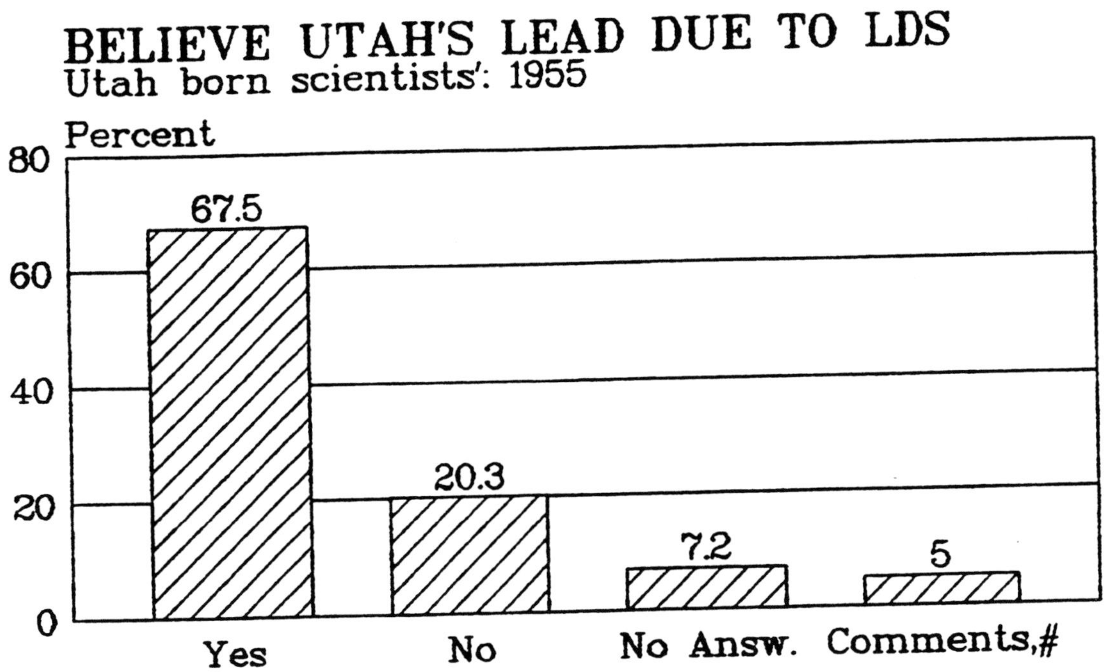

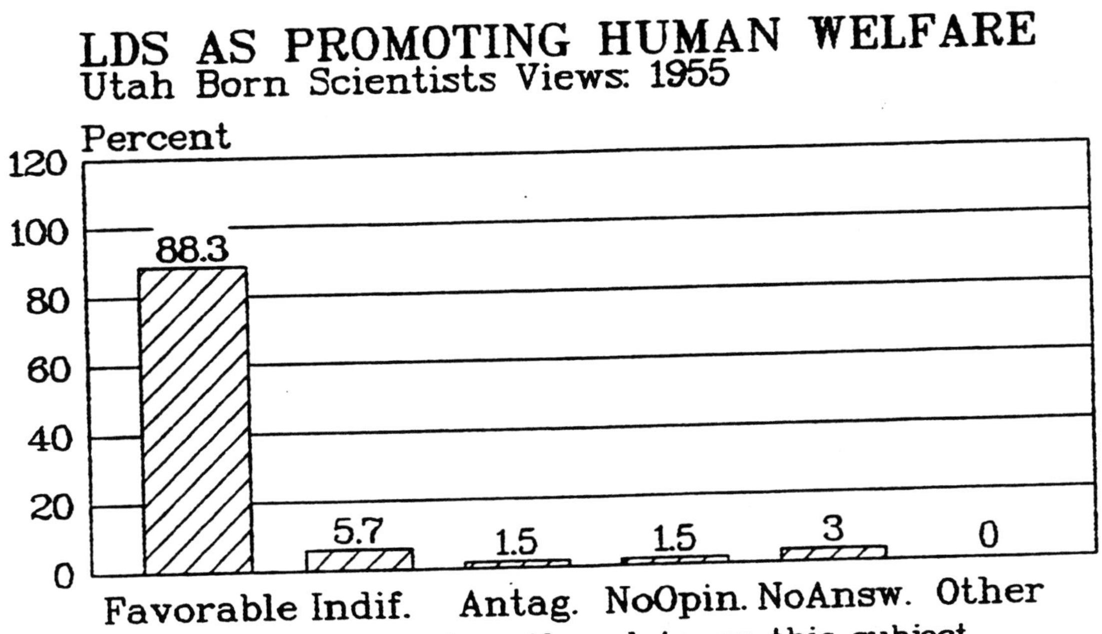

See Table 14 for other data on this subject.

LDS SCIENTISTS: JOS. SMITH AS INSPIRED
1955 Study

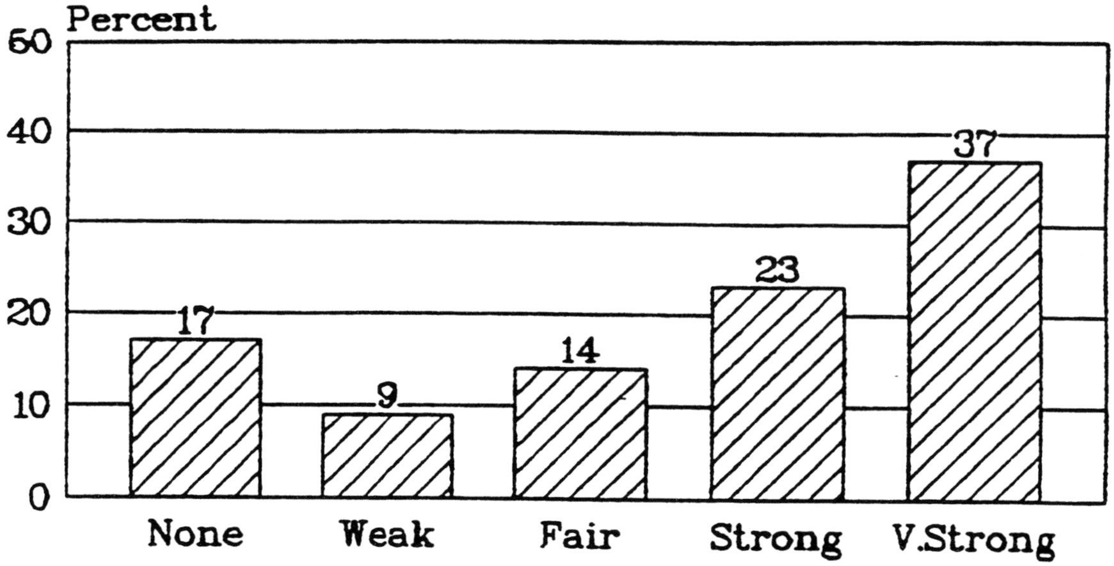

LDS SCIENTISTS: JOS. SMITH INSPIRED
1992 Study

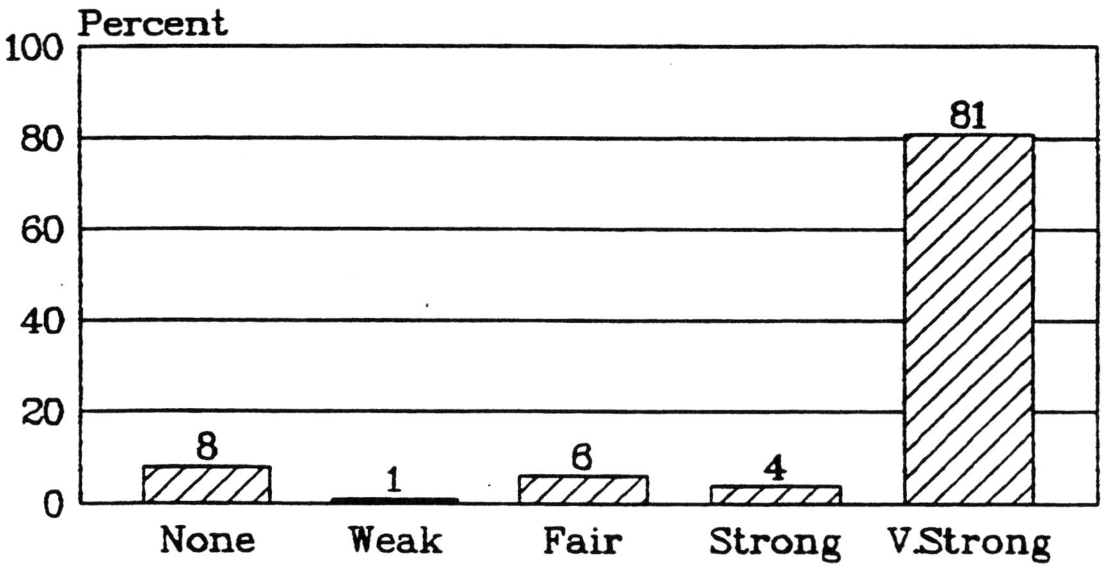

hypothesis that Utah scientists can harmonize their religion and science. It was answered with a resounding "Yes!" for Believers. There is no significant difference in 1955 and 1992 answers for Strong Mormons. It was about 85%. Other Churches' Believers were 64% in 1955 and 77% in 1992. Mormon non-Believers were the largest group by far who indicated they did not harmonize their religion and science, 40% in 1955 and 80% in 1992. The reader may question whether some scientists who say they harmonize, actually do so. What about the 17% of Strong Mormons in 1992 who disagreed that the earth is at least hundreds of millions years old, and the 28% more who said they had No Opinion on this virtually certain scientific knowledge? Have they some harmonizing left to do?

How they go about developing this harmony was the subject of questionnaire items about the role of science in religious conviction and their views about inerrancy of scripture and whether it is to be taken literally.

CHANGE IN PERCENTAGES OF MORMONS WITH STRONG CONVICTION

On items reported from this point on, there were **certainly significant** changes from 1955 to 1992. Very important to the question of whether the Mormon Church can reasonably be called a science-harmony religion was whether the scientists it produces believe in it.

Their conviction was shown by answers to the question, "Please show the strength of your conviction that Joseph Smith, Jr., was inspired by God in the formation of the Mormon Church." The choices were (1)No such conviction; (2)Weak; (3)Fair; (4)Strong; and (5)Very Strong.

For non-Mormons the choices were the same but on the statement, "Please indicate the strength of your conviction that Jesus of Nazareth is a divine person of the Godhead."

Mormons who had any strength of belief in Joseph Smith always had as strong or stronger belief in Jesus as divine.

The Mormon scientists answered as follows on the conviction of Joseph Smith as inspired by God in the formation of the Church of Jesus Christ of Latter-day Saints:

1955: No Such or Weak, 26%; Fair, 14%;Strong, 23%; Very Strong, 38%.
1992: No Such or Weak, 9%; Fair, 6%;Strong, 4%; Very Strong, 81%.

In the study of the Utah born scientists 41 years ago, there was a hint of an increase of Strong Believers. Younger scientists showed a tendency to be stronger in belief than older ones. (Table 18, 3)

We do not believe our data shows why this increase in Strong Mormons occurred over these two generations. It went from 60% in the Strong and Very Strong categories to 85%. In 1955 the Very Strong were less than twice the Strong. In 1992 the Very Strong were about 20 times the numbers of Strong. Later in this chapter we will depart from data and speculate on some factors involved in this increase.

To be analytical, there seem to be only three possible meanings to this data. (1) The commitment to key Mormon belief has truly risen 41% among Mormon scientists; or (2) the zeal to make their "testimony" known on a survey has risen; or (3) Mormon scientists have more zeal to let their beliefs be known to a researcher seen as a public university professor emeritus (1992) than to a doctorate graduate student (1955). (Or some unknown combination of these three.) Shear speculation is (3), with no basis in fact known to us, (1) and/or (2) are the probable meanings. Either or both are complimentary to the Mormon Church programs.

When the percentages of Strong Mormon scientists are translated into numbers, they mean that there are about 1400 Strong Mormon scientists who were graduates of the Utah universities and listed in 1990 American Women of Science, based on this 1992 study.

Whatever the causes, the increase of overwhelmingly Strong "testimonies of Christ" by the Mormon scientists was also testimony to the credibility of Mormonism for some highly educated, professionally competent minds.

FIELDS OF SCIENCE

These Utah scientists were in at least fifty fields of science. There were Strong Mormons in each field except a few containing only one respondent. A few fields had somewhat more Strong Mormons than other fields. Two fields were over-represented among the total Mormons by double and triple. (See Appendix B, "Reliability of the Study" for description of how fields were used to adjust "weightings" to increase reliability by withdrawing, randomly, calculated percentages of questionnaires returned from chemists and physicists. This adjustment lowered a little, not significantly, the numbers of Strong Mormons and Mormon Literalists.)

Chemistry was the most over-represented and Physics the next. We cannot resist wondering if this had anything to do with the fact that two world-renown Mormon scientists, Harvey Fletcher and Henry Eyring, were respectively physicist and chemist and well known in Mormondom as Strong in the faith. On one of our surveys, the person cited as having most influenced respondents in their science-religion thinking was Henry Eyring.

THE ROLE OF SCIENTIFIC REASON IN RELIGIOUS CONVICTION

That use of scientific reason or logical thinking as a means to religious conviction has a **minor** role in religious conviction elicited among Strong Mormons 16% agreement in 1955 but 45% in 1992. (Table 34) That the scientific viewpoint and method should be held in very high regard and given a **major** role in all convictions produced 59% agreement in 1955 but only 36% in 1992. Non-Mormons had 61% agreement in 1992. (No data for non-Mormons as a group in the 1955 study.) (Table 35)

That religious conviction should come primarily from answers to prayers, miraculous healing, and statements from religious authorities had, among Strong Mormons, only 19% agreement, 55% disagreement in 1955 but 42% agreement and 40% disagreement in 1992. Both times there were more than 20% who had no opinion or wrote in amendments, most of which were striking out a part of the statement before agreeing with it. The part most often deleted was "statements from religious authorities". The factor most often added was the "Holy Spirit". A major role for the "Holy Spirit" was written in by noticeable numbers of Mormon scientists.

We have no data as to why this shift to less confidence in science relative to the spiritual evidence occurred, but it is consistent with the few other notable changes to be discussed later in this chapter.

On belief in God, the results showed small change over the years in question. The change among Mormons was to a bit more belief in God. Among all categories of Mormon scientists, 1992, agreement was 97%. This is higher than for the average of Americans. In contrast, among non-Mormon Utah scientists it was 58% agreement, with about 40% of No Opinion. (Table 41)

Agreement that God is now limited by realities in the nature of things, such as man's "free agency", was heavily a position of Mormons, 65% among Strong ones in 1955, 38% in 1992. Among Other Churches' Believers it is near zero both times. Why the Mormons have moved in the direction of the non-Mormons over the years, we do not know. (Table 43)

Do you believe that God commonly acts directly in events on earth, that is, that

REASON MINOR ROLE IN CONVICTION
LDS Strong Believer Scientists: 1955

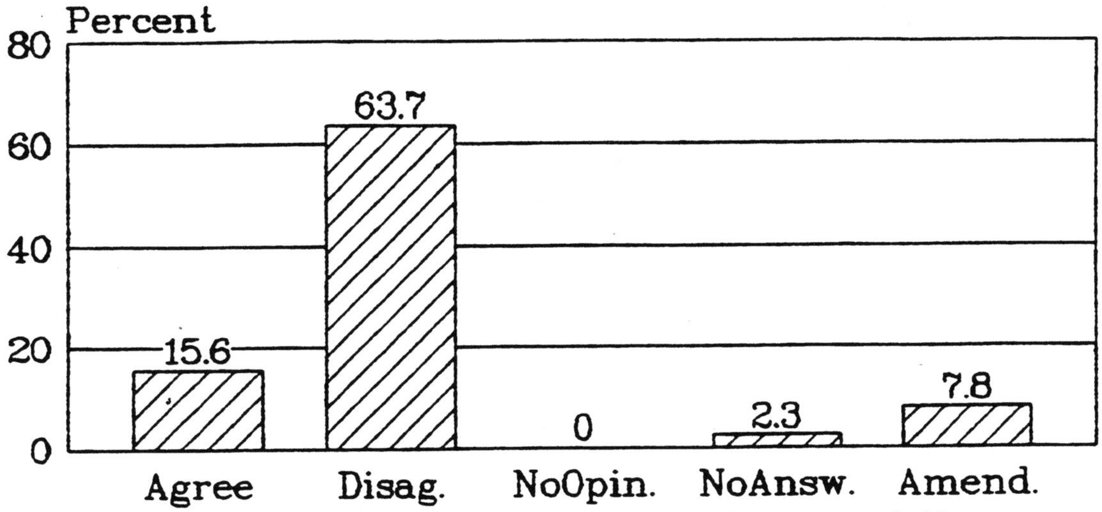

Table 34 has more data on religious convictions.

REASON MINOR ROLE IN CONVICTION
LDS Strong Believer Scientists: 1992

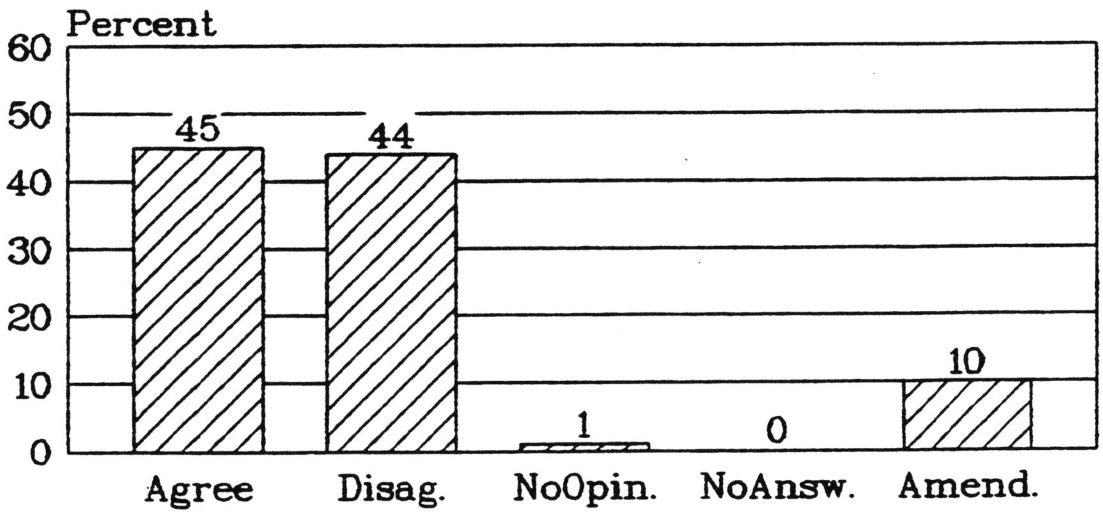

Table 34 has more data on religious convictions.

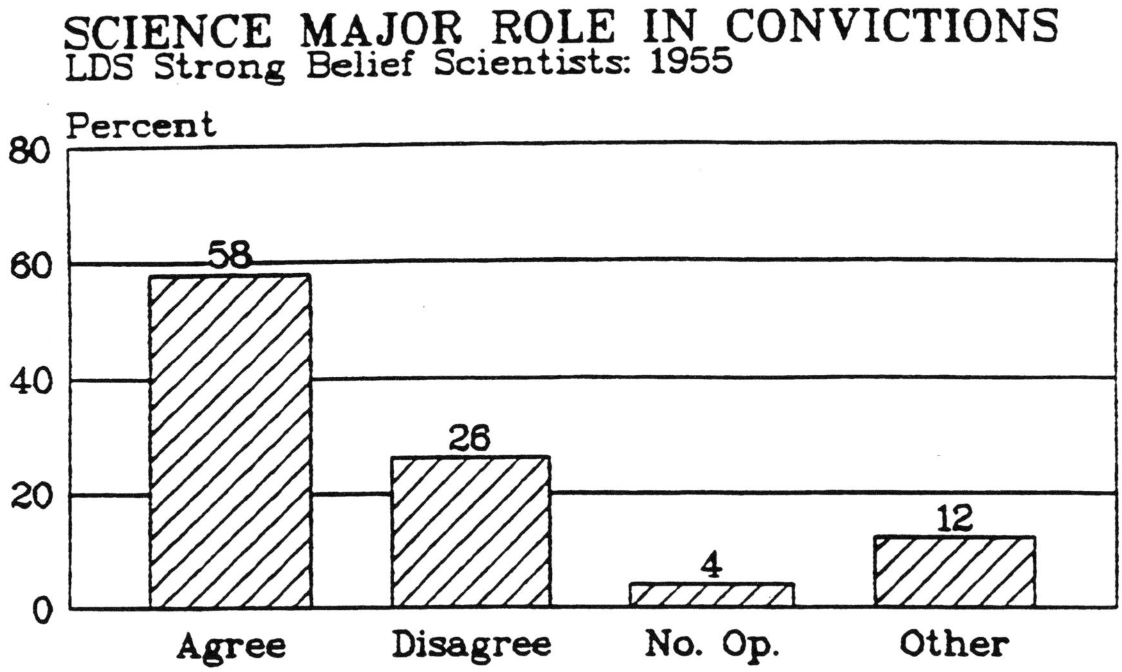
SCIENCE MAJOR ROLE IN CONVICTIONS
LDS Strong Belief Scientists: 1955
Percent
80
60
40
20
0
58
26
4
12
Agree
Disagree
No. Op.
Other

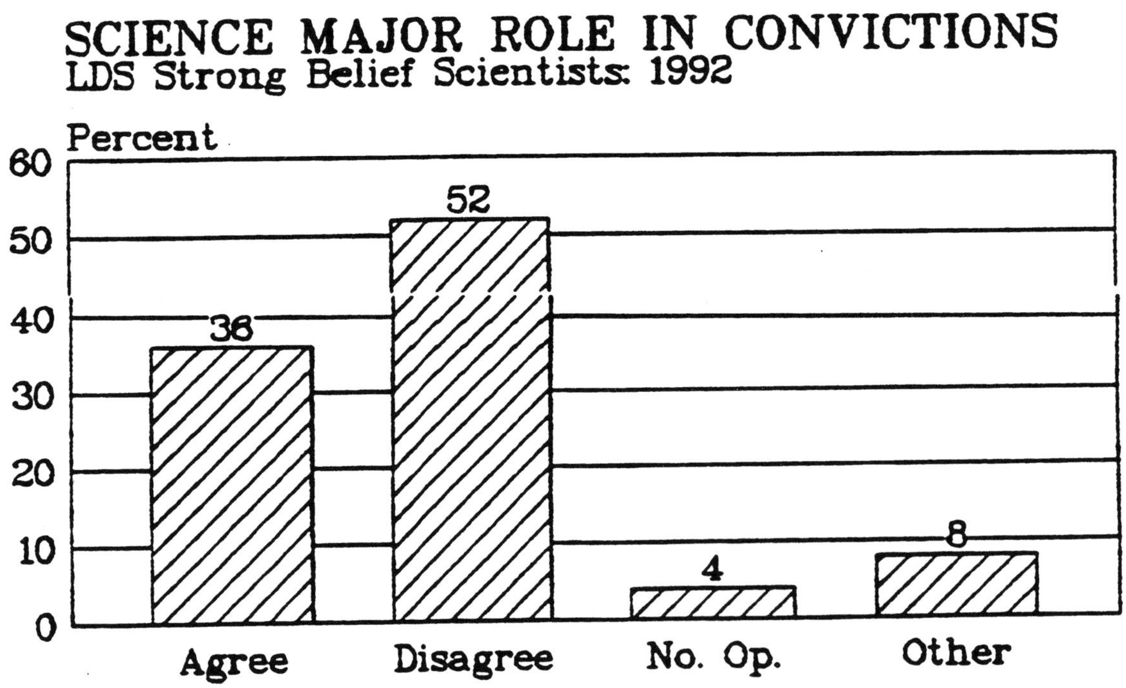
SCIENCE MAJOR ROLE IN CONVICTIONS
LDS Strong Belief Scientists: 1992
Percent
60
50
40
30
20
10
0
36
52
4
8
Agree
Disagree
No. Op.
Other

EVOLUTION A METHOD OF GOD: 1955
Strong Believer LDS Scientists

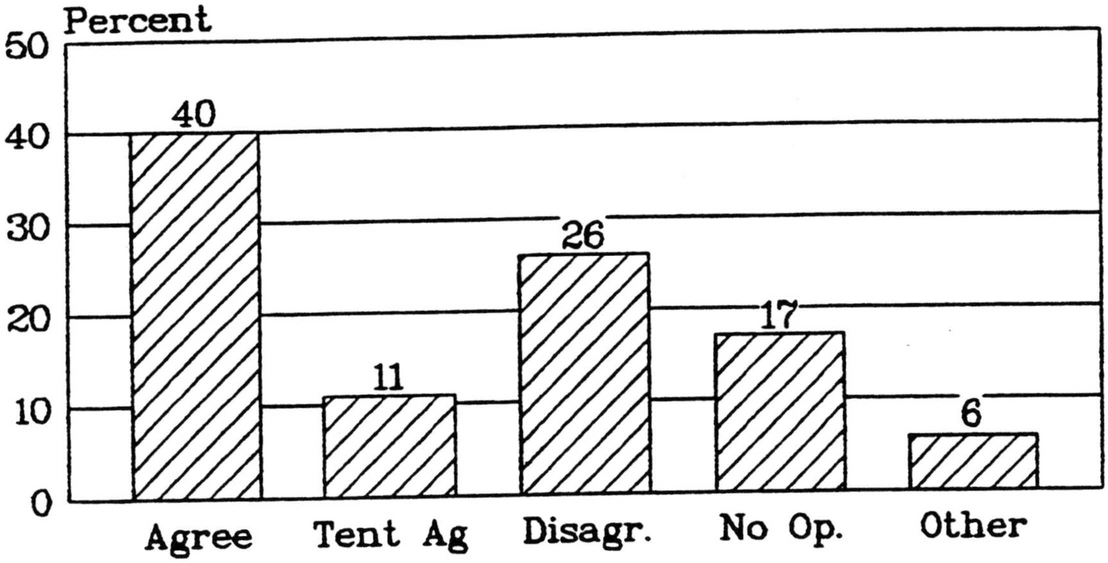

EVOLUTION A METHOD OF GOD: 1992
Strong Believer LDS Scientists

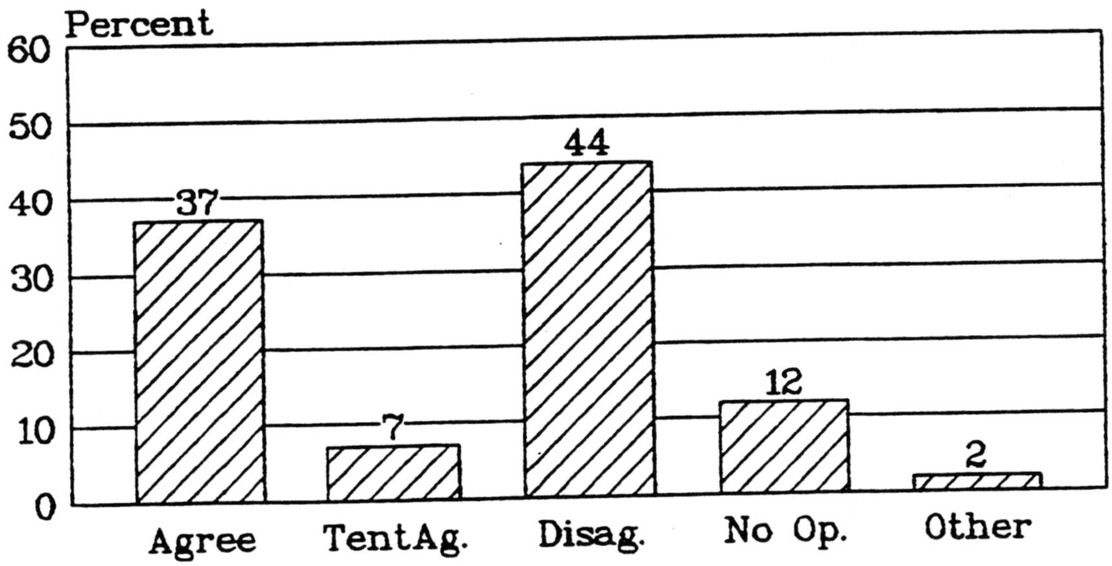

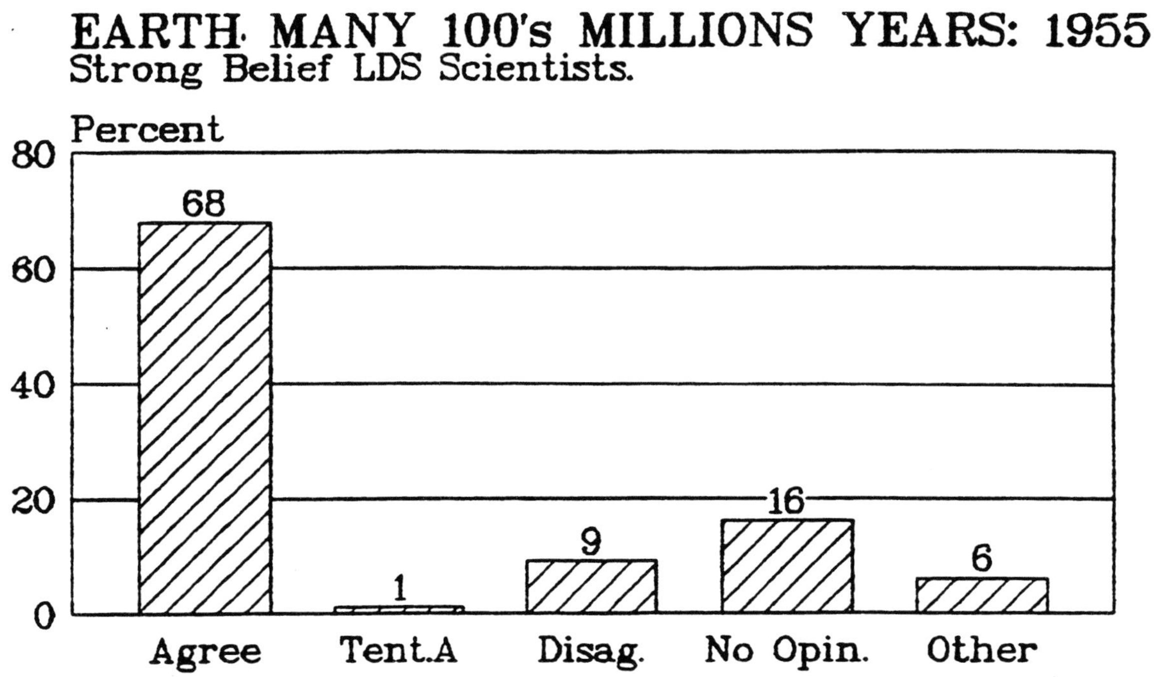
EARTH MANY 100's MILLIONS YEARS: 1955
Strong Belief LDS Scientists.
Percent
80
60
40
20
0
68
1
9
16
6
Agree
Tent.A
Disag.
No Opin.
Other

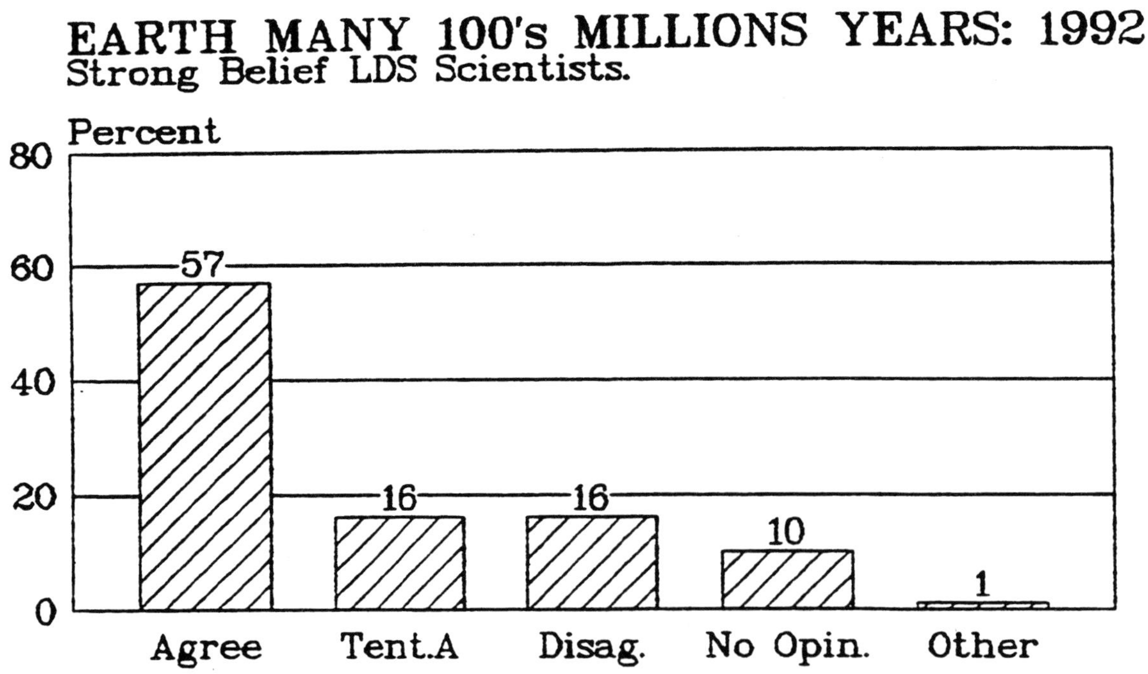
EARTH MANY 100's MILLIONS YEARS: 1992
Strong Belief LDS Scientists.
Percent
80
60
40
20
0
57
16
16
10
1
Agree
Tent.A
Disag.
No Opin.
Other

God often intervenes in human affairs? "Yes", replied 23% of Strong Belief Mormons in 1955, "yes" 85% in 1992! Of non-Mormons in 1991, the "yes" answers were 30%. One might suppose that Mormons thought He intervened between 1955 and 1992! One might guess these interventions included the growth of Israel, the rapid spread of Mormonism, the revelation opening the Priesthood to blacks, the dissolution of the Communist bloc, and other answers to prayers.

THE AGE OF THE EARTH

Do you believe that the earth took at least many hundreds of millions of years to create?

1955: Strong Mormons, Agree, 68%; Tent. Agree, 1%;
Disagree, 10%; No Opinion, 16%; Other, 5%.
1992: Strong Mormons, Agree, 57%; Tent. Agree, 16%;
Disagree, 16%; No Opinion ,10%; Other, 1%.
1955: Other Churches' Agree, 36.%; Tent. Agree, 28%;
Disagree 16%, No Opinion, 8%, Other, 12%.
1992: Other Churches' Agree, 78%; Tent. Agree, 11%;
Disagree 11%.

Both in 1955 and 1992 there was total agreement with the "hundreds of millions of years" from all Utah scientists whose fields require and provide accurate knowledge of the earth's age. **No** geologists, for instance, came in against the "hundreds of millions of years", though most of them were Strong Mormons. Why their disagreeing colleagues in other fields did not consult them, the specialists, before forming opinions, we can only guess. (Table 22)

That God created man's mortal body, probably by making many small progressive changes in life forms over millions of years, that is, "evolution" was probably God's process, produced the following responses: (Table 24)

1955: Strong Mormons: Agree, 9%; Tent. Agree, 41%;
Disagree, 26%; No Opin., 15%; Other, 9%.
1992: Strong Mormons: Agree, 35%;Tent. Agree, 7%;
Disagree, 44%; No Opin., 12%; Other, 2%.
1955: Other Churches': Agree, 20%; Tent. Agree, 36%;
Disagree, 28%, No Opin, 8%; Other, 8%.
1992: Other Churches': Agree, 78%; Tent. Agree, 11%;
Disagree, 11%.

Of Strong Mormons in the fields that study the history of life forms, 95% agreed that evolution was probably God's process.

Evolution by chance and selection instead of by God's design was opposed totally in both studies by Strong Mormons and 80% of Other Churches' Believers in 1955, 87% in '92. Belief that the species were special creations of God and did not arise from the process called "evolution"? It rose among Strong Mormons.

1955: Strong Mormons: Agree, 31%;Disagree, 47%;
No Opinion, Other 22%
1992: Strong Mormons: Agree, 60%;Disagree, 30%;
No Opinion, 10%.
1955: Other Churches': Agree,20%;Disagree, 68%;
No Opinion, 12%.
1992: Other Churches':Agree, 22%;Disagree, 67%;
No Opinion, 11%.

The Hardy data cited earlier showed that scientists came from "liberal" Protestant faiths much more than from the "fundamentalist" (like Southern Baptist). They are centers of anti-evolution, so-called Creation Science. Why Mormons have tended toward them, who were among Mormonism's historically most obvious antagonists, one can only guess.

ERRANCY OR INERRANCY OF THE MORMON SCRIPTURES

The questions about the "Standard Works" were pertinent mostly for Mormons, because non-Mormons are seldom readers of these Mormon scriptures, except the Bible. That the "Standard Works" are all inspired but each contains **some human errors** was agreed to by 86% of Strong Mormons in 1955 but only 70% in 1992. (Table 45)

The other side of this question, that the "Standard Works" contain **no errors** except Bible mistranslation, found 14% of Strong Mormons in agreement in 1955, but 30% in 1992. With No Opinion on this were about 8%, Other (with comments) 9% in 1955, 20% in 1992. (Table 44). This was consistent with the other changes over the years toward views we labeled Literal and from those called Interpretive. It was not so consistent with the answers on the method by which they read the Scriptures, because few said "Literally". Most checked "Interpret them with Reason". A doctrine of inerrancy pushes toward disharmony in the minds of reasonable people if, in truth, there exist in scriptures internal contradictions or inconsistencies with scientifically known reality. If the inconsistencies can be the result of human imperfection in writers or translators, not of mistakes by God, problems between religion and science are greatly reduced, as Chapter II showed.

With the movement toward the Literal in the past forty years as shown by the data, Mormonism as a religion harmonizing with science was in a little less favorable light than it used to be. This is assuming that the Literal which affirms a "young" earth and anti-evolution promotes an antagonism, not a harmonizing, with science. However, the belief of Strong Mormon scientists in the fields which specialize in studying the age of the earth is heavily, almost, in fact, unanimously, against the idea that the earth is only thousands of years old. And Strong Mormon scientists in the fields that study the history of life forms are, with few exceptions, believers in evolution as God's probable method of creating living creatures. So there was still substantial harmonizing, regardless.

The 64% of Strong Mormons who said they "Interpret them (the scriptures) with reason" showed no movement toward the "Literal" over the years in question. This supports the hypothesis that Utah scientists harmonize by using the Interpretive method, just as did the earlier study. But there was, in the specifics, oddly, a movement toward the Literal instead, which would support the hypothesis less well, as noted above.

For instance, there was the movement on the age of the earth from 69% Interpretive in 1955 to 56% in 1992, away from evolution as God's method of 50% in 1955 down to 37% in 1992, and toward Special Creation from 31% favoring in 1955 to 60% in 1992.

Obviously a number of Strong Mormon scientists who did not circle "Take them literally" as their method of reading nevertheless take them literally enough to **disbelieve** that the earth is hundreds of millions of years old, literally enough to believe in Special Creation of the "kinds" instead of evolution.

WHY DID THE CHANGES, 1955 TO 1992, OCCUR?

In the case of the age of the earth and of the probability of evolution, it might be speculated by some that Literalism became more tenable because they believe that scientific evidence for an "old" earth and for evolution has become weaker in recent years. For them, apparently, it has, relative to strength of faith in religious Literalism.

SCRIPTURES INSPIRED, NOT INERRANT
LDS Strong Belief Scientists: 1955

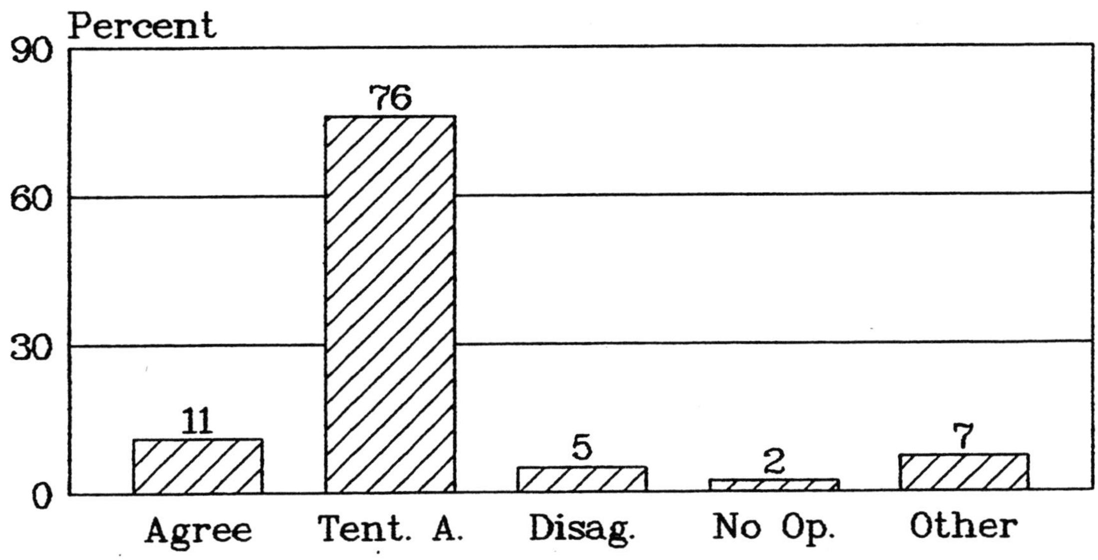

SCRIPTURES INSPIRED, NOT INERRANT
LDS Strong Belief Scientists: 1992

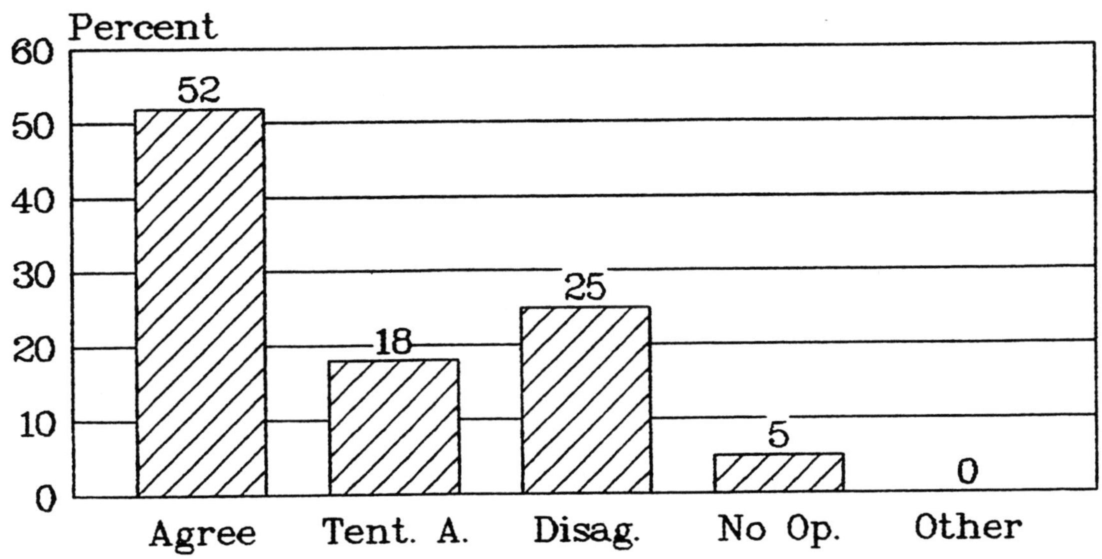

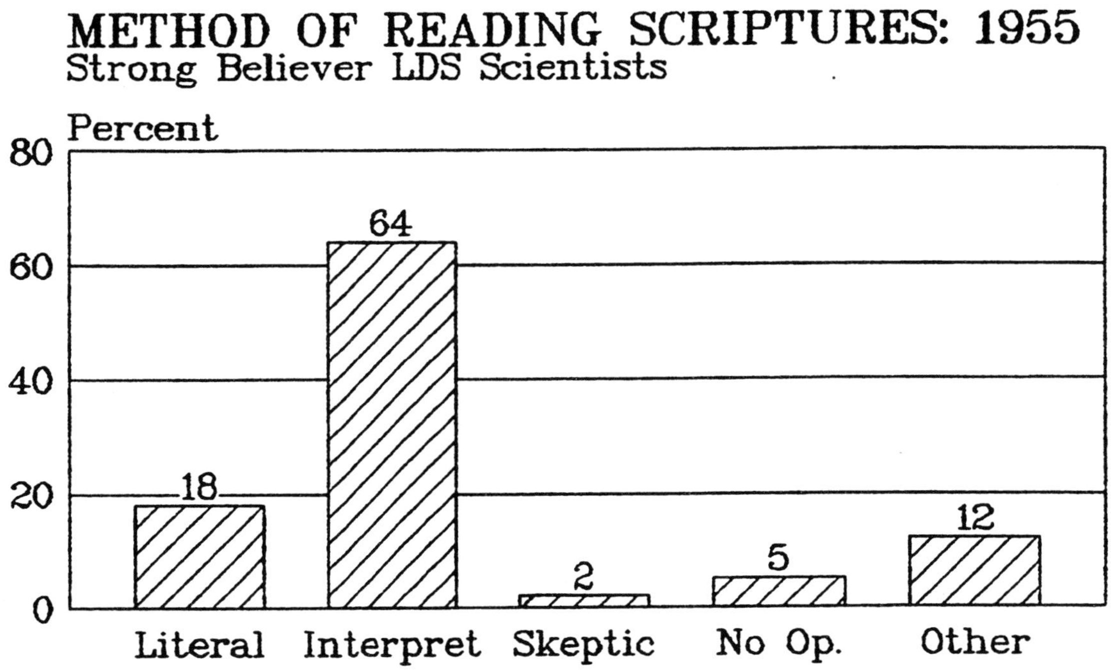
METHOD OF READING SCRIPTURES: 1955
Strong Believer LDS Scientists
Percent
80
60
40
20
0
64
18
2
5
12
Literal
Interpret
Skeptic
No Op.
Other

METHOD OF READING SCRIPTURES: 1992
Strong Believer LDS Scientists
Percent
80
60
40
20
0
57
8
1
5
9
21
Literal
Interpret
Skeptic
No Op.
Other
Combine

But in reality in those years the evidence for the "aged" earth and for evolution has accumulated, not diminished. The Strong Mormon scientists in the fields that specialize in the evidence are as firmly convinced of the "aged" earth and of evolution as they ever were. Any who believe that scientific evidence for these views has become weaker over these years are clearly out of their fields and lack credibility.

One specific instance of new evidence for evolution since 1955 was the amazing and continuing discoveries in the world of the double helix, DNA, and technical comparisons of animal and human DNA, which augment impressively the evidence for evolution. Phenomenal developments in genetic engineering have occurred as a result.

Evidence against dogmatic philosophical "Darwinism", with its insistence that all living things came from chance and natural selection, has indeed developed over these years. They are represented well in Darwin on Trial by P. E. Johnson, a Berkeley law professor. The book itself, though not the evidence and arguments, is too recent (1991) to have influenced the scientists of this study.

Johnson describes a confrontation at the Wistar Institute between mathematician D. S. Ulam and Darwinists. Ulam used the "Statistical monstrosity" approach to **deny** that an eye, say, could have occurred by chance and natural selection.

Johnson also cites French mathematician Schutzenberger who entered the discussion on Ulam's side. These were approaches much like the earlier one noted in Chapter II of Charles Guye. In short, in addition to chance, creation seems to have required at least pre-existing intelligence involved in generating laws of functional design.

Darwinists replied, in effect, that the eye, say, did come about, nevertheless, and evolution by chance and selection is the only theory that now explains it. As I understand the matter, the mathematicians remained truly unrefuted, and their weakness was only lack of a theory to replace Darwinism--unless they, adopted "Special Creation", which they, in fact, emphatically rejected.

Johnson in his last paragraph of the book says, "Exposing Darwinism to possible falsification would not imply support for any other theory, certainly not any pseudoscientific theory based on a religious dogma."[3] The evidence accumulated by Johnson was not to injure evolution but only challenge the dogmatic incorporation of it into the inflexible chance and selection mold. He simply rejects the closure against inquiry insisted upon by doctrinaire Darwinists.

There has, then, been accumulating evidence that the deification of chance in evolution is, as George Bernard Shaw called it, "Nineteenth century rubbish." Shaw also believed in the broader view of evolution as did the hundreds of scientists in our study who view it as God's means of creation.

Such insights **against** mere chance and mere natural selection could have helped move scientists from a "no God needed here" stance to believing an evolutionary process requiring God, i.e., intelligence and plan. This may have encouraged some scientists into reach of "Believing" faith, which did occur over these years.

We are lured into further speculation as to why the increase in strength of religious belief has occurred. Our data did not give the answers. The closest they came was a look at what has occurred in the religious beliefs of Utah scientists who are other than Mormon. Has their religious commitment also increased in this period? The studies showed that it has not by one measure and has by another. While the percent of non-Mormons who were Believers in Christ has not increased, the proportion of Very Strong Believers in Christ compared to Strong was the same pattern as among the Mormons, namely, decided movement toward the Very Strong from the merely Strong. In 1955 Strong among them were equal in numbers to Very Strong. In 1992 the Very Strong were triple the number of Strong. However, the numbers of Mormon Very Strong were ten times the merely Strong.

Something seems to have happened to Mormons that did not happen among other Utah scientist graduates. This brings us to the limits of our data. They do not show answers to us. All they do is surprise us with the level, the unmistakably increased level, of religious commitment in this group of Ph.D., mostly, men and women of science.

Perhaps accounting for such movement away from scientific views as occurred, the authorities on science and religion of the older generation, Dr. Widtsoe, Dr. Talmage, and Dr. Merrill, who were scientists in the governing Quorum of the Twelve of the Church, departed this sphere. Two later Church leaders more recently wrote opinions on Mormonism and science which were strongly of the Literal type. One wrote an impressive compendium of Mormon ideas.[5]

Recent books by Mormon General Authorities (Some of Elders Neal Maxwell, and Dallin Oaks, and Presidents Marion D. Hanks and Gordon Hinckley come to mind)[6] have disclaimers saying that they are not official views of the Church but personal opinions. (Of course, for Mormons the published opinions of Apostles are weighty, whether official or not.) The Literalistic writers in point did not, however, do this. Perhaps they felt it unnecessary, believing that Mormons should know that books by the Authorities are not necessarily official doctrine. Anyway, one put the "young" earth, special creation, anti-evolution, literalist views in the compendium of Mormon ideas. We have met many good Mormons who quote this book as if it were "the" truth, which it was not necessarily. Of course, a beguiling aspect was that much of it is surely Mormonism, and the anti-science ideas, which are not, were inserted with no warning as to their questionable nature, in fact, with unqualified endorsement. I supposed that they influenced many Mormon teachers and reinforced such medieval and sectarian views as are still current, though not doctrinal, in Mormondom.

Against this supposition, however, the data from Strong Believer Mormon scientists themselves do **not** show the changes to be much caused by following Mormon writers who happened to be unscientific. In a double-checking questionnaire mailed in early 1992 there were most of the same questionnaire items of the present study, and same method of sampling, except that an item was added like the 1955 study had, namely, "Authors who have most influenced your Science-religion ideas." Of the respondents (this was also a representative response producing reliable results), 64% gave some answer on this item. Of those who answered, the largest single response was "Dr. Henry Eyring" (the world renown theoretical chemist and Strong Mormon.)

Other Mormon writers of similar viewpoints, such as Apostle-scientist Dr. Widtsoe, were mentioned by 37% of respondents. Only 5%, by contrast, listed the late two Elders who were Literalists or writers of similar views. The data we have from the scientists questions the influence of those writers in particular. We still seem to lack solid answers as to the causes of the changes toward the Literal.

The changes ought not be attributed to the Mormon Church having announced that the earth is only some thousands of years old. At the time of the early study it had no such doctrine and it does not now. As a leading Strong Believer Mormon scientist writer on science and religion, Dr. Frank B. Salisbury, Professor of Plant Pathology at Utah State University, wrote in 1974, "Although various General Authorities have taken various stands, the official position of the Church has always been that we must not take an official position."[7] Dr. William Lee Stokes, formerly head of the Geology Department of the University of Utah, also found this to be the case.[8] (Dr. Salisbury and Dr. Stokes are both Very Strong Believer Mormons, as both their books and answers to our questionnaire show.)

That there is no official Mormon doctrine also applies, as our Chapter II found, to God-directed evolution. Of course, a Godless, chance, evolution was clearly against Church doctrine. The recent (1992) article on "Evolution" in the Encyclopedia of Mormonism quotes the First Presidency of Heber J. Grant as stating "Leave geology, biology, and anthropology, no one of which has to do with the salvation of the souls of mankind, to scientific research . . . "

They also affirmed that Mormon doctrine includes that man is the child of God, formed in the divine image and endowed with divine attributes, and that the primal parents of our race were named Adam and Eve.

Evolution, with God's hand, can be part of the "how" of creation and eliminate any need to reject the knowledge of evolutionary science. The author of the Encyclopedia article, Wm. E. Evenson, stated, "The scriptures tell why man was created, but they do not tell how . . . "[9]

We have some bases for forming hypotheses, more or less informed guesses, about what caused the changes in a few Mormon scientists' convictions. Here are some, suggested by events that occurred in these forty years in the Mormon world. Let us take up now the question of why the Mormon scientists now believe Very Strongly in much larger percentages than before. It is probably true, but we are not offering data here to support it, that the Mormon educational system has been more effective in the years affecting the present scientists than in the years that would have come to bear on the development of earlier generations.

The L.D.S. Institutes of Religion near colleges and universities have become more numerous, now above 300, and possibly more effective in promoting Mormon belief. The high school seminaries have become more widespread and attendance higher, in both numbers and percentages of available young Mormon people. The increased belief of the scientists has been at least concomitant with rapid growth of the Church, intense missionary work, and its spread far beyond the boundaries of Utah. Almost all the Strong Believer Mormon scientists indicated on the questionnaire that they were active in the Church between ages 18 and 24. It is our guess that most of them were missionaries during this time, an activity which is generally believed to strengthen belief in the Church.

Let us proceed with the speculative. Perhaps the frightening nuclear threat (a real probability of the "end of the world"), and the movements against sexual morality with their frightening problems of rearing good Mormon children in a more wicked society, motivated more passionate commitment than did more settled times. One socio-psychological principle says that people with a religious ideology under attack react by believing in it even more strongly. In some ways Mormons are under less attack than earlier. We had opposition during our entire history. But it was heavily from other Christians and Republicans (in the latter half of the 1800's), people who had value systems ostensibly much like Mormons. Now there are dire threats from evil systems of "antivalues" rampant in movies, TV, teen-culture music (so-called). Irresponsible sex, mind damaging drugs, ghastly humanity demeaning violence, and gross materialistic greed show capacity to destroy the entirety of religious morality and civilized life itself. (George Bernard Shaw deplored in his day what he called "unscrupulous corybantics and anacreontics". In his day they may have been mild compared to now).[10]

The Mormons may have resolved to take a stance of Very Strong faith to resist the wicked world and protect their children from its onslaughts by means of devout adherence to the Gospel.

The movement toward more literalistic use of scripture brings the Mormon scientists to percentages now that divide more like the Seminary teachers reported in the early study and less like the scientists did then. No doubt those seminary teachers did educate in religion many of these scientists. And only the scientists whose fields gave them overwhelming evidence against reading scripture too narrowly and literally resisted the medieval interpretations. Or so we might speculate.

It is possible that some Mormons feel themselves more in "common cause" with ultra-conservative Catholics and fundamentalist Protestants than they used to be. This "common cause" would be what they call "anti-liberalism". In emotionally leaning this way, the Mormons who did so may have absorbed the medieval religious ideas on the earth's age and evolution. This may be about 20% of Mormons (but no doubt far less scientists) judging from some unpublished polls in Utah and Arizona.

On the other hand, we know from our studies reported in this book that almost all non-Mormon Utah scientists who are church goers are mainline Protestants and believe in the aged earth and evolution as God's probable method. Very few indeed of the Other Churches' Believers were Conservative or Southern Baptists or evangelicals, but almost all of the few who were held "young earth" and Special Creation views.

MORE SPECULATIONS ON THE CHANGES SINCE 1955

Steve Allen, the well known "polymath", who came to my close attention when he received an honorary doctorate from his Alma Mater, Arizona State University, recently added another book, Dumbth, to his other fifty plus.[11] It is about the need for improved thinking. He testified that "Some religions are far more sensible than others." He questions any religion so lacking a truthful spirit that it has doctrine that the earth is only thousands of years old. On this point a religion would be "guilty of serious dumbth." Of course, as we have seen, Mormonism has no such doctrine, even if some members believe this way. **But, in contrast, the number of Strong Mormon scientists who believe in the "aged" earth is approximately 800 in 1992**. As we noted in Chapter II, at least three Mormon Apostles also thought so.

One might ask, "Why is the thinking of a number of Mormon scientists, those in fields independent of earth age evidence, going against an "old" earth?". That the earth is very old is general knowledge among almost all educated people except persons under overpowering religious influence from literal views.

We realize that, in the eternal perspective of salvation, whether one believes the earth is aged or young, could seem trivial, except to those certain scientists entrusted to study and know such things. Maybe most of us can get along quite well without knowing. It is something about which people, unless they presume to be scientifically literate, can state "No opinion" as an honest answer. But stating as true in the physical world something that one has not studied carefully seems to me either careless, naive, or of a questionable spiritual nature. After all, truth for Mormons is a "knowledge of things as they are", and that which "is more or less than this is the spirit of that evil one who was a liar from the beginning".[12] I know this may seem too demanding an ethic, even for Saints. Many of us have felt this problem, I suppose, as we struggle to improve.

This moves toward the personal, so let me say something about my background at this point. Along with other undergraduate studies, I took two geology classes at University of Utah, hiked the Wasatch range, southwest Wyoming mountains, and the Grand Canyon. I rubbed shoulders with oil geologists for nine years. So when Allen wrote that belief in a "young" earth is a kind of "dumbth", I said, "Amen".

Another personal anecdote may be appropriate. The Hawaii Campus of Brigham Young University was being evaluated by an accreditation team of the Western College Association for its crucial first possible accreditation. Dr. Bill Priest of the team, a national leader in college administration, challenged me, asking, in effect, "Dr. Wootton, this is the college of a very strict church: no smoking, no drinking, no sex. It seems fundamentalist. So do you allow your science department to teach evolution?"

I replied that if any professor in our biological science department did **not** teach the theory of evolution, I would seriously question his competence.

Dr. Priest asked if the Church believed that God used evolution to establish creatures. I replied that it does not believe so, or otherwise, officially. Members can choose. I referred to some of my doctoral findings, now stated in this book, about how many Mormon scientists are both staunch members and believers in evolution.

He noticed that I said "members can choose". He asked if top leaders could choose, and whether we could conceivably get a leader over the Church who opposed the teaching of evolution. My answer was, "Possibly". Dr. Priest then asked what I would do if that leadership expected me to have our biology teacher stop teaching any evolution.

I replied that this was a hypothetical situation, which I did not believe would occur. But Dr. Priest continued to question what I would do if I were asked to 'shut down' our biology professor on evolution. I said I would answer honestly, but not meaning to presume any special courage, because I didn't think it would come up. "I wouldn't do it."

He asked whether that might not cost me this job. I said that in that case, I would work elsewhere. That was the end of his inquiry. I never knew whether my answers on this had any effect on the outcome. But the full accreditation was granted with considerable commendation to the college from the committee. (Accreditation teams ought to care about academic integrity and freedom to teach.)

Interesting was the fact that the accreditation society, the Western College Association, only a few years later, came under the directorship of an able, active Mormon who was our Dean of Instruction at the Hawaii Campus of Brigham Young University when I was there, Dr. Kay J. Andersen.

SUSPECT REASONING : "OUT OF FIELD"

In juxtaposition to the case of Strong Mormon Geologists who affirmed an "aged" earth, almost **none** of the believers in Special Creation of the species were in fields that study the species. For instance, while most Utah biologists are Strong Mormons, we found none who believe in Special Creation as against evolution. It was more a belief of engineers and others whose fields have almost nothing to do with knowledge of the facts supporting evolution. There were many who were not deterred by this fact from holding opinions which contradict the knowledge of other fellow Strong Mormons' in their fields.

We suppose that almost everyone learns to reason well in his or her own field. But some seem to slight the rules of reason when forming opinions about conclusions in someone else's field. This is not to cast doubt on the high level of competence in their own fields. That is established, and that is their business. And they would rightly resent any impugning of their competence.

This may leave one wondering, however, where was rational or even empathic judgment about the competence of their brothers in geology, biology, and other related sciences? To be a Strong Mormon it isn't even necessary, religiously, by doctrine. This has been shown beyond question by the responses reported in this book. **Being a Very Strong Mormon was compatible in 1992 with belief in a very aged earth and in evolution as apparently God's method of creating species. And while this was close to 100% true of those in the fields that study the earth and its creatures, it was also true of many Mormon scientists, no matter what their fields.** The statistics establish that there are probably at least 400 Strong Mormon scientists for evolution and 800 for the aged earth.

What we may be seeing is additional evidence of the known cognitive phenomenon that people who are competent thinkers in their specialties are not necessarily good reasoners about matters beyond their fields, pathetic as this may be. Two careful researchers, Nisbett and Ross, presented many scientific studies about the abilities of intelligent well-educated people to form correct social judgments. These are in Human Inference: Strategies and Shortcomings of Social Judgment.[13] Their overall conclusion is that we, whom they call "lay scientists", generally are as apt to be wrong as right in our social judgments. It is shocking insight. If you doubt this, I recommend reading their book. Of course, judgments about the age of the earth and evolution are not social judgments. But I suppose it should be easier to be correct about these physical matters, than the social. But many of the Mormon scientists are mistaken, nevertheless. Either those who believe in the "aged" earth are mistaken or those who believe otherwise are in error. Who more likely uses the scientific method in geology, the geologists or, say, are against it are correct. Who uses the scientific method in studying living creatures, the biologists or, say, the metallurgists? This does not imply that there are no Strong Mormon engineers and metallurgists who believe in the "aged" earth or in evolution. Our responses show there are. But not in as large percentages as some other fields. **Strong Mormon geologists and biologists are almost 100% in agreement that the earth is "aged" and that evolution is probably God's method of creating the species.**

The inference strategy which Nisbett and Ross identify as most often leading to error in social judgments may well explain the errors of the scientists who hold erroneous opinions out of their fields. It is the strategy of judging by what is readily, currently, available as opinion in one's own head (the "availability heuristic") instead of seeking truth by scientific method. This might well apply to the "young earth" and anti-evolution scientists. They have the opinions in their heads from church teaching sources, or elsewhere, which they have not bothered to test by the scientific method. Once again, the scientists who **do** use the scientific method, and therefore are likely to be most correct, in geology and biology are, particularly, geologists and biologists!

This ends my speculations in this book about the changes in Utah scientist beliefs from 1955 to 1992 which this study found.

NEW DATA MOSTLY UPHELD MORMON HARMONY IDEA

The new data still upheld the original hypothesis. However, one might not have supposed that two generations later Mormon scientists would have moved at all toward disbelief in the "aged earth" or evolution. I would have guessed that the percentages would remain stable or move more toward the "Interpretive". And I was surprised by the **extent** of the movement toward ever more Strong Belief by Mormon scientists in Jesus as Divine and Joseph Smith as inspired. The 1955 data was itself very favorable to the Church. And I questioned my study at one point, which caused me to replicate it and to turn it over to the scrutiny of an expert pollster at Arizona State University, Dr. Bruce D. Merrill, Director of the Media Research Center of the Walter Cronkite School of Journalism.

The data were reliable enough, but Science is humbling. It has the admirable truth testing method of being replicable. "They also serve who merely stand and wait." Or replicate. One needs humility when faced by the many disciplining rules of the scientific method. (A case can be made that scientists, by expectation, use more careful and demanding tests for truth than do religionists, at least religionists who avoid scientific method.) Anyway, this study can be tested by replication, and I will gladly help, if asked.

IMPORTANCE OF RELIGION REVISITED: CONCLUSION

The importance of some religion to the welfare of society was affirmed by many voices, mostly adverse witnesses, in Chapter I. They expressed hope that improved religion would harmonize with science and have credibility and also spiritual strength. We return to this theme to round out the book with views of the renown secular philosopher-economist Robert L. Heilbroner. I quote him not because he necessarily has status with religionists, but because he probably has not. I bring him as an "adverse witness" testifying of the need for more religion in our future.

SECULAR EXPERT SAYS RELIGION NEEDED

Because of predicted dire conditions in the world, he said "some kind of religion must replace the spiritual emptiness of industrial civilization . . . the absence of religion is the sapping force of Western industrial civilization." He believed that there will be an effort to find some new religious basis for the civilization to come. But he is also very apprehensive that the free inquiry on which science is based would have a hard time making its peace with the tradition and ritual that would likely develop.

He wrote, in the same context as the quotations above, "I am against religion, for science...I find myself very much like the king's messenger."[14] If Heilbroner could see the ascendance of a religion provided for us by the Lord, that supports freedom and science among other truths, he might **not** consider its arrival such "king's messenger" bad news. Many scientists, as Saints & Scientists reports, consider its arrival indeed the very "Good News".

CONCLUSION: MORMONISM SUPPORTS SCIENCE; SCIENTISTS ARE BELIEVERS

The results of the 1992 study of scientist graduates of Utah universities confirmed every part of the 1955 study, except for the changes we just discussed. The Utah Mormon culture is still the most highly productive of scientists, first place among the states, leading by 21% the second place.

Almost all the Mormon scientists believe the Church was responsible for Utah's lead and contributed significantly to their own achievements. Eight-five percent of Strong Mormons believe they harmonize their religion and science. A majority assert "Interpretive" rather than "Literal" positions on issues of science and religion, although a reduction from the earlier study. Most of the Utah educated scientists, even the non-Mormons and the merely Nominal Mormons, viewed the Church favorably as an institution for human welfare. Almost none appeared "antagonistic". An impressive 85 percent of Mormons are Strong Believers in Jesus as the Christ and Joseph Smith as a prophet. **This study thus affirms about 1,400 testimonies of the truth of the Gospel.**

Mormonism excels as a religion that supports science. This book establishes this beyond doubt. Mormon Church leaders were quoted to that effect. Mormonism built a fine and accessible public school system and universities highly productive of doctorates. The scientists noted many distinctive religious doctrines which encourage mental development and service. Mormonism produced the kind of value system, family solidity, and healthy living style that are known to facilitate achievement. And so, as a result, Utah outperforms all other states in total productivity rate for scientists.

It is remarkable that Mormonism did all this, not as its essential purpose, which I understand to be empowerment and enlightenment by the "Holy Spirit of truth" for the eternal exaltation of humanity, but as a corollary of the spiritual aims.

Our quest has been deeply rewarding. We hope you also found it uplifting, since the figures represented inspiring human lives and showed new aspects of a true religion, a fundamental faith that promotes science.

CHAPTER NOTES

PREFACE

1. Alfred North Whitehead, Science and the Modern World, N. Y., 1925, p. 180.
2. Aubrey A. Douglass, Modern Secondary Education, N. Y., 1938, p. 258.

CHAPTER I

1. Will Durant, The Story of Civilization, Vol. VI, "The Reformation", N. Y., 1957, p 939.
2. Bertrand L. Conway, The Question Box, N. Y., 1929, p. 181.
3. Alfred North Whitehead, Science and the Modern World, N. Y., 1925, p. 180.
4. George Allen Morgan, What Nietzsche Means, Cambridge, 1941, p. 76.
5. George Bernard Shaw, Everybody's What's What, N. Y., 1944, p. 363.
6. Ibid., p. 154.
7. Ibid., p. 232.
8. Ibid., p. 332.
9. Ibid., p. 360.
10. Upton Sinclair, The Profits of Religion, Pasadena, 1918, p. 286, p. 301, p. 312.
11. John W. Draper, The History of the Conflict Between Religion and Science, N. Y., 1896, p. vii.
12. Joseph Fielding Smith, Man, His Origin and Destiny, Salt Lake City, 1954, p. 139.
13. Martin J. Scott, Things Catholics Are Asked About, N. Y., 1927, p.246.
14. Whitehead, op. cit., p. 180.
15. Shaw, op. cit., p. 362.

CHAPTER II

1. Andrew D. White, A History of the Warfare of Science with Theology in Christendom, N. Y., 1896.
2. Draper, op. cit.
3. White, loc. cit.
4. H. H. Lane, Evolution and the Christian Faith, Princeton University, 1923, p. 51.
5. Conway, op. cit., p. 181.
6. Conway, op. cit. p. 179, p. 181.
7. Ibid.
8. Conway, op. cit., p. 182.
9. Conway, op. cit., p. 181.
10. Draper, op. cit., p. 360.
11. Whitehead, op. cit., 181.
12. Lane, op. cit.
13. J. A. Thomson, Science and Religion, N. Y., 1877.
14. A. Winchell, Reconciliation of Science and Religion, N. Y., 1877.
15. W. A. Whitehouse, Christian Faith and the Scientific Attitude, N. Y., 1952.
16. C. E. DeM. Sajous, Strength of Religion as Shown by Science, Philadelphia, 1926.
17. James Y. Simpson, Landmarks in the Struggle Between Science and Religion, N. Y.
18. Harry Rimmer, The Harmony of Science and Scripture, Berne, Indiana, 1940, p. 55.
19. Widtsoe, op. cit., p. 134.
20. Smith, op. cit. p. 463.
21. Journal of Discourses, 13:61.
22. Talmage, James E., First Book of Nature, S.L.C., 1888, p.233.
23. John A. Widtsoe, Evidences and Reconciliations, Salt Lake City, 1943, p. 125.
24. Joseph Fielding Smith, Man, His Origin and Destiny, Salt Lake City, 1954.
25. White, op. cit. p. ix.
26. Draper, op. cit., p. x.
27. Ibid., p. 363.
28. Ibid., p. 365.
29. Simpson, op. cit., p.12.
30. White, op. cit., p. 141.
31. White, op. cit., p. 154.
32. Lane, loc. cit.
33. Conway, op. cit., p. 182.
34. Simpson, op. cit., p. 91.
35. White, op. cit., p. ix.
36. J. G. Crowther, The Social Relations of Science, N. Y., 1941, p. 322.
37. Whitehead, op. cit., p. 182.

38. Shaw, op. cit., p. 362.
39. Conway, op. cit., p. 35.
40. John Henry Evans, *Joseph Smith, An American Prophet*,
N. Y., 1936, p. 351.
41. Smith, op. cit., p. 8.
42. John A. Widtsoe, *Discourses of Brigham Young*, Salt Lake City, 1925, p. 397.
43. Robert Millikin, *Science and Life*, loc. cit.
44. Shaw, op. cit., p. 64.
45. LeCompte Du Nouy, *Human Destiny*, N. Y., 1947, p. 34. 46. Conway, op. cit., p. 115.
47. Walsh, op. cit.
48. Scott, op. cit., p. 246.
49. Widtsoe, *Discourses*, op. cit., p. 397.
50. Widtsoe, *Evidences*, op. cit., p. 125, 127.
51. Smith, op. cit., p. 139.
52. Rimmer, op. cit., p. 55.
53. Conway, op. cit., p. 72.
54. Ibid., p. 182.
55. Widtsoe, op. cit., p. 110.
56. Ibid.
57. Ibid., p. 111.
58. Ibid., p. 112.
59. Smith, op. cit. p. 419.
60. Ibid., p. 422.
61. Lane, op. cit., p. 180.
62. Conway, op. cit., p. 69.
63. Ibid., p. 70, 71.
64. Ibid., p. 69.
65. *Journal of Discourses,* 14:115.
66. Talmage, op. cit., p.233.
67. James E. Talmage, *The Earth and Man*, Salt Lake City, 1931, p.3.
68. J. Reuben Clark, Jr., *On the Way to Immortality and Eternal Life*, Salt Lake City, 1949, p. 202.
69. *Pearl of Great Price*,"The Book of Abraham", Chap. iv.
70. Widtsoe, op. cit., p. 134.
71. 3 Peter 3:8.
72. Widtsoe, op. cit., p. 136.
73. Ibid., p. 138.
74. Smith, op. cit., p. 463.
75. Bruce McConkie, *Doctrines of Salvation*, Vol 1, Salt Lake, 1954.
76. Whitehead, op. cit., p. 181.
77. Lane, op. cit., p.51.
78. Sajous, op. cit., p. 250, 243.; Lane, op. cit., p. 189, 198-99.
79. Scott, op. cit., pp. 253, 255.
80. Ibid., p. 257.
81. Conway, op. cit., p. 8.
82. Ibid., p. 9.
83. Ibid., loc. cit.
84. Ibid., p. 10.
85. Ibid.
86. Talmage, op. cit. p. 4.
87. Widtsoe, op. cit., p. 149.
88. Ibid., p. 156.
89. Ibid., p. 155.
90. Ibid.
91. Smith, op. cit., p. 132.
92. Ibid., p. 133.
93. Ibid., p. 213.
94. McConkie, op. cit., p. 141.
95. Ibid., p. 143.

CHAPTER III

1. Scott, op. cit., p. 251.
2. Albert Einstein, *Pageant*, "My Faith", August, 1950, p., 35.
3. *Time*, August 31, 1953, p. 48.
4. Paul Blanchard, *American Democracy and Catholic Power*, Boston, 1949, p., 38.
5. Hardy, Kenneth, "Social Origins of American Scientists and Scholars", *Science*, 185 (Aug. 9, 1974):497-506.

6. Harvey C. Lehman and Paul A. Witty, Scientific Monthly, "Scientific Eminence and Church Membership", December, 1931, pp. 544-549.
7. R. H. Knapp and H. B. Goodrich, Origins of American Scientists, University of Chicago Press, 1952, p. 23.
8. Conway, op. cit., p. 64, p. 68.

CHAPTER IV

1. Discourses of Brigham Young, p. 387, p. 395.
2. Albert Einstein, Pageant, "My Faith", August, 1950, p.35.
3. The Improvement Era, February, 1939, p. 94.
4. George Bernard Shaw, address before American Academy of Political Science. Complete reference presently unknown to author.
5. Samuel Smucker, The Religious, Social, and Political History of the Mormons, N. Y., 1858, p. 454.
6. John A. Widtsoe, Salt Lake City, 1943.
7. Frank B. Salisbury, Creation, Deseret Book, Salt Lake City, 1976.
8. William Lee Stokes, Joseph Smith and the Creation, Salt Lake City, 1991. See also The Creation Scriptures, 1979; So God Created Man, 1988; Evolution? The Scriptures Say Yes!, 1988. Dr. Stokes assumes the nearly literal meaning of the scriptures, is a scientist and scholar, and with an agreeable spirit shows their harmony.
9. Encyclopedia of Mormonism, "Science and Scientists", MacMillan, N. Y., 1992, p. 1274.
10. Richard T. Wootton, Religious Orientations of Utah Scientists Related to Certain Problems of Latter-day Saint Church Education, doctoral thesis, University of Utah, 1956.
11. Salisbury, op. cit., p.44.
12. E. L. Thorndike, Science, "Men of Science", August 16, 1940, p. 26.
Why Dr. Thorndike chose "white population", I can only guess. I chose it in later studies because Utah has almost totally white population, so, for comparison to other states, I wanted a level field. This may seem to imply that including non-whites would have handicapped the standing in scientist production for some other states. Although I regret possible racist interpretations, it has been the situation. But this can be ascribed to educational and other cultural opportunity deficits largely imposed by whites in the past. It implies, if anything, that American society now owes special opportunity to blacks as remedy and will benefit by doing so. Of course, there have been and are some outstanding black scientists, in spite of general past (we hope definitely past), maltreatment of some blacks by some whites.
13. Zabel, H. E., "Statistical Abstract of American Men of Science, 10 edition." (paper sent to R.T. Wootton, September 28, 1965.)
14. Kenneth R. Hardy, "Social Origins of American Scientists and Scholars." Science 185 (Aug. 9, 1974):497-506.
15. Unpublished letter to R. T. Wootton.
16. DeBoer, Ray L., "A Historical Study of Mormon Education and the Influence of Its Philosophy on Public Education in Utah" (unpublished doctoral dissertation, University of Denver, 1951.)

(No notes for Chapter V)

CHAPTER VI

1. Times and Seasons, 5:758, Nauvoo, Illinois, 1845.

CHAPTER VII

1. Salisbury, Frank B., Creation, Salt Lake City, 1976, p.51.

CHAPTER VIII

1. Historical Statistics of the U. S., Part 1, U. S. Department of Commerce, Washington, D. C., pp 24-37.
2. Hardy, op. cit., p.497.
3. Johnson , P.E., Darwin on Trial, Washington, D.C., 1991, p. 38-39.
4. New Testament, Matthew 7:20
5. McConkie, Mormon Doctrine, Salt Lake City, 1979
6. Hinckley, Gordon, Faith the Essence of True Religion, Salt Lake City, 1989; Oaks, Dallin, The Lord's Way, Salt Lake City, 1991; Hanks, Marion D., Bread Upon the Waters, Salt Lake City, 1991.
7. Salisbury, op. cit., p. 109.
8. Stokes, Wm. Lee, So God Created Man, Salt Lake City, 1988, p.iii.
9. Encyclopedia of Mormonism, N. Y., N. Y., 1992, p. 478.
10. Shaw, op.cit. p. 232.
11. Doctrine & Covenants, 93:24-26.
12. Allen, Steve, Dumbth, Buffalo, N. Y., p. 265.
13. Nisbett & Ross, Human Inference: Strategies and Shortcomings of Social Judgment, Englewood Cliffs, N. J.
14. Wade, Nicholas, "Robert L. Heilbroner: Portrait of a World Without Science", Science, Aug. '74, p. 599.

INDEX

T

U-W

Y-Z

APPENDIX A

TABLES

Table 1

Churches in Which Respondents Stated at Least Nominal Membership

	Number of Scientists	Percentage of Scientists	1992
Latter Day Saint	214	75.9	71%
Methodist	9	3.2	2
Episcopal	9	3.2	2
Presbyterian	9	3.2	2
Baptist	0	0	1
Unitarian	7	2.5	4
Catholic	3	1.1	2
Lutheran	0	0	4
Orthodox	0	0	2
Other	13	4.6	2
None	18	6.3	8
Total	**282**	**100%**	**100%**

Table 2

Conviction that Jesus is a Divine Person of the Godhead

Numbers are percentages

	No Such	Weak	Fair	Strong	V Strong	No Answer
Utah Scientists	19.9	8.2	11.3	19.2	34.3	7.1
Other Churches' Believers	0	0	32	32	36	0
1992	0	0	0	33	66	1
LDS Believers - 1992	0	0	0	8	85.5	1
Episcopal	11.1	11.1	33.4	22.2	22.2	0
Methodist	33.4	33.3	0	22.2	11.1	0
Presbyterian	22.2	22.2	33.4	11.1	11.1	0
Unitarian	71.4	14.3	14.3	0	0	0
Catholic	0	0	0	0	100	0
None	77	5.7	0	5.7	0	11.6
Other	53.8	0	7.7	23.1	0	15.4
LDS Scientists	11.7	7	11.2	21.5	43.5	5.1
Nominal LDS	43	25	16	8	0	8

Table 3

Conviction that Joseph Smith was Inspired by God in the Formation of the Church of Jesus Christ of Latter-day Saints

Numbers are percentages

	No Such Conviction	Weak	Fair	Strong	V Strong	No Answer
Utah Born Scientists	33.0	7.8	11.7	17.4	28.0	2.1
Other Churches' Believers	68.0	4.0	12.0	0	0	16.0
LDS Scientists	16.9	8.8	14.0	22.9	36.9	0.5
1992	8.0	1.0	6.0	4.0	81.0	0.0

Table 4

Conviction that the Church of Jesus Christ of Latter-day Saints is the Only Authoritative Church of Christ on the Earth Today

Numbers are percentages

	No Such Conviction	Weak	Fair	Strong	V Strong	No Answer
Utah Born Scientists	41.5	9.6	7.8	13.5	25.5	2.1
Other Churches' Believers	80.0	9.0	8.0	0	0	4.0
LDS Scientists	25.7	12.1	10.3	18.7	32.7	0.5
1992	6.0	3.0	6.0	4.0+	81.0+	

Table 5

Did They Believe that Religion and Science are so Far Removed from Each Other That No Attempt is Logically Necessary to Harmonize Them

Numbers are percentages

	Yes	Partially	No	No Opinion	No Answer	Other
Utah Scientists	(Not Tabulated)					
Other Churches	20.0	56.0	16.0	0	4.0	4.0
in 1992	0	11.0	78.0	11.0	0	0
Nominal LDS	21.8	16.4	43.6	10.9	5.5	1.8
in 1992	60.0	20.0	20.0	0	0	0
LDS Fair Believers	6.7	13.3	76.7	3.3	0	0
LDS Strong Believers	3.1	10.0	87.0	2.3	0	0
in 1992	6.0	11.0	76.0	7.0	0	0

Table 6

Did They Believe that Their Church Doctrine and Science Can Be Logically Harmonized?

Numbers are percentages

	Yes	Partially	No	No Opinion	No Answer
Utah Born Scientists	61.0	22.7	10.7	2.6	3.0
Other Churches	68.0	20.0	4.0	0	8.0
Nominal LDS	14.5	41.0	34.5	4.0	6.0
LDS Fair Believers	53.3	43.3	3.4	0	0
LDS Strong Believers	87.0	13.0	0	0	0

(This Question was not asked in 1992)

Table 7

Did They Logically Harmonize Their Church Doctrine and Science in Their Own Philosophy of Life?

Numbers are percentages

	Yes	Partially	No	No Opinion	No Answer
Utah Born Scientists	61.0	21.6	13.3	1.8	2.3
Other Churches	64.0	28.0	4.0	0	4.0
1992	78.0	22.0	0	0	0
Nominal LDS	20.0	36.4	40.0	1.8	1.8
1992	0	0	80.0	20.0	0
LDS Fair Believers	56.7	36.7	3.3	3.3	0
LDS Strong Believers	86.8	13.2	0	0	0
1992	83.0	15.0	1.0	0	0

Table 8

Did They Believe that Utah's Per Capita Lead in Production of Men of Science is Somehow Attributable to L.D.S. Church Influence?

Numbers are percentages

	Yes	No	No Answer	Number of Comments
Utah Born Scientists	67.5	20.3	7.2	5
Other Churches	26.0	48.0	13.0	13
Nominal LDS	56.4	30.8	5.5	7.3
1992	40.0	60.0	0	8
LDS Fair Believers	76.7	10.0	6.7	3.3
LDS Strong Believers	89.8	4.7	4.7	.8
1992	86.0	8.0	6.0	3

Table 9

Did They Believe that Their Own Church Contributed Significantly to Their Professional Achievements?

Numbers are percentages

	Yes	No	No Answer	Number of Comments
Utah Born Scientists	55.7	38.7	3.9	1.8
Other Churches' Believers	44.0	48.0	4.0	4.0
1992	22.0	55.0	11.0	Some: 12.0
Nominal LDS	27.3	67.3	3.6	1.8
1992	0	80.0	Some: 20	0
LDS Fair Believers	56.7	40.0	3.3	0
LDS Strong Believers	85.3	10.1	3.9	.8
1992	68.0	8.0	Some: 24	

Table 10

Did They Attend Church Meetings Regulary Until 18 Years of Age?

Numbers are percentages

	Yes	No	No Answer
Utah Born Scientists	75.5	23.0	1.5
Other Churches' Believers	52.0	44.0	4.0
Nominal LDS	67.3	30.9	1.8
LDS Fair Believers	83.3	13.3	3.4
LDS Strong Believers	88.4	11.6	0

Item not in 1992 Questionaire.

Table 11

Were They Active in Their Church as an Officer, Teacher, or Missionary Between the Ages of 10 and 24?

Numbers are percentages

	Yes	No	No Answer	Other
Utah Born Scientists	50.8	48.6	.3	.3
Other Churches' Believers	28.0	68.0	4.0	
1992	33.0	60.0	3.0	3.0
Nominal LDS	32.7	67.3		
1992	20.0	80.0		
LDS Fair Believers	60.0	40.0		
LDS Strong Believers	73.6	26.4		
1992	87.0	11.0	2.0	

Table 12

Were They Active Members of Their Church?

Numbers are percentages

	Yes	No	Partially	No Answer
Utah Born Scientists	55.7	40.8	0.7	2.8
Other Churches' Believers	60.0	20.0	4.0	16.0
1992	100.0			
Nominal LDS	10.8	88.2		
1992	100.0			
LDS Fair Believers	46.7	43.3	3.4	6.6
LDS Strong Believers	91.2	7.2	0.8	0.8
1992	97.0	3.0		

Table 13

Percentages of Utah Born Scientists in Various Church Positions

Numbers are percentages

	Stake Leaders (1)	Ward Leaders (2)	Other Church Offices (3)	None
Utah Born Scientists	(Not Tabulated)			
Other Churches' Believers			16.0	84.0
Nominal LDS			5.5	94.5
LDS Fair Believers	6.7		30.0	63.3
LDS Strong Believers	32.6	7.8	37.2	22.5

(Question not asked in 1992)

Table 14

Attitude toward the Church as an Institution for Promoting Human Welfare

Numbers are percentages

	Favorable	Indifferent	Antagonistic	No Opinion	No Answer	Other
Utah Born Scientists	88.3	5.7	1.5	1.5	3.0	
Other Churches' Believers	56.0	24.0	4.0	4.0	8.0	4.0
1992	78.0	22.0				
Nominal LDS	87.3	7.3	1.8	1.8	1.8	
1992	60.0	40.0	0			
LDS Fair Believers	100.0					
LDS Strong Believers	99.2	.8				
1992	93.0	2.0	0		1.0	4.0

Table 15

Utah Scientists in Various Fields of Science

Numbers are percentages

	Physical	Agricultural	Biological	Social	Other	No Answer
Utah Born Scientists	53.5	9.2	29.1	7.1	.4	.7
Other Churches' Believers	72.0		20.0	4.0		4.0
Nominal LDS	41.8	9.1	34.5	10.9	3.6	
LDS Fair Believers	46.7	13.3	33.3	3.3		3.3
LDS Strong Believers	52.7	13.2	25.6	7.0	.8	.8

Table 16

Latter-day Saint Scientist Conviction, by Field, that Joseph Smith was Inspired by God in Forming the Latter-day Saint Church

Numbers are percentages

	No Such Conviction	Weak	Fair	Strong	Very Strong
Chemistry	17.0	6.0	11.0	22.0	44.0
Agriculture	11.1	3.7	11.1	22.3	51.8
Biology	12.0	8.6	22.4	20.7	36.3
Physics	19.0	9.7	14.3	14.3	42.7
Geology	6.8	13.4	26.6	33.2	20.0
Social Sciences	43.6		12.4	25.0	19.0

(In 1992, the numbers in *Strong* and *Very Strong* are so high, 85%, that the above type of breakdown has little significance. The few Mormon less than Strong are almost all in psychology and biology.)

Table 17

Extent of Emotional Troubling During Changes of Science-Religion Beliefs

Numbers are percentages

	Intensely	Somewhat	No	No Answer
Utah Born Scientists	6.7	30.9	41.5	19.9
Other Churches' Believers	12.0	28.0	32.0	28.0
Nominal LDS	3.6	30.9	54.5	11.3
LDS Fair Believers	3.3	56.7	26.7	13.3
LDS Strong Believers	7.8	27.1	45.0	20.2

(In 1992 no questions asked about *Troubling*)

Table 18

Number of Years in Science by Percentages

Number of Years in Science:	10+	15+	20+	25+	30+	35+	40+	45+
Utah Born Scientists	.7	14	26(41)	22(63)	18(80)	8(89)	5(94)	6
Other Churches' Believers	8	4	20(32)	12(44)	32(76)	8(84)	8(92)	8
Nominal LDS		11	23(35)	22(56)	18(75)	15(89)	4(93)	7
LDS Fair Believers		17	39(47)	13(60)	17(77)	3(80)	13(93)	7
LDS Strong Believers	2.3	15	23(40)	30(70)	16(85)	6(92)	4(95)	5

(Not calculated for 1992)

Percentages in this table are to the nearest unit..
Numbers in parentheses are cumulative percentages.

Table 19

The Earth was Created in a Relatively Short Period of Time, That is, in Some Thousands of Years

Numbers are percentages

Legend: **A - Tentative Agreement** **D - Tentative Disagreement**
AA - Positive Agreement **DD - Positive Disagreement**

	A	AA	D	DD	No Opinion	No Answer	Amended
Utah Born Scientists	5.4	1.8	37.0	41.7	3.6	5.8	4.7
Other Churches' Believers	8.0	12.0	32.0	32.0	4.0	12.	
Nominal LDS			47.3	47.3	1.8	3.6	
LDS Fair Believers	3.3		33.3	53.3		3.3	6.8
LDS Strong Believers	10.2	2.4	41.2	31.2	3.4	5.5	5.5
LDS Seminary Teachers	25.0	9.6	19.2	25.0	19.2		1.9

(Question not asked in 1992)

Percent contradictory answers between this item and item 17(b): Scientists, 1.1 %; teachers, none.

Table 20

Classifications of Scientists who Believed Positively That the Earth was Created in a Relatively Short Period of Time, that is, in Some Thousands of Years

Field of Science:		**Religion:**	
Petroleum Engineering	1	Unitarian	1
Biochemistry	1	Latter-day Saint	3
Astronomy	1	Presbyterian	1
Biology	2		

Total number: 5

Percent of all Utah Born Scientists: 1.8 per cent.

(Not applicable to 1992 questions)

L.D.S. SEMINARY TEACHERS SURVEY

All Seminary teachers of the Salt Lake City area were sent questionnaires in 1955 with most items identical to those sent to the Utah born scientists in 1955.

They received a cover letter explaining the relationship of their survey to that of the scientists and assuring them of anonymity.

These were mostly "early morning" Seminary teachers at junior high schools and high schools. They also included "released time" school-day Seminary teachers.

The response was eighty-seven percent of the questionnaires completed and returned.

No survey of Seminary teachers was made for the 1992 study.

Table 21

Classifications of Scientists who Believed Tentatively That the Earth was Created in a Relatively Short Period of Time, that is, in Some Thousands of Years

Field of Science:		Religion:	
Instrumentation	1	Latter-day Saint	14
Chemical	4	Congregationalist	1
Agricultural	5		
Metallurgical	1		
Biological	4		

- Total number: 15

Percent of all Utah Born Scientists: 5.3 per cent.
(Not applicable to 1992 questions)

Table 22

The Earth Took at least Hundreds of Millions of Years to Create

Agreement: "Interpretive"

Numbers are percentages

Legend: A - Tentative Agreement; AA - Positive Agreement; D - Tentative Disagreement; DD - Positive Disagreement

	A	AA	D	DD	No Opinion	No Answer	Amended
Utah Born Scientists	36.0	36.8	6.8	2.5	7.5	4.3	6.0
Other Churches' Believers	28.0	36.0	4.0	12.0	8.0	12.0	
1992	78.0		11.0		11.0		
Nominal LDS	38.2	41.4	5.5	3.6	1.8	4.0	5.4
1992	100.0						
LDS Fair Believers	33.3	46.7	10.0			3.3	6.7
LDS Strong Believers	42.1	26.4	7.0	2.3	11.6	4.7	6.9
1992	73.0		17.0		9.0		
LDS Seminary Teachers	25.0	13.5	28.8	9.6	21.2		1.9

(1992 did not provide A, AA, D, DD. 1992 agreement is A+AA, etc.)

Table 23

Man's Body did not Evolve in any Fashion from Simpler Species and is Not Biologically Related to Them

Agreement: "Literal"

Numbers are percentages

Legend: **A - Tentative Agreement** **D - Tentative Disagreement**
AA - Positive Agreement **DD - Positive Disagreement**

	A	AA	D	DD	No Opinion	No Answer	Amended
Utah Born Scientists	10.6	5.3	33.0	35.1	6.4	3.5	5.3
Other Churches' Believers	4.0	8.0	32.0	48.0	8.0		
Nominal LDS	3.6		32.7	54.5		3.6	7.3
LDS Fair Believers	3.3		46.7	43.4	2.0	3.3	
LDS Strong Believers	20.9	11.6	32.6	12.2	11.6	2.3	3.3
LDS Seminary Teachers	17.3	50.0	13.5	7.7	5.8	1.9	3.8

(No identical question in 1992)

Percent contradictory answers between this item and item 17(d): Scientists, 5 %; Teachers, 7.7%.

Table 24

God Created Man's Mortal Body, Probably Making Many Small Progressive Changes from Simple to More Complex Forms over Millions of Years

Agreement: "Interpretive"

Numbers are percentages

Legend: **A - Tentative Agreement** **D - Tentative Disagreement**
AA - Positive Agreement **DD - Positive Disagreement**

	A	AA	D	DD	No Opinion	No Answer	Amended
Utah Born Scientists	19.9	11.7	33.0	16.0	7.1	5.7	6.6
Other Churches' Believers	36.0	20.0	24.0	4.0	8.0	4.0	4.0
1992	11.0	78.0	11.0				
Nominal LDS	27.3	3.6	27.3	5.5	23.6	3.6	7.3
1992	80.0		11.0				
LDS Fair Believers	50.0	23.0			16.7	3.3	6.7
LDS Strong Believers	41.1	8.5	20.2	6.2	15.5	1.6	
1992	7.0	35.0	44.0		12.0		2.0
LDS Seminary Teachers	13.5	7.7	25.0	38.5	9.6	1.9	3.8

Table 25

It is not Known Whether a God Made Man. The Species, Including Man, Probably Came Through General Evolution by the Process of Chance and Selection, Rather than by Intelligent Design

Agreement: "Skeptical"

Numbers are percentages

Legend: **A - Tentative Agreement** **D - Tentative Disagreement**
AA - Positive Agreement **DD - Positive Disagreement**

	A	AA	D	DD	No Opinion	No Answer	Amended
Utah Born Scientists	19.9	11.7	33.0	16.0	7.7	5.7	6.0
Other Churches' Believers	12.0	8.0	36.0	24.0	4.0	8.0	8.0
Nominal LDS	43.6	23.6	12.7	3.6	7.3	5.0	3.6
LDS Fair Believers	13.4	3.4	40.0	9.9	20.0	6.7	6.6
LDS Strong Believers	2.3	1.5	29.5	49.6	5.1	5.4	6.2

Table 26

Other Species Than Man also had a Creation as Distinct Species and are Unrelated by Biological Lineage from the Simpler to the More Complex

Agreement: "Literal"

Numbers are percentages

Legend: **A - Tentative Agreement** **D - Tentative Disagreement**
AA - Positive Agreement **DD - Positive Disagreement**

	A	AA	D	DD	No Opinion	No Answer	Amended
Utah Born Scientists	14.5	3.2	40.8	24.5	6.4	5.7	4.9
Other Churches' Believers	16.0	4.0	32.0	36.0		12.0	
1992	22.0	0.0	67.0		11.0		
Nominal LDS	5.5	43.6	36.4	5.4	7.3	1.8	
1992	0		100.0				
LDS Fair Believers	10.0	3.3	56.7	26.7		3.3	
LDS Strong Believers	24.8	6.2	38.0	8.5	10.9	3.9	8.17
1992	20.0	36.0	31.0		7.0		6.0
LDS Seminary Teachers	38.5	23.1	15.4	5.8	15.4	1.9	

Percent contradictory answers between this item and item 17(g): Scientists, 8.9 %; Teachers, 11.5%.

Table 27

The Species Other than Man were Created by God, Probably by Making Many Small Changes from Simple to More Complex, Over Millions of Years

Agreement: "Interpretive"

Numbers are percentages

Legend: **A - Tentative Agreement** **D - Tentative Disagreement**
AA - Positive Agreement **DD - Positive Disagreement**

	A	AA	D	DD	No Opinion	No Answer	Amended
Utah Born Scientists	39.6	8.9	16.7	6.0	5.7	14.9	7.8
Other Churches' Believers	32.0	16.0	20.0	12.0	4.0	16.0	
Nominal LDS	25.5	9.1	29.1	7.2	14.5	7.3	7.3
LDS Fair Believers	63.3	10.0	3.3	3.3	16.7	3.3	
LDS Strong Believers	48.8	7.8	14.0	3.1	14.7	3.9	7.7
LDS Seminary Teachers	17.3	9.6	28.8	23.1	15.4	1.9	3.8

(No identical question in 1992)

Percent contradictory answers between this item and item 17(f): Scientists, 8.9 %; Teachers, 11.5%.

Table 28

Classifications of Scientists who Believed Positively That Other Species Than Man also had a Creation as Distinct Species and are Unrelated by Biological Lineage from the Simple to the More Complex

Field of Science:		**Religion:**	
Petroleum Engineering	1	Latter-day Saint	9
Biochemical	1	Unitarian	1
Astronomical	1		
Instrumentation	1		
Chemical	3		
Agriculture	1		
Social	1		
Biological	1		

Total number: 10

Percent of all Utah Born Scientists: 3.5 per cent.
(No data base in 1992 from which to derive this table.)

Table 29

Classifications of Scientists who Believed Tentatively That Other Species Than Man also had a Creation as Distinct Species and are Unrelated by Biological Lineage from the Simple to the More Complex

Field of Science:		Religion:	
Biological	8	Latter-day Saint	36
Chemical	9	Congregationalist	1
Agricultural	8	Methodist	2
Metallurgic	1	None	1
Petroleum Engineering	1		
Engineering and Physics	1		
Civil Eng. & Meteorological	1		
Geological	3		
Social	2		
Physics	4		
Chemical Engineering	1		
Engineering	1		

Total number: 40

Percent of all Utah Born Scientists:14.0 per cent.

Table 30

The Flood of Noah Covered the Top of Ararat at least 15 Cubits (Not less than 26 feet) Deep and the Whole Earth Correspondingly, as Literally Described in Genesis in the Bible

Agreement: "Literal"

Numbers are percentages

Legend: **A - Tentative Agreement** **D - Tentative Disagreement**
AA - Positive Agreement **DD - Positive Disagreement**

	A	AA	D	DD	No Opinion	No Answer	Amended
Utah Born Scientists	8.2	0.4	37.6	21.3	24.1	5.3	2.5
Other Churches' Believers	16.0	4.0	40.0	16.0	16.0	8.0	
Nominal LDS	1.8		32.7	36.4	21.8	1.8	5.5
LDS Fair Believers			43.3	23.3	30.0	3.3	
LDS Strong Believers	15.5		34.9	7.0	31.0	6.2	4.6
LDS Seminary Teachers	38.5	19.2	21.2	9.6	9.6		1.9

(No identical question in 1992)

Table 31

Classifications of Scientists who Believed Tentatively That the Flood of Noah covered the Top of Mount Ararat at least 15 Cubits (Not Less than 26 Feet) Deep and the Whole Earth Correspondingly, as Literally Described in Genesis in the Bible

Field of Science:		Religion:	
Petroleum Engineering	1	Latter-day Saint	20
Biological	5	Unitarian	1
Chemical	10	Congregationalist	1
Metallurgical	2	Methodist	1
Agricultural	2	Catholic	1
Engineering	1		
Physics	1		
Organic Chemical	1		
None Listed	1		
Social	1		

Total number: 24
Percent of all Utah Born Scientists: 8.5 per cent.
(No flood data in 1992)

Table 32

The Flood of Noah was Reality, but the Details Must be Interpreted Differently than Given Literally in Genesis

Numbers are percentages

Legend: **A - Tentative Agreement** **D - Tentative Disagreement**
AA - Positive Agreement **DD - Positive Disagreement**

	A	AA	D	DD	No Opinion	No Answer	Amended
Utah Born Scientists	47.5	6.0	9.9	3.2	21.7	4.3	7.4
Other Churches' Believers	56.0	16.0	16.0	4.0	4.0	4.0	3.6
Nominal LDS	32.7	7.3	12.7	7.0	32.7	3.6	
LDS Fair Believers	70.0	10.0			13.3	6.7	
LDS Strong Believers	51.9	4.7	12.4		17.0	3.1	10.9
LDS Seminary Teachers	32.7	11.5	38.5	13.5	3.8		
(No flood data in 1992)							

Percent contradictory answers between this item and item 17(h): Scientists, 2.5%, Teachers 7.2%

Table 33

There was Not Necessarily any Such Flood as Described in Genesis

Numbers are percentages

Legend: **A - Tentative Agreement** **D - Tentative Disagreement**
AA - Positive Agreement **DD - Positive Disagreement**

	A	AA	D	DD	No Opinion	No Answer	Amended
Utah Born Scientists	25.9	5.9	38.7	5.7	14.2	7.8	1.8
Other Churches' Believers	20.0		28.0	16.0	16.0	4.0	
Nominal LDS	40.6	9.1	16.4	3.8	16.4	10.3	3.6
LDS Fair Believers	16.6		6.7	43.3	26.7	6.7	
LDS Strong Believers	14.7		65.1	8.5	11.6	5.4	1.6
LDS Seminary Teachers			36.5	63.5			
(No flood data in 1992)							

Table 34

Use of Scientific Reason or Logical Thinking as a Means of Religious Conviction Should have a Minor Role, if Any

Agreement: "Literal"

Numbers are percentages

Legend: **A - Tentative Agreement** **D - Tentative Disagreement**
AA - Positive Agreement **DD - Positive Disagreement**

	A	AA	D	DD	No Opinion	No Answer	Amended
Utah Born Scientists	16.5	1.8	50.4	17.0	3.5	5.8	5.0
Other Churches' Believers	32.0	8.0	32.0	12.0	4.0	12.0	
1992:	22.0		56.0		11.0		11.0
Nominal LDS	16.4	3.6	40.0	21.8	5.5	7.2	5.5
1992:	40.0		40.0		20.0		
LDS Fair Believers	13.3		66.7	10.0	3.3	6.7	
LDS Strong Believers	14.0	1.6	60.5	13.2		2.3	7.8
1992:	45.0		44.0		1.0		10.0
LDS Seminary Teachers	32.7	3.8	40.4	17.3	1.9	1.9	1.9

Percent contradictory answers between this item and item 17(l): Scientists, 3.5%, Teachers 3.8%

Table 35

The Scientific Viewpoint and Method Should be Held in Very High Regard and Given a Major Role in All Convictions

Agreement: "Interpretive"

Numbers are percentages

Legend: **A - Tentative Agreement** | **AA - Positive Agreement** | **D - Tentative Disagreement** | **DD - Positive Disagreement**

	A	AA	D	DD	No Opinion	No Answer	Amended
Utah Born Scientists		18.1	17.7	2.1	2.8	4.3	8.5
Other Churches' Believers				12.0			
1992	56.0		22.0		22.0		
Nominal LDS	49.1	25.5	10.9	1.8	1.8	5.4	5.5
1992	80.0		20.0				
LDS Fair Believers	63.3	16.5	10.0		3.3	3.3	3.3
LDS Strong Believers	48.0	10.0	20.0	6.0	4.0		12.0
1992	36.0		52.0		4.0		8.0
LDS Seminary Teachers	36.5	5.8	34.6	15.4	3.8		3.8

Percent contradictory answers between this item and item 17(k): Scientists, 3.5%, Teachers 3.8%

Table 36

Religious Conviction Should Come Primarily from Answer to Prayers, Miraculous Healing, and Statements from Religious Authorities

Agreement: "Literal"

Numbers are percentages

Legend: **A - Tentative Agreement** | **AA - Positive Agreement** | **D - Tentative Disagreement** | **DD - Positive Disagreement**

	A	AA	D	DD	No Opinion	No Answer	Amended
Utah Born Scientists	10.3	1.1	42.9	19.1	8.5	7.1	9.0
Other Churches' Believers	20.0	8.0	36.0	4.0	20.0	8.0	
1992	22.0		67.0				11.0
Nominal LDS	7.3	3.3	34.5	25.5	20.0	5.5	3.5
1992	0		60.0		20.0		20.0
LDS Fair Believers	3.3	3.3	70.0	10.0	3.3	3.3	6.7
LDS Strong Believers	17.1	1.6	45.0	10.1	9.1		17.1
1992	45.0		38.0				15.0
LDS Seminary Teachers	22.0	15.1	41.8	9.6	1.9		9.6

Table 37

Religious Conviction Should Come Primarily from Logical Thinking Upon the Facts of History, the Existing World, the Fruits of Religion, and Personal Experience

Agreement: "Interpretive"

Numbers are percentages

Legend: **A - Tentative Agreement** **D - Tentative Disagreement**
AA - Positive Agreement **DD - Positive Disagreement**

	A	AA	D	DD	No Opinion	No Answer	Amended
Utah Born Scientists	52.8	17.0	8.2	1.0	3.9	5.0	12.1
Other Churches' Believers	36.0	28.0	12.0	8.0		12.0	4.0
Nominal LDS	52.7	20.0	5.5		9.0	7.3	5.5
LDS Fair Believers	60.0	16.5			3.3	6.7	13.3
LDS Strong Believers	54.3	11.6	13.2	0.8	0.8	2.3	17.0
LDS Seminary Teachers	46.2	21.2	17.2	5.8	1.9	1.9	5.8

(No comparable question in 1992)

Table 38

God Commonly Acts Directly in Events of the Earth, That is, He Constantly Intervenes in Human Affairs

Agreement: "Literal"

Numbers are percentages

Legend: **A - Tentative Agreement** **D - Tentative Disagreement**
AA - Positive Agreement **DD - Positive Disagreement**

<table>
<tr><th></th><th>A</th><th>AA</th><th>D</th><th>DD</th><th>No Opinion</th><th>No Answer</th><th>Amended</th></tr>
<tr><td>Utah Born Scientists</td><td>12.8</td><td>1.8</td><td>46.1</td><td>13.1</td><td>10.3</td><td>5.7</td><td>9.6</td></tr>
<tr><td>Other Churches' Believers</td><td>20.0</td><td>8.0</td><td>40.0</td><td>8.0</td><td>4.0</td><td>8.0</td><td>12.0</td></tr>
<tr><td>1992</td><td colspan="2">78.0</td><td colspan="2">22.0</td><td></td><td></td><td></td></tr>
<tr><td>Nominal LDS</td><td>7.3</td><td></td><td>36.4</td><td>20.0</td><td>20.0</td><td>10.8</td><td>5.5</td></tr>
<tr><td>1992</td><td colspan="2">0.0</td><td colspan="2">80.0</td><td></td><td></td><td>20.0</td></tr>
<tr><td>LDS Fair Believers</td><td>10.0</td><td></td><td>63.3</td><td>6.7</td><td>13.6</td><td>3.3</td><td>3.3</td></tr>
<tr><td>LDS Strong Believers</td><td>20.2</td><td>3.1</td><td>48.1</td><td>7.8</td><td>3.9</td><td>4.7</td><td>12.4</td></tr>
<tr><td>1992</td><td>13.0</td><td>66.0</td><td colspan="2">15.0</td><td>5.0</td><td></td><td>1.0</td></tr>
<tr><td>LDS Seminary Teachers</td><td>25.4</td><td>5.8</td><td>61.5</td><td>15.4</td><td></td><td></td><td>1.9</td></tr>
</table>

Percent contradictory answers between this item and item 17(p): Scientists, 2.8%, Teachers 3.8%

Table 39

God Does Not Commonly Intervene in Human Affairs: Man's Life on Earth is Largely Shaped by Man's Own Agency

Numbers are percentages

Legend: **A - Tentative Agreement**, **AA - Positive Agreement**, **D - Tentative Disagreement**, **DD - Positive Disagreement**

	A	AA	D	DD	No Opinion	No Answer	Amended
Utah Born Scientists	54.3	11.0	11.0	1.8	8.2	4.6	8.5
Other Churches' Believers	48.0	12.0	16.0		8.0	12.0	4.0
Nominal LDS	43.6	20.0	5.5		18.2	10.9	1.8
LDS Fair Believers	79.2	6.6	3.3		6.7	3.3	
LDS Strong Believers	57.4	6.2	18.6	3.1	1.6	2.3	10.9
LDS Seminary Teachers	51.9	25.0	17.3	5.8			

(No comparable question in 1992)

Table 40

There is a God Who is Creator, But He Never Intervenes on Earth Now

Agreement: "Skeptical"

Numbers are percentages

Legend: **A - Tentative Agreement**, **AA - Positive Agreement**, **D - Tentative Disagreement**, **DD - Positive Disagreement**

	A	AA	D	DD	No Opinion	No Answer	Amended
Utah Born Scientists	5.3	0.7	47.2	12.1	19.9	7.4	7.1
Other Churches' Believers	8.0		52.0	12.0	8.0	16.0	4.0
Nominal LDS	3.6	3.6	25.5	7.3	45.5	10.9	3.6
LDS Fair Believers	13.3		50.0		26.7	3.3	6.7
LDS Strong Believers	1.6		65.9	17.8	3.9	4.7	6.2
LDS Seminary Teachers			30.8	67.3			1.9

(No comparable question in 1992)

Table 41

God is Completely Unknown to Man

Agreement: "Skeptical"

Numbers are percentages

Legend: **A - Tentative Agreement**, **AA - Positive Agreement**, **D - Tentative Disagreement**, **DD - Positive Disagreement**

	A	AA	D	DD	No Opinion	No Answer	Amended
Utah Born Scientists	8.2	3.2	48.2	16.2	6.0	14.9	3.5
Other Churches' Believers	0.0	4.0	56.0	20.0	4.0	16.0	0.0
Nominal LDS	16.4	5.5	23.6	5.5	32.7	12.7	3.6
LDS Fair Believers	60.0	3.3	16.7	6.7			
LDS Strong Believers	0.0	0.8	64.3	28.7	2.3	2.3	0.8
LDS Seminary Teachers			25.0	75.0			

(No comparable question in 1992)

Table 42

God Can and May do Anything Whatsoever, No Matter How Seemingly Impossible and Contradictory to Present Logic, Science, or Facts as Seen by Man

Agreement: "Literal"

Numbers are percentages

Legend: **A - Tentative Agreement**, **AA - Positive Agreement**, **D - Tentative Disagreement**, **DD - Positive Disagreement**

	A	AA	D	DD	No Opinion	No Answer	Amended
Utah Born Scientists	23.4	4.3	25.9	11.3	17.4	7.1	9.6
Other Churches' Believers	24.0	12.0	12.0	4.0	20.0	20.0	8.0
Nominal LDS	12.7	3.6	29.1	20.0	27.2	7.3	
LDS Fair Believers	33.3		26.7	13.3	20.0	6.7	
LDS Strong Believers	33.3	3.9	28.7	5.4	7.0	5.4	15.5
LDS Seminary Teachers	30.8	19.2	30.8	15.4	1.9		1.9

(No comparable question in 1992)

Percent contradictory answers between this item and item 17(t): Scientists - 12.1%; Teachers - 26.9%

Table 43

God is Now Limited to Some Extent by Realities in the Nature of Things in the Universe, Including Man's Free Agency

Numbers are percentages

Legend: **A - Tentative Agreement** **D - Tentative Disagreement**
AA - Positive Agreement **DD - Positive Disagreement**

	A	AA	D	DD	No Opinion	No Answer	Amended
Utah Born Scientists	38.3	6.0	13.8	3.5	24.8	10.3	4.3
Other Churches' Believers	16.0		20.0	24.0	20.0	16.0	4.0
1992	100.0						
Nominal LDS	18.2	1.8	12.7	5.5	43.6	14.5	3.6
1992	20.0	20.0	40.0				20.0
LDS Fair Believers	43.6	6.6	26.7		16.7	3.3	3.3
LDS Strong Believers	9.0	56.0		15.0	14.0		6.0
1992	11.0	36.0	36.0		11.0		6.0
LDS Seminary Teachers	42.3	30.8	9.6	13.5		1.9	1.9

Table 44

The "Standard Works" are the Word of God, Entirely Without Error, Except for Mistranslation in the Bible

Agreement: "Literal"

Numbers are percentages

Legend: **A - Tentative Agreement** **D - Tentative Disagreement**
AA - Positive Agreement **DD - Positive Disagreement**

	A	AA	D	DD	No Opinion	No Answer	Amended
Utah Born Scientists	6.7	6.0	0.7	54.6	17.8	8.2	6.0
Other Churches' Believers	8.0	4.0	36.0	12.0	20.0	16.0	4.0
1992	22.0		67.0		11.0		
Nominal LDS	0.0	0.0	56.4	25.5	14.5	1.8	
1992	0.0		80.0		20.0		
LDS Fair Believers	3.3		82.5	6.6		6.6	
LDS Strong Believers	13.2	0.8	60.5	7.8	3.9	4.7	9.3
1992	37.0		40.0		6.0		17.0
LDS Seminary Teachers	23.1	13.5	42.3	13.5		3.8	3.8

Table 45

The "Standard Works" are All Inspired by God, but Each May Reflect Some Human Error and Limitation because They are in Man's Language

Agreement: "Interpretive"

Numbers are percentages

Legend: **A - Tentative Agreement** **D - Tentative Disagreement**
AA - Positive Agreement **DD - Positive Disagreement**

	A	AA	D	DD	No Opinion	No Answer	Amended
Utah Born Scientists	50.4	6.7	14.2	7.1	11.7	4.6	5.0
Other Churches' Believers	24.0	16.0	12.0	4.0	24.0	20.0	
1992	11.0	78.0	0.0		11.0		
Nominal LDS	23.6	1.8	30.9	12.7	23.6	5.4	1.8
1992	0.0		60.0		40.0		
LDS Fair Believers	73.3	3.3	13.3	0.0	6.7	3.3	
LDS Strong Believers	75.0	11.0	5.0		2.0		7.0
1992	18.0	52.0	25.0		5.0		
LDS Seminary Teachers	46.2	26.9	17.3	9.6			

See text in Chapter VI for comments on lines 3 & 5.

Table 46

The "Standard Works" are Nothing but the Thoughts of Men and Thus May Contain Many Errors

Agreement: "Skeptical"

Numbers are percentages

Legend: **A - Tentative Agreement** **D - Tentative Disagreement**
AA - Positive Agreement **DD - Positive Disagreement**

	A	AA	D	DD	No Opinion	No Answer	Amended
Utah Born Scientists	16.0	8.9	42.6	11.7	11.0	7.1	2.5
Other Churches' Believers	4.0	8.0	24.0	12.0	28.0	24.0	
Nominal LDS	40.0	16.4	12.7		16.4	9.1	5.5
LDS Fair Believers	10.0		63.3	3.3	16.7	6.7	
LDS Strong Believers	1.6		65.9	23.3	3.1	3.9	2.3
LDS Seminary Teachers			30.8	69.2			

(Item not on 1992 questionaire.)

Table 47

Scriptures in the "Standard Works" Must be Literally Interpreted Without Effort to Stretch Them to Fit Supposed Facts or Theories of Science

Agreement: "Literal"

Numbers are percentages

Legend: **A - Tentative Agreement**, **AA - Positive Agreement**, **D - Tentative Disagreement**, **DD - Positive Disagreement**

	A	AA	D	DD	No Opinion	No Answer	Amended
Utah Born Scientists	10.3	1.8	48.6	11.7	11.0	10.6	5.7
Other Churches' Believers	12.0	4.0	20.0	20.0	16.0	24.0	4.0
Nominal LDS	9.1	1.8	38.2	14.5	21.8	10.9	3.6
LDS Fair Believers	10.0		73.3	6.7	3.3	6.7	
LDS Strong Believers	14.7	2.3	56.6	3.9	5.4	7.8	9.3
LDS Seminary Teachers	36.5	13.5	32.7	11.5	5.8		

(Item not on 1992 questionaire.)

Table 48

Interpretation of the Words of Scripture Should be Somewhat Flexible to Harmonize with Logical Thinking or Scientific Reasoning

Agreement: "Interpretive"

Numbers are percentages

Legend: **A - Tentative Agreement**, **AA - Positive Agreement**, **D - Tentative Disagreement**, **DD - Positive Disagreement**

	A	AA	D	DD	No Opinion	No Answer	Amended
Utah Born Scientists	56.0	6.0	9.6	2.1	11.0	8.9	5.7
Other Churches' Believers	40.0	12.0	12.0	12.0	8.0	12.0	4.0
Nominal LDS	47.3	7.3	3.6		25.5	11.9	5.5
LDS Fair Believers	80.0	6.6	6.7	3.3	3.3		
LDS Strong Believers	61.2	3.9	15.5	1.6	2.3	7.0	8.5
LDS Seminary Teachers	32.7	9.6	42.3	9.6	1.9	3.8	

(Item not on 1992 questionaire.)

Table 49

Most Statements by the President of the Latter-day Saint Church are the Infallible Word of God, Official Latter-day Saint Doctrine

Numbers are percentages

Legend: **A - Tentative Agreement** **D - Tentative Disagreement**
AA - Positive Agreement **DD - Positive Disagreement**

	A	AA	D	DD	No Opinion	No Answer	Amended
Utah Born Scientists	14.9	2.1	48.6	17.0	7.1	6.7	3.2
Other Churches' Believers			28.0	28.0	24.0	16.0	4.0
Nominal LDS	1.8		58.2	21.8	12.7	5.4	
LDS Fair Believers	3.3	3.3	80.0		10.0	3.3	
LDS Strong Believers	31.8	3.1	46.5	4.7	3.1	5.4	5.4
LDS Seminary Teachers	28.8	13.5	38.5	9.6	3.8	1.9	3.8

(Item not on 1992 questionaire.)

Table 50

The Word of God, Official Latter-day Saint Doctrine, is Found only in the Scriptures or in Pronouncements by the President of the Church Explicitly as Revelation

Numbers are percentages

Legend: **A - Tentative Agreement** **D - Tentative Disagreement**
AA - Positive Agreement **DD - Positive Disagreement**

	A	AA	D	DD	No Opinion	No Answer	Amended
Utah Born Scientists	24.5	2.5	29.8	15.2	15.2	9.2	3.2
Other Churches' Believers	8.0	4.0	32.0	20.0	20.0	16.0	
Nominal LDS	1.8		36.4	18.2	29.1	10.9	3.6
LDS Fair Believers	30.0		36.7	3.3	16.7	13.3	
LDS Strong Believers	45.0	3.9	27.9	7.0	9.3	3.1	3.9
LDS Seminary Teachers	34.6	21.2	26.9	13.5	1.9		

(Item not on 1992 questionaire.)

Table 51

Nothing from Scripture or Church Authorities is Revelation from God

Agreement: "Skeptical"

Numbers are percentages

Legend: **A - Tentative Agreement**, **AA - Positive Agreement**, **D - Tentative Disagreement**, **DD - Positive Disagreement**

	A	AA	D	DD	No Opinion	No Answer	Amended
Utah Born Scientists	9.8	6.7	46.8	14.5	13.8	6.4	1.4
Other Churches' Believers	4.0	8.0	36.0	12.0	20.0	16.0	4.0
Nominal LDS	21.8	9.1	16.4		38.2	10.9	3.6
LDS Fair Believers	6.7		76.7		10.0	6.7	
LDS Strong Believers	2.3		65.9	28.7	1.6	0.8	
LDS Seminary Teachers			32.7	67.3			

(Item not on 1992 questionaire.)

Table 52

No Church is Divinely Authorized

Agreement: "Skeptical"

Numbers are percentages

Legend: **A - Tentative Agreement**, **AA - Positive Agreement**, **D - Tentative Disagreement**, **DD - Positive Disagreement**

	A	AA	D	DD	No Opinion	No Answer	Amended
Utah Born Scientists	18.1	9.9	41.8	12.1	12.1	5.3	0.4
Other Churches' Believers	24.0	20.0	16.0	12.0	12.0	16.0	
Nominal LDS	45.5	12.7	7.3	1.8	27.3	3.6	1.8
LDS Fair Believers	3.3		60.0	3.3	23.3	10.0	
LDS Strong Believers	3.9	0.8	65.9	22.5	3.9	2.3	
LDS Seminary Teachers			26.9	73.1			

(Item not on 1992 questionaire.)

Table 53

No Church is the ONLY Divinely Authorized One

Numbers are percentages

Legend: **A - Tentative Agreement**   **D - Tentative Disagreement**
AA - Positive Agreement   **DD - Positive Disagreement**

	A	**AA**	**D**	**DD**	**No Opinion**	**No Answer**	**Amended**
Utah Born Scientists	31.2	11.3	30.5	11.0	8.5	6.0	0.4
Other Churches' Believers	36.0	24.0	12.0	12.0	4.0	12.0	
Nominal LDS	61.2	16.2	1.8		12.7	7.3	
LDS Fair Believers	40.0		23.3	3.3	23.3	10.0	
LDS Strong Believers	13.2	0.8	57.4	22.5	3.1	3.1	
LDS Seminary Teachers	5.8		12.2	69.2	1.9	1.9	

(Item not on 1992 questionaire.)

Table 43 is omitted (redundant).

Table 55

Comparison of Scientists and Seminary Teacher Questionnaires Containing One or More of "Interpretive" or "Literal" Answers in the Total Science-Religion Section (All of them 17) of the Questionnaire

Individual Questionnaire With:		**Utah Scientists Percent**	**L.D.S. Believers Percent**	**Seminary Teachers Percent**
1 Belief	"Literal"	22.7	22.0	5.8
1 Belief	"Interpretive"	2.9	3.1	7.7
2 Beliefs	"Literal"	9.4	12.0	11.5
2 Beliefs	"Interpretive"	3.6	3.8	3.8
3 Belief	"Literal"	17.7	15.1	13.5
3 Belief	"Interpretive"	10.0	3.8	9.6
4 Beliefs	"Literal"	8.3	7.5	7.7
4 Beliefs	"Interpretive"	12.9	7.5	21.2
5 Belief	"Literal"	3.9	3.1	15.4
5 Belief	"Interpretive"	13.6	7.5	9.6
6 Beliefs	"Literal"	3.3	3.8	9.8
6 Beliefs	"Interpretive"	10.8	10.	15.4
7 Belief	"Literal"	3.9	3.8	13.5
7 Belief	"Interpretive"	12.2	15.1	9.6
8 Beliefs	"Literal"	1.6	0.6	9.6
8 Beliefs	"Interpretive"	12.9	16.9	11.5
9 Belief	"Literal"	0.6	0.6	9.6
9 Belief	"Interpretive"	12.9	18.2	5.8
10 Beliefs	"Literal"	0.0		1.9
10 Beliefs	"Interpretive"	5.7	8.1	1.9
11 Belief	"Literal"	0.0		
11 Belief	"Interpretive"	1.8	3.1	3.8

Table 56

Comparison of Utah Born Scientists and Latter-day Saint Seminary Teachers as to Who Have Answered More Toward One Viewpoint than the Other

Six or More Answers Numbers are percentages	Utah Scientists	L.D.S. Believer Scientists	Seminary Teachers
"Literal"	11.0	8.1	42.3
"Interpretive"	56.3	74.2	48.0

As judged by having 6 or more answers of one viewpoint.

Table 57

Scientists as to Whether They Changed Their Opinions on Any Beliefs of Item 17 as They Matured

Numbers are percentages

	Yes	No	No Answer	Other
Utah Born Scientists	70.9	21.7	6.7	0.7
Other Churches' Believers	52.0	20.0	20.0	8.0
Nominal L.D.S.	83.6	10.9	3.6	1.8
L.D.S. Fair Believers	80.0	13.3	6.7	
L.D.S. Stong Believers	68.2	22.5	7.8	0.8

Table 58

Percentages of Respondents as to When Changes in Science-Religion Beliefs Took Place

Numbers are percentages

Before 14	14 - 18	18 - 22	22 - 30	After 30	No Answer	Process Continual
1.8	2.1	7.4	34.0	6.7	34.4	12.1

Table 59

Percentages of Total Changes from Various Science-Religion (Item 17) Beliefs as Indicated by Respondents

	Percentage Changes from		
	"Literal"	"Interpretive"	"Skeptical"
Utah Born Scientists	52.9	35.2	12.0
Nominal L.D.S.	52.6	33.4	13.0
L.D.S. Stong Believers	49.0	39.0	12.0

Table 60

Percentages of Respondents Stating Various Extent of Emotional Troubling During Changes of Science-Religion Beliefs

Numbers are percentages

	Intensely	Somewhat	Not Troubled	No Answer
Utah Born Scientists	6.7	30.9	41.5	19.9
Other Churches' Believers	12.0	28.0	32.0	28.0
Nominal L.D.S.	3.6	30.9	54.5	11.3
L.D.S. Fair Believers	3.3	56.7	26.7	13.3
L.D.S. Stong Believers	7.8	27.1	45.0	20.2

Table 61

Percentages of Total Changes from Various Science-Religion Beliefs Indicated by Respondents with Varying Degrees of Emotional Troubling

Numbers are percentages

	Percentage Changes from		
	"Literal"	"Interpretive"	"Skeptical"
Intensely Troubled	53.0	41.0	6.0
Somewhat Troubled	54.0	32.0	13.0
Not Troubled	53.0	35.0	12.0

APPENDIX B

REPRESENTATIVENESS OF THE RESPONSES

REPRESENTATIVENESS OF THE RESPONSES, 1955

The response of Utah born scientists to the questionnaire of the 1955 study was 63 percent. This was about the same as the average for 204 Doctoral questionnaires from Teacher's College, Columbia University. It was the same as the response to a published study of scientists by Visher, whose letter and questionnaire were close to the same length as the ones used in this study.

It is not known with certainty whether the data shown on the returned questionnaires would hold true for those who did not respond. Was the non-response just from putting it aside and not getting back to it? Or was it related in a significant way to some scientists' status or beliefs? For instance, have some "Believing" members of the Mormon Church been reluctant to support the study for fear it would be negative about their Church? Have some scientists of other faiths neglected to answer because the study was primarily about Mormons? Have some scientists who were once Latter-day Saints but were now only nominal members refrained from answering for fear the study would be unfair in some way? In wording the letter and questionnaire I tried to minimize any biased reactions.

The problem was not whether some chance number of each of such groups had failed to return the questionnaire; it was whether reactions more confined to one group would render the statistics given by the returns too inaccurate to be relevant to the problems of the study.

I needed methods of approximating the percentages of (1) the non-Mormons, (2) the "Believing" Mormons, and (3) the nominal Mormons which could not reflect any reactions of the scientists themselves to the questionnaire. Two methods for making this approximation were found. One was the use of a brief questionnaire addressed to the Mormon Branch Presidents in the areas of the Utah born scientists whose present addresses were in the missions of the Church. The directory of the Church was used to obtain addresses of the Branch Presidents where the scientists lived.

The name of the scientist in his area was sent to the Branch President. He was asked to check a simple one-page questionnaire whether he knew the mentioned scientist to be a member of the Church, whether he believed him to be an active member, and whether he considered him to be a "Believer" or not.

Of the 66 Branch Presidents to whom the questionnaires were sent, 59 returned them completed, an 86.3 percent response. Lack of information on the scientists living in the areas of the 14 percent who did not respond did not likely affect this check significantly one way or the other. This was because it was a relatively small percentage and because the status of the scientists living in the areas unreported would not likely have any connection to the failure of the Branch President to respond.

This response gave reports on 166 scientists of the 206 judged to be living in the missions of the Church. Results of this check were as follows, compared to the data from the questionnaires returned by the scientists themselves.

Comparison of Numbers of Latter-day Saints among Utah Born Scientists as Reported by Branch Presidents and as Reported by Scientists Questionnaires

	L.D.S. on branch Records	No record but known to be L.D.S.	Active Members	Are they L.D.S. Believers? Yes	No	Don't Know
Branch Presidents	59	9	60	62.6	21.6	15.8
Scientists	75.9 (Classifying themselves as L.D.S.)		64	72.8		

It appeared from this comparison that the 63 percent response from the scientists' questionnaires was substantially representative of all Utah born scientists living in the mission fields, as far as proportions who were Active, and who were Believing were concerned. The scientists' questionnaires showed only 7.9 percent higher percentages of Mormons, 4 percent higher of Active, and 9.8 percent higher of Believing than did the Branch Presidents.

We do not know whether the scientists living in the Stakes (the better organized areas) of the Mormon Church would have been more or less inclined toward the Church than those living in the missions. If they would be, then the scientists' questionnaire response would come still closer to being representative of the whole group of Utah born scientists.

Another approximation, though less reliable, of the representativeness of the response was whether scientists of any one field responded more or less than would be expected compared to the percentages in the nation generally in that field. This would be an indicator only if Utah born scientists divide by fields the same as those nationally and if the field is significantly related to being either a Mormon and/or a Believer.

Among the Utah respondents there were distinctly less in agriculture than were the American scientists as a whole, 9.2 percent for the respondents and 14.7 percent for the national total.

Fields of Science of All American Men of Science Compared to Fields for Respondents in this Study

	Physical Sciences	Agricultural Sciences	ABiological Sciences	Social Sciences
American Men of Science	44.2	14.7	35.6	5.4
Questionnaire Respondents	48.6	9.2	34.0	7.1

An uninformed guess might have been that Utah born scientists would have been more in agriculture, but as can be seen in the above table, this was not true.

One might have guessed that agriculture would contain larger percentages of Believers than fields more directly connected to the science-religion conflicts. From the data of this study, this seems to be true. Those in agriculture showed 51.8 percent in the Very Strong Believer category, compared to 20 percent of those in geology and 19 percent of those in social sciences, the lowest in Very Strong Believers. Those in agriculture, to look at the other side of the coin, had only 11.1 percent with No Such Conviction (that Joseph Smith was inspired by God) compared to 19 percent of those in physics and 43.6 percent of those in social science.[4] Since the percent in agriculture who responded was below the national percent of scientists in agriculture, and since agriculturalists were the strongest Believers, there is no evidence here of an under response by non-Believers. And the percent response from those in social science among the Utah born was above the national percentages in social science. Utah either produces relatively more social scientists or they have over-responded to this survey. This suggests, if anything, that non-Believers responded more heavily, since social scientists contain more non-Believers and less Strong Believers.

These two above checks on representativeness, particularly the check with the Branch Presidents, seemed to show that the 63 percent response from Utah born scientists was representative of the whole group of Utah born scientists. There seems to be no evidence that any significant categories of the Utah scientists, say, non-Mormons, Strong Believer Mormons, or merely nominal Mormons is misrepresented in the responses. The data received were regarded by the dissertation committee as sufficiently representative to justify the major findings and conclusions of the study, particularly that scientific minds can harmonize Mormonism and science.

REPRESENTATIVENESS OF THE RESPONSES, 1992.

In science when one replicates a previous study, it is important to replicate in every relevant detail. In every way I could control, the 1992 study was a replication of the 1955. Both were mailed questionnaires with cover letters of very similar approach. For almost all questionnaire items, the wording was identical. The size of response, 65%, was only two percent higher.

There were differences I could not control. The receiver of a mailed survey can be influenced by how he perceives the competance and integrity of the researcher. In 1955 I was identified only as a doctoral student at the University of Utah. In 1992 I was identified only as an Emeritus Professor of Arizona State University. In both cases one might or might not have guessed that I was born in Utah and at least nominally a Mormon.

The other differences beyond my control were in the scientist population itself and in the changes in the world during the span of time. Whatever changes in responses these made were essentially what the study was trying to discover rather than being contaminants.

As was true of the 1955 study, the percentage responding was typical, 65%, of successful mailed questionnaire studies. All these other studies have subject matter that have nothing to do with my study. So the 65% response figure most probably comes from other factors than the subject matter, the researcher, or the subject population. These factors can be recipients who habitually ignore mailed questionnaires, who have the questionnaire and/or its return envelop lost in the "piles of papers", who intend to do it someday. Some have moved and the mail fails to catch up. There are many reasons why some questionnaires do not come back, in any study, that have nothing to do with the study itself. This was the percentage who did not respond to my studies in 1955 and 1992.

Nevertheless, I made another type of test of reliability, one which analyzes the breakdown in one's responses compared to items where the breakdown of the total subject population is known from other sources. I could make two tests. First, one based on the fields of science. Second, one based on responses from a part of the subject population whose key beliefs are already discernible by other means than the questionnaire in comparison to questionnaire answers.

I searched the on-line data base American Men and Women of Science and tabulated the fields of science for my total subject population. Then I compared this to the tabulated fields of science of the respondents. They were essentially the same, except for a much larger response from chemists and physicists. To adjust for this, I selected out the questionnaires returned from chemists and physicists, and randomly removed the number of over-responses. I used the corrected list for the statistical tabulations (using SPSS) which I have reported.

I had also tabulated my results uncorrected, that is, with the excessively large response from chemists and physicists included. Corrected and uncorrected, the results came out significantly the same, except that the corrected results showed slightly less tilt toward the Literal. It did not change the percentages between Strong Mormons or Nominal Mormons. The corrected results showed slightly more non-Mormons. The corrected results did not require any changes in the conclusions of the study.

Another test was available. It bears directly on the point of whether non-responses represent significant numbers of those **other than** Strong Mormons. This point is important because the percentage of Strong Mormons was likely the most notable finding of the study.

I tabulated responses, by postmarks, from the Salt Lake area, the Brigham Young University area (Orem, Springfield, Provo), and "all others". There was a glaring difference in the overall tabulations of questionnaire answers when so compared. In the Salt Lake area and the "all others" areas, the figures showed 30% non-Mormons and 15% Nominal Mormons. The figures for the B.Y.U. area, however, showed 100% Strong Mormon--no non-Mormons, no other than Strong Mormons, **yet the percent of non-response was the same**.

Apparently Mormons can also just set questionnaires aside, lose them, etc. (This conclusion, of course, assumes that almost all of the B.Y.U. area scientists are Strong Mormons. So Strong Mormons responded, as we know, but other Strong Mormons also, in the same percentages put them aside, lost them, etc. The non-responses were apparently the usual random neglects and not mainly non-Mormons and Nominal Mormons holding out. Or could it be that in the B.Y.U. area scientists who are other than Strong Mormons avoid questionnaires like a plague, but in other geographical areas they do not? I don't think so.

The data reported for the respondents of the 1992 study are representative of the Utah university graduates who are scientists listed in the 1990 edition of American Men and Women of Science sufficiently to justify the conclusions of this book. And the evidences of changes between the two studies are particularly dependable because they have nothing to do with the percent of responses, which were essentially the same in both studies.

Both the 1955 and 1992 studies were done by the same researcher, using the same methodology, with similar cover letters (see Appendix C), and identical questionnaire items. The clear differences between 1955 and 1992 were the nature of the scientist populations themselves, which was what the studies were about and reported with care.

The design, data handling, and conclusions of the 1955 study were examined and approved by the doctoral committee. The replication was by a professor who has examined many doctoral studies as chair and member of graduate committees.

Furthermore, Dr. Bruce Merrill, Director of the Media Research Center of the Walter Cronkite School of Journalism at Arizona State University, approved the replication design and suggested the tests by fields of science and the corrections by weightings. He also noted the test provided by the Provo area.

Furthermore, the conclusions rest upon large and obvious differences. None of them are close calls. I believe no probable margin of error would close those gaps enough to invalidate the conclusions. The results of the studies are reliable. The differences shown between 1955 and 1992 are real.

APPENDIX C

LETTERS AND QUESTIONNAIRES OF THE STUDIES

LETTER SENT WITH QUESTIONNAIRE TO UTAH BORN SCIENTISTS

Dear Dr.   :

Your native state, according to Dr. Edward L. Thorndike of Columbia University, is unique as a producer of scientists, as you may know. It produced twice as many scientists per capita as the average state and 30 percent more per capita than the second place state, as listed in the 1938 American Men of Science.

A similar study of the 1949 volume which has been made as part of my doctoral thesis indicates that in the decade since Thorndike's study Utah has increased its lead by 28 percent. (522 Utah born scientists are listed.)

Since your native state is unusual in production of scientists, Utah born scientists themselves appear to be an indispensable source of opinion and fact on the religion-science controversy. Church educators may seek to build belief and activity of young people in the churches while at the same time increasing their appreciation of science. But is it possible to do both? And if it is, does it seem to require a certain orientation in science and religion rather than some other orientation?

To obtain and interpret viewpoints from this important source is a necessary part of my doctoral thesis. The enclosed questionnaire is to obtain the information believed to be most essential for additional light on the questions above.

You need not sign the questionnaire, since some responses may involve confidential beliefs. No attempt of any kind will ever be made to identify any questionnaire with a particular scientist.

Your indispensable help will be greatly appreciated. If you request, the results of this study will be sent to you shortly after it is finished as a token of my gratitude.

Sincerely,

Richard T. Wootton

RTW/js
Enclosure

P.S. The time required to complete the questionnaire is only 10 minutes, and the study cannot succeed without this help, so please answer now if you can.

RELIGIOUS ORIENTATION QUESTIONNAIRE

1. Your field of science:
2. Approximate number of years you have been in the field of science since receiving bachelor's degree:
3. Would you say that you attended church meetings regularly until 18 years of age?
4. Were you active in your church as an officer, teacher, or missionary between the ages of 18 and 14?
5. Do you believe Utah's per capita leads in production of Men of Science is somehow attributable to Latter-day Saint influence?
Yes______ No______ In what ways?______________________________
6. Do you believe that your church contributed significantly to your professional achievements? Yes______ No______
In what ways?______________________________
7. Church in which you have at least nominal membership__________
8. Would you say that you are now an active member of your church?
____
9. State your present church position or office:______________
10. What would you say is the strength of your conviction that Jesus of Nazareth is a divine person of the Godhead?
No such conviction_____ Weak_____ Fair_____ Strong_____
Very Strong______
11. What is your attitude toward the Church of Jesus Christ of Latter-day Saints as an institution for promoting human welfare?
Favorable___ Indifferent___ Antagonistic___ No Opinion___
Since a substantial number of Utah scientists will likely be at least nominal members of the L. D. S. Church, the remainder of the questionnaire has some questions more pertinent to L. D. S. members than to others. If others complete the questionnaire in spite of this, it will be greatly appreciated.
12. Do you believe that your church doctrine and science can be logically harmonized? Yes_____ Partially_____ No_____
No Opinion_____
13. Do you believe that you logically harmonize your church doctrine and science in your own philosophy of life?
Yes_____ Partially_____ No_____ No Opinion_____
14. Do you believe that the fields of religion and science are so far removed from each other that no attempt is logically necessary to harmonize them? Yes_____ Partially_____ No_____
No Opinion_____
15. What would you say is the strength of your conviction that Joseph Smith, Jr. was inspired by God in the formation of the Church of Jesus Christ of Latter-day Saints?
No Such Conviction_____ Weak_____ Fair_____ Strong_____
Very Strong_____
16. What would you say is the strength of your conviction that the Church of Jesus Christ of Latter-day Saints today is the only authoritative Church of Jesus Christ on the earth today?
No Such Conviction_____ Weak_____ Fair_____ Strong_____
Very Strong_____

17. Following is a list of various beliefs which relate to the

religion-science controversy. Please indicate by a check in the appropriate column opposite each belief your agreement, disagreement, or absence of opinion on each belief (a) through (dd) below.
Please use a single check to indicate Tentative agreement or Tentative disagreement. Use double check marks to indicate Positive agreement or Positive disagreement.
PLEASE AMEND ANY BELIEF BELOW TO MAKE IT REPRESENT MORE ACCURATELY YOUR OPINION BEFORE CHECKING IT--IF NECESSARY.

	Agree	Dis-Agree	No Opinion
(a) The earth was created in a relatively short period of time, that is, some thousands of years.			
(b) The earth took at least hundreds of millions of years to create.			
(c) Man's body did not evolve in any fashion from simpler species and is not biologically related to them.			
(d) God created man's mortal body, probably by making many small progressive changes from simple to more complex forms over millions of years.			
(e) It is not known whether a God made man. The species, including man, probably came through general evolution by the processes of chance and selection rather than by intelligent design.			
(f) Other species than man also had a creation as distinct species and are unrelated by biological lineage from the simpler to the more complex.			
(g) The species other than man were created by God, probably by making many small changes from simple to more complex, over millions of years.			
(h) The flood of Noah covered the top of Mount Ararat at least 15 cubits (not less than 26 feet) deep and the whole earth correspondingly, as literally described in Genesis in the Bible.			
(i) The flood of Noah was a reality but the details must be interpreted differently than given literally in Genesis.			
(j) There was not necessarily any such flood as described in Genesis.			
(k) Use of scientific reason or logical thinking as a means to religious conviction should have a minor role.			

(l) The scientific viewpoint and method

should be held in very high regard and given a major role in all convictions. ---------------------

(m) Religious convictions should come primarily from answers to prayers, miraculous healing, and statements from religious authorities. ---------------------

(n) Religious conviction should come largely from logical thinking upon the facts of history, the existing world, the fruits of religion, and personal experience. ---------------------

(o) God commonly acts directly in events on the earth, that is He constantly intervenes in human affairs. ---------------------

(p) God does not commonly intervene in human affairs; man's life on earth is largely shaped by his own agency. ---------------------

(q) There is a God who is creator but He never intervenes on earth now. ---------------------

(r) God is completely unknown to man. ---------------------

(s) God can and may do anything whatsoever, no matter how seemingly impossible and contradictory to present logic, science, or facts as seen by man. ---------------------

(t) God Himself is now limited to some extent by realities in the nature of things in the universe, including man's free agency. ---------------------

(u) The "Standard Works" are the word of God entirely without error, except for mistranslation in the Bible. ---------------------

(v) The "Standard Works" are all inspired by God but each may reflect some human error and limitation because they are in man's language. ---------------------

(w) The "Standard Works" are nothing but the thoughts of men and thus may contain many errors. ---------------------

(x) Scriptures in the "Standard Works" must be literally interpreted without effort to stretch them to fit supposed facts or theories of science, with the exception of obvious figures of speech. ---------------------

(y) Interpretation of the words of scriptures should be as flexible as language permits (that is, somewhat flexible) to harmonize with logical thinking or scientific reasoning. ---------------------

(z) Most conference statements by the President of the L.D.S. Church are the infallible word of God, official L.D.S. doctrine. ---------------------

(aa) The word of God, official L. D. S.

doctrine, is found only in the scriptures or in pronouncements given by the President of the Church explicitly as revelation. ---------------------

(bb) Nothing from scriptures or church authorities is the word of God. ---------------------

(cc) No church is divinely authorized. ---------------------

(dd) No church is the only divinely authorized one. ---------------------

(ee) If you wish, add below beliefs which you hold and consider particularly important in addition to the above to portray your general viewpoint on the religion-science problem: (You may use the back of page for additional comment. Those touching your field of science would be most helpful.)

18. As you matured did you change your opinion on any of the above beliefs?

19. If you changed your opinion on some, will you please circle the letter in the list under 17 above which identifies the belief from which you changed.

20. At about what age did most of the changes occur?

21. Were some of these changes emotionally troubling to you?
Intensely______ Somewhat________ No_____

22. Please list the writers, teachers, or speakers whom you recall offhand helping you the most to form your philosophy of science and religion.

November 22, 1991

Dear Scientist Graduate of a Utah University:

Utah produced, per capita, about 30% more scientists than the second place state, which was Idaho. (Surveys of American Men of Science, 1938, 1949, and 1956.) I am now bringing this type of study up to date using the 1990 American Men and Women of Science.

Utah's remarkable standing stimulated me years ago to make a study, with indispensable help from the scientists, of the orientations of those scientists to science-religion issues. My doctoral thesis at the University of Utah was based on that study. (I'll send you a summary of it, if you request.)

The number of scientists listed in American Men and Women of Science has increased 140% since 1949. What has happened to Utah's lead over these years? And what has changed in the religious orientations of Utah scientists? Please help me find out and report to you.

You can be part of producing a valuable set of data for scholarly publication and for your interest. Please answer the enclosed one sheet questionnaire. A stamped return envelop is provided for your convenience. The extra self-addressed card is for you to request separately the results of this anonymous study. (An individual's name cannot be associated with the questionnaire answers.)

A Professor Emeritus of Arizona State University, I recently retired as Chair of the Department of Educational Administration and was previously Director of Special Projects for the university President John Schwada.

This will be an objective study, reliably reported, with complete documentation kept available. The current address labels are a statistically determined **random sample** of scientists graduated from a Utah university, and who are in the AMWS 17th edition CD-ROM database. **Therefore, a high level of response is important**. I am doing this at my own expense. I also will see that it is distributed to you, key libraries and available for publication in scholarly journals. With your **indispensable** help, the data will be interesting.

The earlier study was unique--the only statistical study of any scope on Mormon science-religion issues approved by a university doctoral committee. The results were highly significant statistically and practically. The current **update you are making possible** may be even more so. Sending you the summaries will show some of my deep appreciation to you for participating.

Sincerely,

Richard T. Wootton

RELIGION ORIENTATION QUESTIONNAIRE

Please, as you wish, comment or amend. Questionnaire is brief.

1. Your state of birth:_______________.
2. Your field of science:_______________________________________
Number of years in field of science since Bachelor's Degree:________
3. Church in which you have at least nominal membership:____________

4. Have you changed denominations? 1> Yes. 2> No.
From:______________________________To:______________________________

5. Would you say you are now an active member of your church?______

6. Were you active in your church as an officer, teacher, or missionary between ages 18 and 24?__________________________________

7. Do you believe that Utah's per capita lead in production of <u>Men and Women of Science</u> is somehow attributable to Mormon Church influence?____

8. Do you believe that your church contributed significantly to your professional achievements? 1> Yes.__ 2> Some.__ 3> No.__ 4> No opinion.__ Any comment as to how:____________________________

9. Please indicate the strength of your conviction that Jesus of Nazareth is a divine person of the Godhead. Please circle:
1> No such conviction. 2> Weak. 3> Fair. 4> Strong. 5> Very Strong.

10. Please indicate the strength of your conviction that Joseph Smith, Jr., was inspired by God in the formation of the Mormon Church. Circle: 1> No such conviction. 2> Weak. 3> Fair. 4> Strong. 5> Very Strong.

11. Indicate the strength of your conviction that the Church of Jesus Christ of Latter-day Saints is the only authoritative Church of Jesus Christ on earth today. 1> No such conviction. 2> Weak. 3> Fair. 4> Strong. 5> Very Strong.

12. What is your view of the Mormon Church as an institution for promoting human welfare? 1> Favorable. 2> Indifferent. 3> Antagonistic. 4> No opinion. 5> Other:________________

13. Do you believe that the fields of science and religion are so far removed from each other that no attempt is logically necessary to harmonize them? 1> Yes. 2> Partially. 3> No. 4> No Opinion. Any comment:______________________________________

14. Do you believe that you logically harmonize your church's doctrines and science in your own philosophy of life?
1> Yes. 2> Partially. 3> No. 4> No Opinion.

15. Use of scientific reason or logical thinking as a means to religious conviction should have a minor role, if any.
1> Agree. 2> Disagree. 3> No Opinion. 4> Other:____________

16. The scientific viewpoint and method should be held in very high regard and given a major role in all convictions.
1> Agree. 2> Disagree. 3> No Opinion. 4> Other.____________

17. Religious conviction should come primarily from answers to prayers, miraculous healings, and statements from religious authorities. 1> Agree. 2> Disagree. 3> No opinion.
4> Other:______

18. Do you consider yourself a believer in God, as you define God?
1> Yes. 2> Tentatively. 3> No. 4> No opinion.
5> Other:________

19. Do you believe that God is now limited by realities in the nature of things, such as man's "free agency"?
1> Yes. 2> Tentatively. 3> No. 4> No opinion.
5> Other:_______

20. Do you believe that God commonly acts directly in events on earth, that is, that God often intervenes in human affairs?
1> Yes. 2> Tentatively. 3> No. 4> No opinion.

21. Do you believe that the earth took at least many hundreds of millions of years to create? 1> Yes. 2> Tentatively. 3> No.

22. God created man's mortal body, probably by making many small progressive changes in life forms over millions of years, that is, "evolution" was probably God's process. 1> Agree. 2> Tentatively Agree. 3> Disagree. 4> No opinion. 5> Other:________________

23. The species, including man, probably came through evolution by the processes of chance and selection rather than by design.
1> Agree. 2> Tentatively Agree. 3> Disagree. 4> No opinion.

24. The species of living creatures were special creations of God and did not arise from the process called "evolution". 1> Agree.
2> Tentatively agree. 3> Disagree. 5> No opinion.

25. The "Standard Works" are all generally inspired by God but each contains some human error because they are in man's language.
1> Agree. 2> Tentatively agree. 3> Disagree. 4> No opinion.

26. The "Standard Works" are the words of the Lord and contain no errors, except for mistranslation in the Bible. 1> Agree 2> Disagree 3> No opinion. 4> Other:______________________________

27. Please check which words best represent your method of reading the "Standard Works": 1> Take them literally. 2> Interpret them with reason. 3> View them skeptically. 4> Some combination of these. 5> Other:________________________________. Thank you.

February 19, 1992

Your biography was chosen, by your colleagues, for the 1990 American Men and Women of Science to help, among other things, in studies of what it takes to produce persons of such achievement.

You are a graduate of a Utah university and may be interested in knowing that we have just completed a study of numbers of scientists per million produced by each of the United States. Utah surpasses the second place state, Delaware, by 21%! Please help us a bit to get some answers as to "Why?".

Hypothetically, the Mormon church may be a partial answer. But what are the religions of the scientists from Utah? Were they "active" in their church or not as young people? Are they "active" now? Are they "believers"? Do they think their church significantly contributed to Utah's record and/or to their own careers? Do they believe they harmonize their church with their science? Where does this leave them on such questions as the age of the earth and evolution? I am very curious about this and guess that you might be, too. So let's get some answers!

Please use the enclosed postage paid envelop to return the short questionnaire. We must have a high level of response, as a scientist, you know. You will receive results at my expense and for your interest. Send the request separately if you wish anonymity. Phone, if you like, to 602-831-1632.

You may ask whether this study will be reliable. It has a good chance. I am an Emeritus Professor of Arizona State University, where I was previously a department Chair in the Division of Policy and Leadership. My field is Social Psychology, and I have supervised many a dissertation. More important is the consultant on this project, Dr. Bruce Merrill, Professor in the Walter Cronkite School of Communication, and foremost Arizona political pollster.

An almost identical study was done on the 1949 American Men of Science for a University of Utah doctoral dissertation. (You may guess, by whom?) The results of the study with which you are helping will be compared to the earlier ones. What has changed in our generation? These will be among your results.

They all depend on you and your colleagues completing the questionnaire. Well, it went fine once. We all want to see the answers. Let's do it again now. Please turn to the questionnaire.

Sincerely,

Richard T. Wootton, 985 W. Elliot Road
Suite 5 #45, Chandler, AZ, 85224

RELIGION ORIENTATION QUESTIONNAIRE: Please freely comment or amend.

1. State in which born:____________ 2. Parent Occupation:____________

3. Your field of science:____

4. Church in which you have at least nominal membership:____________

5. Would you classify yourself as an active member?________________

6. Do you believe that Utah's per capita lead in production of Men and Women of Science is somehow attributable to Mormon Church influence?________________

7. Please indicate any strength of your conviction that Jesus of Nazareth is a divine person of the Godhead. Please circle:
1> No such conviction. 2> Weak. 3> Fair. 4> Strong. 5> Very Strong.

8. Please indicate any strength of your conviction that Joseph Smith, Jr., was inspired by God in the formation of the Mormon Church. Circle: 1> No such conviction. 2> Weak. 3> Fair. 4> Strong. 5> Very Strong.

9. Do you believe that you logically harmonize your church's doctrines and science in your own philosophy of life?
1> Yes. 2> Partially. 3> No. 4> No Opinion.

10. The scientific viewpoint and method should be held in very high regard and given a major role in all convictions.
1> Agree. 2> Disagree. 3> No Opinion.
4>Other.____

11. Do you believe that God is now limited by realities in the nature of things, such as man's "free agency"?
1> Yes. 2> Tentatively. 3> No. 4> No opinion.
5>Comment?____

12. Do you believe that the earth took at least many hundreds of millions of years to create? 1> Yes. 2> Tentatively. 3> No.
4> No opinion.
5> Comment:____

13. God created man's mortal body, probably by making many small progressive changes in life forms over millions of years, that is,"evolution" was probably God's process.
1> Agree. 2> Tentatively Agree. 3> Disagree. 4> No opinion.
5> Comment:____

14. The species of living creatures were special creations of God and did not arise from the process called "evolution". 1> Agree.
2> Tentatively agree.
3> Disagree. 4> No opinion.
5>Comment:____

15. Please check which words best represent your method of reading the Scriptures: 1> Take them literally. 2> Interpret them with reason. 3> View them skeptically. 4> Some combination of these.
5>Comment:____

16. Authors who have most influenced your science-religion ideas:

THANK YOU!

EDWARD L. THORNDIKE
501 WEST 120TH STREET
NEW YORK CITY

If it ever is published it will be as a memoir of the Amer. Acad of Arts and Sciences, with all the detailed data.

Dear Mr Martin:

My Boston speech is not yet published.

I know of no work being done on the Mormons. They certainly had courage and devotion to their ideals — and still have, I think.

Yrs truly

E. L. Thorndike

Oct 13, '41

IOWA'S CONTRIBUTION TO AMERICAN MEN OF SCIENCE, SEVENTH EDITION

H. E. ZABEL

The latest directory has appeared during the war when many fields of science are marking time and when we have adopted a policy of interrupting the production of scientists. It thus becomes a landmark and an analysis of the data it presents has special significance.

In this directory Iowa has not only maintained her position among the leading states in production of scientists but has slightly improved this relative standing.

NATIVE SCIENTISTS

Iowa has 258 new native son scientists but has lost 76—56 by death. This makes a net gain of 182 for a total of 1292. In the previous edition, six states had more native scientists than Iowa, Indiana surpassing Iowa by a margin of 4. Now Iowa has surpassed Indiana for sixth position by the same margin.

We may follow a method suggested by Dr. E. L. Thorndike (Science July 1940) for computing the number of scientists per million of population. We then use the 1900 census and find Iowa has 580. Only three states outrank Iowa: Utah 1065, Colorado 657, Vermont 589. On this basis, from 1938 to 1944, Iowa has increased her number of scientists per million of population from 538 to 580. She has passed Connecticut and Massachusetts since the appearance of the 6th edition.

The total number of names in the present edition is 34,114, an increase of 23.2%. Iowa's increase over her very high previous total is 16.4%.

ALUMNI

A better showing is made by the increase of alumni of Iowa colleges, where the total stands at 1064, an increase of 208. This is an increase of 24.3%, slightly above the rate for the entire United States: 23.5%. Only seven states have a larger increase of alumni: Illinois 491, Ohio 460, California 451, Pennsylvania 434, New York 386, Massachusetts 332, and Wisconsin 219.

In figure 2, we have the states arranged according to the totals of their alumni scientists. The entire graph for each state indicates these totals. The shaded part of each graph indicates the amount of the increase since 1938. The rate of increase of Iowa is slightly above the average. Especially large rates of increase will be noted for Illinois, Ohio, California, Minnesota, Texas, and Washington.

Iowa is in ninth position in the total number of alumni scientists

12. Origins of American Scientists by States of Birth: Relevance to Scientist Production

Using the 1938 edition of *American Men of Science* as a source, the late Dr. Edward L. Thorndike conducted a study of scientists by states of birth compared to the white populations of the states.

This study revealed an immense disparity between the states in per capita scientist production. The highest state (Utah) was 14.4 times as high as the lowest (Georgia). The highest state was 30 per cent beyond the second place state (Colorado).

Using the 1949 edition of *American Men of Science* as a source, the present writer did the same kind of study again to see what changes might have occurred in that decade during which the number of scientists listed grew from approximately 28,000 entries to approximately 50,000.

Again a great disparity between the states as scientist producers was revealed. However, the highest state (which was still Utah) was now only 11.7 times as high as the lowest (which was now Arkansas). The highest state was now 32 per cent beyond the second place (which was no longer Colorado but Idaho).

Several studies have been made which shed light on the factors which stimulate scientist production. None of these analyze the differences in scientist production between the various states of the union as a source of information on factors stimulating scientist production.

The present study is a preliminary analysis of what factors seem to be present in the top scientist producer (Utah) which are not present in the less productive states. Several factors seem to be eliminated as the main causative agents in Utah's lead by the fact that several other states not only have the individual factors to an approximately similar degree but even the admixtures of the factors to a similar degree.

No student has reported being able to associate any of the following with Utah's lead:

Higher inherited abilities in its population, climate, types of industry and employment, comparative average or total income, racial stock of its people, or national origins of its people.

Utah has been almost as distinctive for an excellent public school system as for production of scientists, being recognized as first in percentages of young people going to college and highest in average number of years education in its population. Yet its standing in education is not proportionately as far beyond other states as in scientist production.

A most clear and incontestable sociological difference between Utah and other states is the presence and influence of the Mormon Church in that particular state. A study among Utah-born scientists points to the philosophy and influence of the Mormon Church as a likely causative factor in high scientist production. Another study by a non-Mormon student (De Boer, Denver U.) credited Mormon influence with being largely responsible for Utah's high standing in education in general.

RICHARD T. WOOTTON
The Church College of Hawaii
Laie, Oahu, Hawaii

Reprinted from
PROCEEDINGS OF THE HAWAIIAN ACADEMY OF SCIENCE
Thirty-Fourth Annual Meeting • 1958-1959

RELIGIOUS ORIENTATIONS OF UTAH SCIENTISTS RELATED TO CERTAIN PROBLEMS OF LATTER-DAY SAINT CHURCH EDUCATION

(Publication No. 18,708)

Richard Tracey Wootton, Ed.D.
University of Utah, 1956

Chairman: Dr. Dasil A. Smith

An objective of many educators in the Church of Jesus Christ of Latter-day Saints is to stimulate active faith in the Church and to increase appreciation for all truth, including the truths of science.

The purpose of this study was to obtain and interpret certain new data which may aid the educator in evaluating and achieving this objective.

Four hypotheses were set up and questionnaire items framed to obtain a type of data deemed likely to test the hypotheses and to cast light on the two problems mentioned. The hypotheses were:

1. Scientific minds can harmonize science with the Latter-day Saint religion. (Sometimes referred to as the "Science L.D.S. Religion Harmony Hypothesis.")

2. L.D.S. scientist "Believers" have favored "Flexible" viewpoints preponderantly, and have favored the "Flexible" viewpoints much more than did educated Latter-day Saint religion teachers not so cognizant of science. (Sometimes referred to as the "L.D.S. 'Believer' Viewpoint Hypothesis.")

3. A sizeable number of L.D.S. scientists have experienced emotional troubling while attempting to harmonize science and religion. (Sometimes referred to as the "Emotional Troubling Hypothesis".)

4. Utah scientists who had troublesome adjustments have made substantially more changes from "Literal" viewpoints than Utah scientists not so troubled. (Sometimes referred to as the "Adjustment Change Hypothesis".)

The conclusions from the data of this section were as follows:

1. That the first hypothesis was probably substantiated: Scientific minds can harmonize Science and L.D.S. Religion.

2. That the objective of stimulating active faith in the Church and also increasing appreciation for science can apparently be achieved to a significant degree.

3. That L.D.S. Church educators should probably be challenged to seek further improvement in the harmonizing of Science and the L.D.S. Religion, since sizeable percentages of L.D.S. scientists were only Nominal L.D.S., sizeable percentages did not believe Science and the L.D.S. Religion can be harmonized, and sizeable percentages were emotionally troubled during the science-religion adjustment process.

These findings substantiated the hypothesis that L.D.S. scientist "Believers" have favored "Flexible" viewpoints

pages in the dissertation, its cost on microfilm, and the Library of Congress card number.
page. No postage is charged if check or money order accompanies order.

MEN OF SCIENCE . . .

By RICHARD T. WOOTTON

CONCERNING PROFESSOR E. L. THORNDIKE'S INQUIRY INTO THE PRODUCTION OF SUPERIOR MEN.

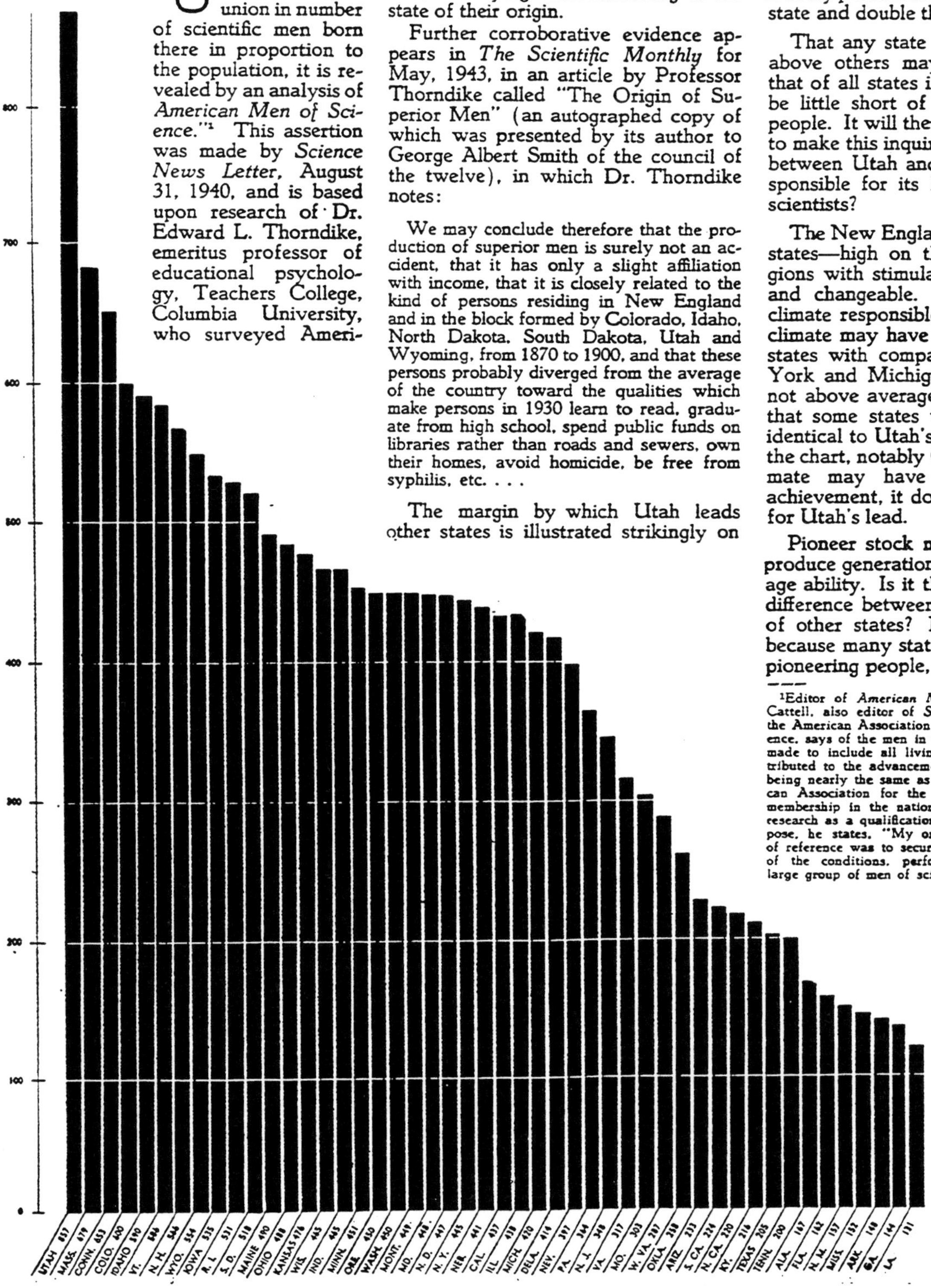

"UTAH leads all of the states of the union in number of scientific men born there in proportion to the population, it is revealed by an analysis of *American Men of Science*."[1] This assertion was made by *Science News Letter*, August 31, 1940, and is based upon research of Dr. Edward L. Thorndike, emeritus professor of educational psychology, Teachers College, Columbia University, who surveyed American scientists for the Carnegie Foundation, classifying them according to the state of their origin.

Further corroborative evidence appears in *The Scientific Monthly* for May, 1943, in an article by Professor Thorndike called "The Origin of Superior Men" (an autographed copy of which was presented by its author to George Albert Smith of the council of the twelve), in which Dr. Thorndike notes:

> We may conclude therefore that the production of superior men is surely not an accident, that it has only a slight affiliation with income, that it is closely related to the kind of persons residing in New England and in the block formed by Colorado, Idaho, North Dakota, South Dakota, Utah and Wyoming, from 1870 to 1900, and that these persons probably diverged from the average of the country toward the qualities which make persons in 1930 learn to read, graduate from high school, spend public funds on libraries rather than roads and sewers, own their homes, avoid homicide, be free from syphilis, etc. . . .

The margin by which Utah leads other states is illustrated strikingly on the chart accompanying this article. It is thirty percent beyond the second place state and double the national average.

That any state would stand so high above others may be surprising, and that of all states it would be Utah will be little short of astounding to many people. It will therefore be worth while to make this inquiry: What differences between Utah and other states are responsible for its higher production of scientists?

The New England and intermountain states—high on the chart—are in regions with stimulating climates, severe and changeable. Is the difference in climate responsible in itself? Although climate may have an influence, several states with comparable climates, New York and Michigan, for example, are not above average. It is also obvious that some states with climates almost identical to Utah's are well below it on the chart, notably Colorado. While climate may have an influence upon achievement, it does not likely account for Utah's lead.

Pioneer stock might be expected to produce generations of more than average ability. Is it therefore an inherited difference between Utahns and people of other states? Probably not, partly because many states were also built by pioneering people, for example, Wash-

[1]Editor of *American Men of Science*, J. McKeen Cattell, also editor of *Science*, the official organ of the American Association for the Advancement of Science, says of the men in the book: "Efforts have been made to include all living Americans who have contributed to the advancement of science, the standards being nearly the same as for fellowship in the American Association for the Advancement of Science or membership in the national scientific societies having research as a qualification." As to the volume's purpose, he states, "My original interest in this work of reference was to secure data for a statistical study of the conditions, performances, traits, etc., of a large group of men of science."

MEN OF ACHIEVEMENT

In a survey comparable to his "Men of Science," Dr. Thorndike went to "Who's Who," "Leaders in Education," and to "American Men of Science" to determine the origin of what he described with the broader term "Men of Achievement." Utah, with 857 such persons born per million white population from 1890 to 1900, led the national average by a wide margin.

ington and Oregon among others, which produce only half as many scientists in proportion as Utah. It could have been the inherited intellect of the particular pioneer people whom the Mormon church attracted to Utah.[2] However, there is no present scientific evidence that Utahns as a whole actually do have higher average native mentality than people of other states.

It appears highly probable that environmental influences are almost wholly responsible for Utah's lead on the chart, leaving this question: What environmental influences?

In years when the men of science were being schooled, the Utah educational system was largely operated by the church, and the relatively high standing of this educational system among the states of the union is well known. Is any superiority of it over those of other states responsible for Utah's lead in production of scientists in proportion to the population?

In the year 1899-1900 (the census year closest to when the men of science were in such schools), eight states were higher than Utah in per capita expenditure for state schools. In percentage of school age enrolled in school, Utah's standing was only .21% greater than the average of the western states. In number in daily attendance per number enrolled, it was only 1.02% above the western average, although 8.75% above the national.

In 1910, the census year closest to when the scientists were in these schools, Utah was not first in number of students and instructors per capita in colleges, universities, and technical schools. Colorado led it by 21.4%, and in expenditure per student and instructor in schools of higher education, Colorado led Utah by 22.4%. Therefore, while Utah had one of the nation's better school systems in these respects, it did not have first place, let alone any lead equal to its phenomenal position in men of science.

If better schools in Utah were responsible for Utah's margin over others in scientists, then apparently it is not because the schools were superior in number of students and instructors or amount spent on education, but could be only because of better teaching or more diligent learning. If schools are the answer, one would still have to look for influences beyond them to explain why the teaching was better or the learning more diligent.

The role of the Mormon church in its development is the most outstanding difference between Utah and other states sociologically. In the year when the average of the men of science were born, about 1895, 75% of Utah's people were Mormons. Almost all phases of the social environment were aspects of Mormon planning. Politics, education, and home life were somewhat shaped to the Latter-day Saint Christian ideal.

A comparison of Utah with other states significantly below it, but having practically all the same possibly influential factors as Utah—same climate, mixed mining and agricultural employment, even higher ranking state schools and college educational systems, and progressive pioneer populace — the same, that is, except for the Mormon church influence which was effective only in Utah, suggests the church as an explanation of its lead. In being the home of the Mormons, as well as in scientist production, Utah is in a class by itself. It seems a reasonable hypothesis that no less than Utah's lead over the second place state could have been caused directly by the influence of the Church of Jesus Christ of Latter-day Saints.[3]

RICHARD T. WOOTTON, '38-'39 editor of the University of Utah *Chronicle* and former missionary to New England, now a corporal in the armed forces, has the young man's inquisitive spirit. About three years ago he read a statement in *Science News Letter* which started him on an investigation promising unusual excitement for the price of some extensive and persistent correspondence. He assembles the returns here, and appends a conclusion or two which may in turn start some inquiries.

AN examination of the 28,000 entries in *American Men of Science* provided a list of the men born in Utah, to whom letters and questionnaires were

(*Concluded on page* 126)

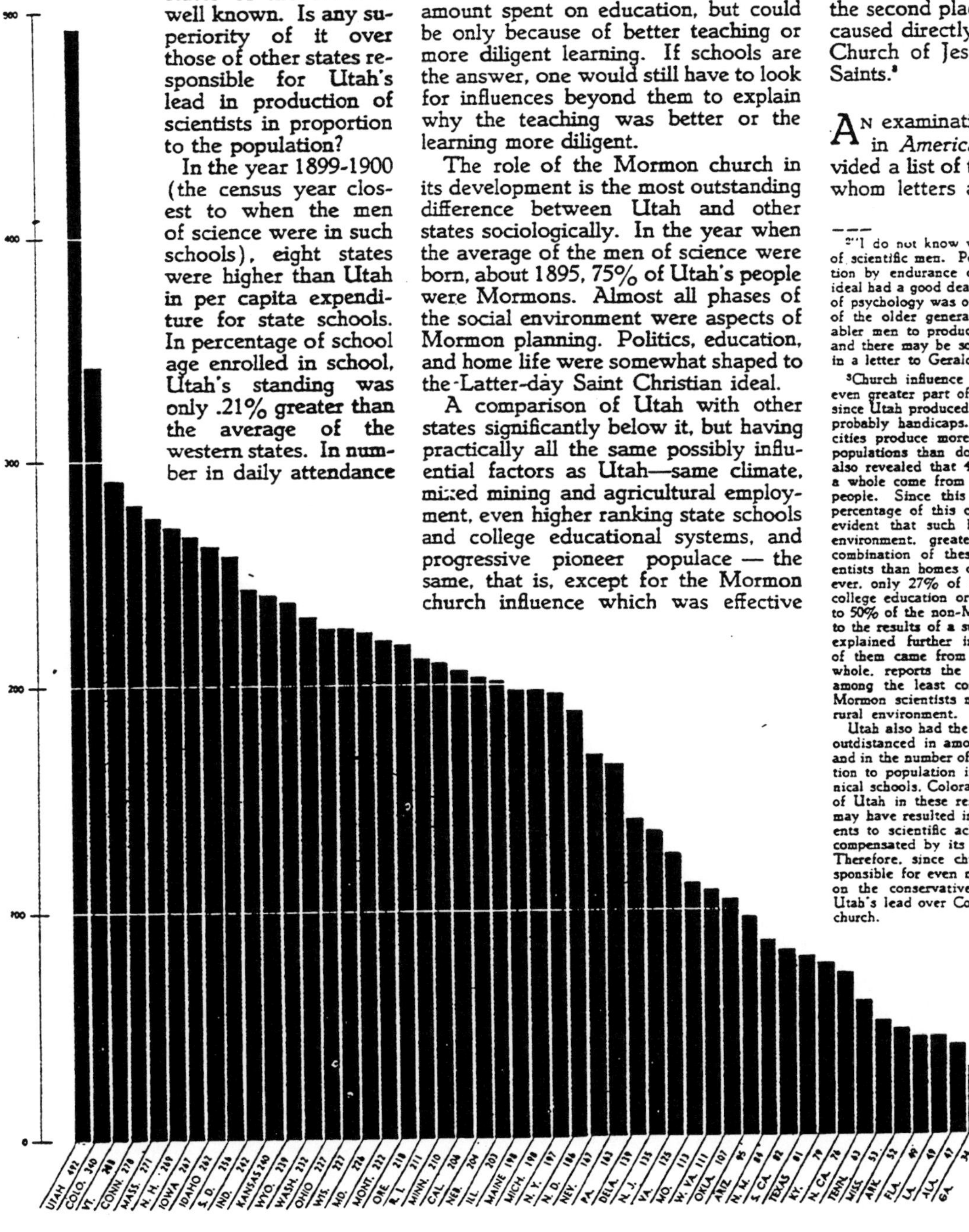

MEN OF SCIENCE

As reported by Dr. E. L. Thorndike, of Columbia University, the number of scientists born in Utah per million population for the period 1890 to 1900, as listed in the 1938 edition of "American Men of Science," represents a lead of thirty percent over the next highest state and is double the national average.

---

[2] "I do not know why Utah was so high in the case of scientific men. Possibly the selection of its population by endurance of tribulation and devotion to an ideal had a good deal to do with it. A Mormon student of psychology was of the opinion that plural marriages of the older generation gave an opportunity for the abler men to produce a larger proportion of children, and there may be something in that." Dr. Thorndike in a letter to Gerald L. Ericksen, chaplain, A.U.S.

[3] Church influence may have been responsible for an even greater part of Utah's total scientist production, since Utah produced under some conditions which were probably handicaps. A study by Cattell showed that cities produce more scientists in proportion to their populations than do rural areas. The same research also revealed that 43% of scientists in the nation as a whole come from homes of business or professional people. Since this is out of all proportion to the percentage of this class in the total population, it is evident that such homes, either by heredity, home environment, greater educational opportunity, or a combination of these factors, produce far more scientists than homes of other vocational classes. However, only 27% of Mormon scientists had parents of college education or professional vocation, in contrast to 50% of the non-Mormon ones from Utah (according to the results of a survey conducted by the writer and explained further in this article), and the majority of them came from farm homes. In the nation as a whole, reports the Cattell survey, farm homes were among the least conducive to scientific achievement. Mormon scientists may have become such in spite of rural environment.

Utah also had the relative handicap of being greatly outdistanced in amount spent per pupil and instructor and in the number of students and instructors in proportion to population in colleges, universities, and technical schools. Colorado being approximately 20% ahead of Utah in these respects. However, church influence may have resulted in these factors ceasing to be deterrents to scientific achievement or may have more than compensated by its influence for their deterent effect. Therefore, since church influence may have been responsible for even more of Utah's standing, it is well on the conservative side to postulate that at least Utah's lead over Colorado was caused by the Mormon church.

(*Continued from page 77*)

sent by the writer in an attempt to check the above hypothesis. It was thought possible in this way to settle important questions which might either disprove or tend to certify the hypothesis.

For example, in Utah in the approximate year of these men's birth, one-fourth of the population was non-Mormon. Is there actually more or less than this percentage of non-Mormons among the scientists from Utah? If there are more in proportion, it would tend to disprove church credit for Utah's lead, while if less, to prove the hypothesis. The questionnaire therefore asked the church affiliation of the Utah scientists.

Next it was necessary to determine whether or not the Mormons among the Utah scientists had actually been exposed to strong church influence or whether they were only nominally Mormon. There seemed three aspects of this to be checked: namely, home influence, church attendance influence, and influence of active individual participation.

The best available check on whether the home was strongly Mormon was taken to be whether or not the parents had testimonies of the divinity of Christ and the church. The scientists were therefore requested to give their opinion as to the testimony of their parents. They were also asked to indicate the number of years they attended church-sponsored meetings regularly, and whether during the formative years of adolescence they participated in the church as teachers, officers, or missionaries.

A check on the resultant attitudes of the scientists themselves toward the church was made by having them indicate their degree of certainty of the divinity of Christ and the church.

The following paragraphs outline the check of the hypothesis made possible by the questionnaire; they must be read carefully, for they are the core of this inquiry:

If the percentage of Mormons in the ranks of Utah scientists is greater than the percentage of Mormons in the Utah population when they were reared;

If many Mormon scientists came from strong Latter-day Saint homes, attended meetings regularly, and were active participants in the program of the church;

If, as a result, many were sufficiently influenced in their lives by the church to have gained testimonies of the divinity of Christ;

If they themselves are convinced that the church contributed significantly to their achievements;

And if there are actually teachings and organizations of the church likely to encourage achievement, particularly in scientific directions—if all of these things were shown to be true by the survey—then the hypothesis would probably be sufficiently certified to warrant the following conclusion:

It is probable that no less than the difference between Utah and the highest non-Mormon state in production of scientists in proportion to population is caused by the influence of the Latter-day Saint Church in the state of Utah.

One hundred and seventy-seven questionnaires were sent, covering the alphabet from A through R. The scientists whose help was sought were generously cooperative, and sixty-two percent answered and returned questionnaires, 50% of the group A through I and 78% of the group J through R. The facts revealed by the greater response of the J-R group correlate very closely with the facts of the A-I group. The percentage response was large enough and sufficiently representative, even in the 50% response group, that additional responses, as received from the 78% response group, did not alter the results. The statistics below are therefore reliable.

The answered questionnaires revealed the following facts; they should be noted in connection with the check of the hypothesis outlined above:

Percentage of Mormons among the Utah Men of Science	83.3
(Contrast this to Mormons in Utah population when these men were born	75.)
Mormon scientists from strong Latter-day Saint homes as indicated by the fact of their parents having testimonies	98.
Mormon scientists who attended church meetings regularly up to 18 years of age	86.
Mormon scientists who participated actively as teachers, officers, or missionaries	72.
Mormon scientists having testimonies of the divinity of Christ	68.
(Non-Mormon Utah-born scientists having testimonies of Christ's divinity	36.3)
Mormon scientists convinced that the church contributed significantly to their achievements	72.

All but one of the hypotheticals used to arrive at the possible conclusion of church credit for Utah's lead are answered clearly in the affirmative by the above statistics. That one is this: Are there teachings and organizations of the church likely to encourage achievement, particularly in scientific lines? The statement of the scientists themselves that they believe the church contributed significantly to their achievements is partial answer to this. Also relevant to this point is the fact that only 37.5% of the non-Mormon scientists, as shown by the writer's survey, thought that their church contributed to their achievements, which suggests that the Mormon church may give teachings and opportunities promoting scientific achievement which are lacking in other churches.[4]

The men of science reared in Utah have given in their replies to the questionnaire some explanations of how church influence could have produced Utah's lead and how it contributed to their own achievements. These indicate that the church does have teachings and organizations likely to encourage scientific achievement, as well as other types of achievement.

As possibly accounting for Utah's position on the chart, a Utah-born scientist now in Washington, D.C., briefly lists the following:

> 1. Mormon doctrine of eternal progress. 2. Encouragement of the church to pursue all lines of truth—i.e., scientific knowledge. "Know the truth and the truth shall make you free." 3. Word of Wisdom—abstinence from alcohol and tobacco.

Pertaining to Utah's lead is this opinion from Manhattan, Kansas:

> In view of the definite interest in education, in scientific experimentation and in cultural and liberal arts as shown by the early leaders of the Latter-day Saints, it seems only a natural consequence that Utah should produce splendid scientists.

A Los Angeles scientist sent this statement:

> Teachings of the church give one a splendid philosophy of life and a strong determination to obtain knowledge. "The glory of God is intelligence" is a most stimulating thought. "Man is saved only as fast as he gains knowledge" is another. Belief that our knowledge gained in this world we take with us to the next is also conducive to struggle for knowledge. I believe the church in this way stimulates young men and women to train their minds. This is an age of science; therefore, in seeking an outlet, more have chosen science than any other field of learning.

A Fort Collins, Colorado, scientist writes:

> One of the fundamentals of the church is to provide each member with a job or responsibility or part in the church's activities. It teaches reliability and honesty and resourcefulness.

This is the view of a Salt Lake City scientist:

> "As man now is, God once was; as God now is, man may become." "Be ye therefore perfect, even as your father in heaven is perfect." The doctrine of intellectual evolution is the essence of Mormon philosophy.

A man of science from Logan, Utah, suggests this reason for Utah's place on the chart:

> Parents of Latter-day Saint youths often make sacrifices they can ill afford to see that their children obtain an education that will qualify them for greater service to mankind, and that will give them greater joy in that service.

Explanations of how the church contributed to their own achievements follow similar lines of thought. A scientist in Orlando, Florida, says it helped him "because of its fundamental philosophy which encourages the development of one's abilities." Another in Ames, Iowa, claims that it aided him in scientific achievement "through constant encouragement of its members."

The dean of commerce of a technological school not in Utah states that the church contributed to his achievements by inculcating a "desire to be of service to my fellow men."

A large number of men of science surveyed made comments such as these quoted. However, space will not now permit printing more than this additional one from a Salt Lake scientist:

> I do not believe the teachings I received were accidental. I think such teachings are general throughout the Latter-day Saint Church. If Utah leads in the production of "men of science," I would expect it to lead by approximately the same percentage in other scholastic fields.

Possibly the scientist is correct in this conclusion, for the Associated Press sent the following story out of Boston, December 7, 1940:

> If there were some sort of "Rose Bowl" contest between states that produce the most smart people per 1,000,000 population, the nod would go to—Utah and Massachusetts. At least so says a report filed here with the American Academy of Arts and Science by Prof. Edward L. Thorndike, Columbia University psychologist. He listed those states in one-two order with respect to producing "men and women of great ability."

Tabulated results of this survey, as shown on the second chart, are published for the first time in this issue of the *Era*, with Dr. Thorndike's permission. Here again Utah has a production in proportion to population double that of the average American state, and its lead over the second place state is still substantial: twenty-two percent. The report mentioned by this press notice was based on an analysis of the volumes *Men of Science, Who's Who,* and *Leaders in Education.*

A comparison of differences between Utah and other states, together with the apparent influence which the church had in the lives of most Mormon scientists as shown by the writer's survey make it appear reasonable that a significant part of Utah's rank as a scientist-producing state could be attributable to the influence of the Church of Jesus Christ of Latter-day Saints.

[4]It should not be supposed, however, that any attempt is made to suggest that all Mormon scientists became such because of the church influence. Indeed, many of them, perhaps a majority, would have been regardless of that influence. The suggestion is that the church probably accounts for no less than the number in proportion to population that Utah has *more* than any non-Mormon state.

ABOUT THE AUTHOR

Richard T. Wootton is emeritus chair of the administration department of the Division of Leadership and Policy of Arizona State University and a professor of social science. Before being chair he was Director of Special Projects for university presidents John Schwada and Russell Nelson and of Financial Aids for G. Homer Durham.

Prior to joining A.S.U. in 1964, he was President of the B.Y.U.-Hawaii Campus and head of its Religion Division, 1959 to 1964. He came as one of its original faculty in 1955 and was then Director of Guidance Services and later Acting Administrator in 1958-59. He was also an instructor in Economics, U. S. History, and New Testament.

In Salt Lake City he was Institute Director for LDS Business College and principal of West High Seminary for the Church Education Department.

He was graduated from the University of Utah with B.S., M. S., and Ed.D. degrees, majoring in political science and administration.

During World War II he served in the Signal Corps in Hawaii, Guam, and Saipan as a cryptographer. After this he was for nine years field manager for Big Piney Oil and Gas Company.

He served in the New England states mission and married Helen Wootton (distant cousin) in the Salt Lake Temple in 1946. They are the parents of William R., Cynthia Rieben, Kathryn Ludeman, Suzanne Rogers, Caroline Alexander, and Lisa Fullmer. At present they have fifteen grandchildren.

In Alma 11th Ward, Chandler, Arizona, he is Employment Specialist and has been a member of High Councils in two stakes.

Richard is the eldest son of J. Tracey Wootton and Luna Chipman of Salt Lake City, Utah.